TEACHING OF
BIOLOGICAL SCIENCE I

TEACHING OF BIOLOGICAL SCIENCE I

Babu Muthuja
M.A., M.A., M.Ed.
Educational Advisor,
Arcot Sri Mahalakshmi Matric Hr. Sec. School,
Villapakkam, Vellore Dist.-632521 T.N.

R. Usharani
M.A., M.Ed.
Principal, Arcot Sri Mahalakshmi Matric Hr. Sec. School,
Villapakkam, Vellore Dist.-632521 T.N.

Er. Harsh Marwah
B. Tech. (Electronics)
Consultant with CISCO

CENTRUM PRESS
NEW DELHI-110002 (INDIA)

CENTRUM PRESS
H.O.: 4360/4, Ansari Road, Daryaganj,
New Delhi-110 002 (India)
Ph.: 23278000, 23261597
B.O.: No. 1015, Ist Main Road, BSK IIIrd Stage
IIIrd Phase, IIIrd Block,
Bangalore - 560 085 (India)
Tel.: 080-41723429
Visit us at: www.centrumpress.com

Teaching of Biological Science I

First Edition, 2009

PRINTED IN INDIA

Printed at Mehra Offset Press, Delhi

Contents

Preface

Biology Science book aims to gather knowledge to B.Ed. (Bachelor of Education) students, who are pursuing their career in the field of Biological Science. The need of this book is to present a clear outline about the use of Biological Science as it has been developed for students with sufficient illustrations to show how the theory is applied in practice with exercises.

This book is really useful for B.Ed. students to learn and prepare themselves for an examination. However, the sections have been prepared so that many of them can be omitted, or condensed to a brief statement of the results, without detriment to later parts of the book.

Author

Unit I

Place, Goals and Objectives of Biology

INTRODUCTION

Biology is the science that deals with living things. It is broadly divided into zoology, the study of animal life, and botany, the study of plant life. Subdivisions of each of these sciences include cytology (the study of cells), histology (the study of tissues), anatomy or morphology, physiology, and embryology (the study of the embryonic development of an individual animal or plant). Also included in biological studies are the sciences of genetics, evolution, paleontology, and taxonomy or systematic, the study of classification.

Pursuing a career in biology can be immensely rewarding and exciting. Studying biology teaches us to ask questions, make observations, evaluate evidence, and solve problems. Biologists learn how living things work, how they interact with one another, and how they evolve. They may study cells under a microscope, insects in a rainforest, viruses that affect human beings, plants in a greenhouse, or lions in the African grasslands. Their work increases our understanding about the natural world in which we live and helps us address issues of personal well being and worldwide concern, such as environmental depletion, threats to human health, and maintaining viable and abundant food supplies.

Biology is the study of life. Alongside physics and chemistry, biology is one of the largest and most important branches of science. At the highest level, biology is broken down based on the type of organism being studied: zoology, the study of animals; botany, of plants; and microbiology, of microorganisms.

Each field has contributed to mankind or the Earth's well-being in numerous ways. Most prominently: botany, to agriculture; zoology, to livestock and protection of ecologies; and microbiology, to the study of disease and ecosystems in general.

Besides classifications based on the category of organism being studied, biology contains many other specialized sub-disciplines, which may focus on just one category of organism or address organisms from different categories.

This includes biochemistry, the interface between biology and chemistry; molecular biology, which looks at life on the molecular level; cellular biology, which studies different types of cells and how they work; physiology, which looks at organisms at the level of tissue and organs; ecology, which studies the interactions between organisms themselves; ethology, which studies the behaviour of animals, especially complex animals; and genetics, overlapping with molecular biology, which studies the code of life, DNA.

The foundations of modern biology include four components: cell theory; that life is made of fundamental units called cells; evolution, that life is not deliberately designed by rather evolves incrementally through random mutations and natural selection; gene theory, that tiny molecular sequences of DNA dictate the entire structure of an organism and are passed from parents to offspring; and homeostasis, that each organism's body includes a complex suite of processes designed to preserve its biochemistry from the entropic effects of the external environment.

The basic picture in biology has stayed roughly the same since DNA was first imaged using x-ray crystallography in the 1950s, although there are constant refinements to the details, and life is so complex that it could be centuries or even millennia before we begin to understand it in its entirety.

But it should be made clear that we are moving towards complete understanding: life, while complex, consists of a finite amount of complexity that only appreciably increases on relatively long timescales of hundreds of thousands or millions of years. Evolution, while creative, operates slowly.

In recent years, much excitement in biology has centered on the sequencing of genomes and their comparison, called genomic, and the creation of life with custom-written DNA programming, called synthetic biology.

Specializations

The specializations may be of greater or lesser interest to us. A few of the specializations related to this field include, but are not limited to:

Anatomy	*Animal Biology*	*Evolutionary Biology*
Epidemiology	Animal Development	Genetics
Bioengineering	Biochemistry	Immunology
Biology	Biological and Life Sciences	Medical Microbiology
Molecular Biology	Biology Teacher	Education Neurobiology
Virology	Biomedical Engineering	Oceanography
Zoology	Biometrics	Parasitology
Marine Biology	Biostatistics	Pathology
Botany	Biotechnology Research	Pre-medical Biology
Radiobiology	Cell and Molecular Biology	Reproductive Biology
Environmental Development	Developmental Biology	Toxicology
Ecology	Entomology	

STUDY OF BIOLOGY

Biology is the study of living things and their vital processes. Because biology covers such a broad area, it has been traditional to separate the study of plants (botany) from that of animals (zoology), and the study of structure of organisms (morphology) from that of function (physiology). Despite their apparent differences, all the subdivisions are interrelated by basic principles, so current practice tends to investigate those biological phenomena that all living things have in common. The advancement of knowledge and technology has resulted in further categorizations that include, but are far from restricted to: cell biology, population biology, ecology, genetics, biochemistry, molecular biology, microbiology, and physical anthropology.

The number of different animal and plant species on earth is estimated at between 2 million and 4.5 million. We are presently killing off species through human action at a faster rate than at any other time, but we are also discovering new oceanic species at an increasing rate. It is not known when the study of biology originated, but it can be safely assumed that early humanoids had some experimental knowledge of the animals and plants around them. One's very survival relied on the recognition of poisonous plants and on the basic understanding of the habits of predators. Many of the earliest records of biology come from the bas-reliefs left behind by the Assyrians and Babylonians. Papyrus and artifacts found in tombs and pyramids indicate that the Egyptians possessed considerable, albeit archaic by today's standards, medical knowledge. There is growing evidence from China and India as early as 2500 BC that there were general practices of therapeutic healing, silkworm use to produce silk, biological control of crops, and agricultural cultivation.

With the arrival of Greek civilization, the study of biology shifted dramatically to a belief that every event has a cause and that a particular cause produces a particular effect. These philosophers of science assumed the existence of a natural law governing the universe; a law that can be comprehended by man through his use of observation and deduction. Although they established the science of biology, their greatest contribution to science was the idea of rational thought. Skipping forward through the rapid evolution of biological advancements to today, recent discoveries concerning hereditary mechanisms and genetic engineering have raised ethical issues beyond our previous imagination, and have potential ramifications that could affect the very existence of life itself. It will be interesting to see what is to come in the future.

With over 7 billion humans on Earth today, and growing explosively. We are rapidly stretching the limits of our planet to sustain life as we know it. Global warming, depleted food sources, desertification, weather pattern changes, shrinking ozone layers, and rising ocean levels are warning signs of these stresses. This is where you can get involved! Whether you enter the doors of biological science or sit on the outside, become informed of the advancements in biology. Make educated choices to support or be critics. Become informed.

BIOLOGY CONCEPTS AND SUPPORTING IDEAS

Semester One will cover:

- The Scientific Method and Safety.
- Chemistry of Biological Processes.
- Cellular Structures and Functions.
- Energy Processes in Living Things.
- DNA and Protein Synthesis.

Conceptual Statement I:
Chemistry of Biological Processes

Living things are made of elements that form biologically important molecules and compounds. Biochemical reactions involving these molecules and compounds form the basis of life processes within cells.

Supporting Ideas

- Through experimentation scientists have discovered that atoms, which are composed of protons, neutrons, and electrons, account for the different properties of the elements.
- Several elements, such as carbon, hydrogen, nitrogen, oxygen, phosphorus, sodium, potassium, sulfur, calcium, and iron, form compounds that are necessary for life.

- Covalent, ionic, and hydrogen bonds result from the underlying structure of elements. These bonds are formed or broken as molecules are assembled or rearranged during metabolism.
- Water is essential to biochemical reactions because of its physical and chemical properties.
- The chemical reactions of life require the maintenance of a narrow range of pH.
- Experiments have shown that carbohydrates, proteins, lipids, and nucleic acids provide the raw materials for the structure and functions of life. These biological polymers are formed through dehydration synthesis.
- Carbohydrates are composed of carbon, hydrogen, and oxygen in a 1:2:1 ratio, which form monosaccharides, disaccharides, and polysaccharides. They are used to store energy and provide support.
- Proteins, formed of amino acids linked together, comprise a chief building material fo organisms and also act as biological catalysts called enzymes.
- Lipids are macromolecules that are insoluble in water. They store energy and are components of cell membranes.
- Nucleic acids are long chains of nucleotides that contain the cell's hereditary information.
- Metabolism includes all the chemical reactions involved in energy production, growth, reproduction, homeostasis, and communication.

Conceptual Statement 2: Cellular Structures and Functions

The cell is the basic unit of structure, function, and organization of all organisms. Certain cell types have organized structures within them called organelles. Each organelle has a specific function to perform in maintaining homeostasis. Our understanding of structure and function of the cell has been a direct result of advances in scientific technology.

Supporting Ideas

- Cumulative historical observations using microscopes and conducting experiments have led to the development of the three principles comprising the cell theory: all living things are made up of cells, life processes occur in cells, and cells come from existing cells.
- Cells can be classified as prokaryotes (which lack membrane-bound organelles) or eukaryotes (which have membrane-bound organelles).
- Eukaryotic cells may have arisen from the joining together of more primitive cell types.
- Advances in centrifugation and fractionation techniques have allowed scientists to determine the functions of individual organelles.
- The nucleus of the living cell directs cellular activity and stores hereditary information.
- Ribosomes, the sites of protein synthesis, are located on rough endoplasmic reticulum and are dispersed throughout the cytoplasm.
- The endoplasmic reticulum is involved in the transport of proteins from the ribosome to the Golgi apparatus.
- The Golgi apparatus packages and transports lipids and proteins for export or distribution throughout the cell.
- The cell membrane, composed of proteins and phospholipids, separates the inside of the cell from its outside environment and as a semipermeable membrane, it regulates what enters and leaves the cell.
- There are several ways in which substances are transported across cell membranes: diffusion (passive transport and osmosis), active transport, and facilitated transport.
- Mitochondria and chloroplasts perform energy transformations in respiration and photosynthesis.
- Cells in the body of multicellular organisms are

arranged in structural and functional groups called tissues: tissues form organs and organs form organ systems.

Conceptual Statement III:
Energy Processes in Living Things

Energy is required to maintain life. All organisms have processes that utilize energy sources to maintain high levels of organization.

- Organisms utilize a series of cyclic energy conversion reactions to meet their needs. Autotrophs convert energy from the sun or energy from inorganic compounds into energy-rich organic compounds. Heterotrophs obtain energy by consuming energy-rich organic compounds from other organisms.
- Experiments have shown that chlorophyll and other pigments in autotrophs absorb light energy and are able to transfer the energy to complex organic reactions.
- Photosynthesis in autotrophs includes a light-dependent stage in which energy is captured. Adenosine triphosphate (ATP) is generated, and free oxygen is released. In the light-independent stage (Calvin Cycle), the energy is used to make glucose from carbon dioxide.
- In cells, ATP acts as an energy-transferring molecule that is repeatedly built up and broken down.
- The products of photosynthesis provide the raw materials for cellular respiration and the products of cellular respiration provide the materials for photosynthesis.
- During cellular respiration, all organisms obtain energy by breaking down the complex chemical compounds in foods and by synthesizing ATP molecules.
- In the absence of oxygen, ATP can still be produced through glycolysis and fermentation.

- Aerobic respiration produces more ATP for cell activity than does anaerobic respiration.

BIOLOGY OBJECTIVES

The Key Objectives in Biology are explained as below, where the student has to understand and perform following things in School and Colleges.

Upon completion of text reading and class teaching course, the student will be able to:

- List unique characteristics that distinguish archaea from bacteria.
- Describe the three-domain system of classification and explain how it differs from previous systems.
- Using a diagram or micrograph, distinguish among the three most common shapes of prokaryotes.
- Indicate where photosynthesis and cellular respiration take place in prokaryotic cells.
- Explain how organization of the prokaryotic genome differs from that in eukaryotic cells.
- List the three main groups of archaea, describe distinguishing features among the groups and give examples of each.
- Explain how the presence of E. coli in public water supplies can be used as an indicator of water quality.
- List the characteristics of protists.
- Describe some major lines of evidence for the endosymbiotic hypothesis.
- List five candidate kingdoms of protists and describe a major feature of each.
- Describe amoeboid movement.
- Describe the function of contractile vacuoles in freshwater ciliates.
- Distinguish between macronuclei and micronuclei.
- Explain how accessory pigments can be used to classify algae and determin phylogenetic relationships among divisions.
- Explain the most widely accepted hypothesis for the evolution of multicellularity.

- List characteristics that distinguish plants from organisms in the other kingdoms.
- Diagram a generalized plant life cycle indicating which generation is the sporophyte/ gametophyte, which individuals are haploid/diploid, where meiosis occurs and where mitosis occurs.
- Distinguish between the categories division and phylum.
- Using the classification scheme presented in the text, list the plant divisions; give the common name for each; and categorize them into nonvascular, vascular seedless and vascular seed plants.
- Provide evidence to defend the position that plants evolved from green algae.
- Describe two adaptations that made the bryophytes' move onto land possible.
- Explain how bryophytes are still tied to water.
- Diagram the life cycle of a moss including gamete production, fertilization, and spore production.
- Describe adaptations of vascular plants, including modifications of the life cycle and modifications of the sporophyte, that have contributed to their success on land.
- Diagram the life cycle of a fern including spore production, gamete production and fertilization.
- Point out the major life cycle differences between mosses and ferns.
- Describe the adaptations of seed plants that have contributed to their success on land.
- Describe the life history of a pine and indicate which structures are part of the gametophyte generation and which are part of the sporophyte generation.
- Point out the major life cycle differences in ferns and pines.
- Distinguish between pollination and fertilization.
- Describe how the needle-shaped leaves of pines and firs are adapted to dry conditions.
- Compare the life cycles of mosses, ferns, conifers, and flowering plants in terms of:

  - Dominant life cycle stage (gametophyte/sporophyte)
  - Whether they are homosporous or heterosporous
  - Mechanism of gamete transfer
- Describe some refinements in vascular tissue that occurred during angiosperm evolution.
- Explain how evolution of the flower enhanced the reproductive efficiency of angiosperms.
- Identify the following floral structures and describe a function for each:

  a. Sepals
  b. Petals
  c. Stamens
  d. Carpels
  e. Filament
  f. Anther
  g. Stigma
  h. Style
  i. Ovary
- Define fruit and explain how fruits are modified in ways that help disperse seeds.
- Diagram the generalized life cycle of an angiosperm, identify which structures are haploid, and explain how it differs from the life cycle of a pine.
- Explain the process of double fertilization and describe the fate of the polyploid nucleus.
- Explain how an angiosperm seed differs from that of a pine.
- Explain how animals may have influenced the evolution of terrestrial plants, and vice versa.
- List characteristics that distinguish fungi from organisms in other kingdoms.
- Explain how fungi acquire their nutrients.
- Explain how non-motile fungi seek new food sources and how they disperse.
- Describe the basic body plan of a fungus.
- Distinguish among fungi and list some common examples of each.
- Provide evidence for both sides of the debate on whether symbiosis in lichens is parasitic or mutualistic.

- Describe the ecological importance of lichens.
- Explain why fungi are ecologically and commercially important.
- List characteristics that distinguish animals from organisms in the other kingdoms.
- Distinguish between radial and bilateral symmetry.
- Outline the major phylogenetic branches of the animal kingdom, which are based upon grade of organization; symmetry and embryonic germ layers; absence or presence of a body cavity; and protostome-deuterostome dichotomy.
- Distinguish among acoelomate, pseudocoelomate and coelomate.
- Distinguish between spiral and radial cleavage; determinant and indeterminate cleavage; schizocoelous and enterocoelous.
- Compare developmental differences between protostomes and deuterostomes including:
  a. Plane of cleavage c. Fate of the blastopore
  b. Determination d. Coelom formation
- List at least nine phyla of the kingdom Animalia.
- Compare and contrast several characteristics of the phyla Porifera, Cnidaria (Coelenterata), Platyhelminthes, Nematoda,and Annelida
- List some examples of members for each of the phyla in objective # 54.
- Given a diagram or dissection specimen of an earthworm, identify the following structures; mouth, pharynx, esophagus, crop, gizzard, intestine, aortic arches, dorsal blood vessel, and ventral nerve cord.
- Identify the function of the structures listed in objective.
- Describe the following systems in the earthworm; locomotion, excretion, nervous, transport, reproduction, and respiration.
- Define the term hermaphrodite.
- List several characteristics of the phyla Molluca, Echinodermata, and Arthropoda.

- List several examples of members of each of the phyla above in objective 59.
- Given a diagram or a dissected specimen of a grasshopper, identify the following structures; antennae, compound eyes, typanum, ovipositor, mandibles, esophagus, crop, gizzard, stomach, gastric caeca, intestine, and anus.
- Identify the function of the structures listed in objective 61 above.
- Describe the following systems of the grasshopper; excretory, nervous, reproductive,locomotion, transport, and respiratory.
- Explain the difference between open and closed circulatory systems.
- List several characteristics of the phylum Chordata.
- Explain what is meant by a notocord.
- List several examples of invertebrate Chordates.
- Define each of the following terms; tetrapods, poikilotherms, and homeotherms.
- List five classes of vertebrate Chordates and several examples of members of each class.
- compare and contrast heart structure, temperature regulation, reproduction, and respiratory mechanisms in the five classes of vertebrate Chordates.
- List several characteristics of the bony fish.
- List several characteristics of the Amphibians.
- List several characteristics of the reptiles.
- List several characteristics of the birds.
- List several characteristics of mammals.
- Distinguish between monotreme, marsupial, and placental mammals and list examples of each.

BIOLOGY IN SCHOOL

No subject is moving faster than Biology. With recent advances in our knowledge of genetics, the sequencing of the human genome, and a fierce world-wide debate raging over evolution, stem cell research, cloning, GM crops and many other topics – there is no greater time to be studying Biology. There is no better Department in England than the award-winning department at School.

The Biology Department consists of full time teachers and one lab technician. Our main objective is to enthuse the pupils to love Biology through encouraging independent thought and analysis, and extensive opportunities for practical work. The Department is superbly resourced, with all the latest practical equipment and each laboratory is equipped with a digital projector and interactive whiteboards.

Pupils learn better through doing rather than listening or watching someone else demonstrate an experiment. Our philosophy is to make the subject as hands- on as possible. This is taken to an extreme at A level - our aim is to get pupils out into the field as much as possible to experience real Biology during our field trips.

Biology is a huge field with a lot of diversity, ranging from the study of biologically significant atoms to the study of entire ecosystems. Biologists are also employed in a lot of different fields.

An example of this range of work includes: working on engineering bio-molecules, working on forensic crime scenes, studying the taxonomic relationships of spiders, investigating exotic diseases, teaching science courses, helping local governments make ecological decisions, working in museums, practicing medicine, running diagnostic labs, studying animal habitats in the rain forest canopy, and planting indigenous plants in a devastated ecosystem.

With such a variety in careers, it is not surprising that there would be a large variety in academic training. Many of these fields have very specific post-graduate programs, such as Medical school, Optometry, or Veterinarian medicine.

Some biology careers such as pharmaceutical sales, technical writer, or laboratory technician require no formal post-graduate education. However, the majority of professional biology careers that are not health related require post-graduate degrees, either a Masters degree (M.S.) or a doctorate degree.

WHY BIOLOGY IS DIFFERENT

INTRODUCTION

It may have occurred to you at one time or another that there are some subtle differences between Biology as a science and Chemistry, Physics, and Mathematics. Obviously, the main difference is that Biology deals with living organisms, but the ramifications of this fact go beyond just the subject matter, because it also affects the nature of the scientific methods employed by biologists.

The evolutionary biologist has written extensively on the philosophical implications of evolutionary biology and has discussed what he sees as the fundamental points that should be incorporated into a philosophy for the biological sciences. That these principles have not been recognized more clearly is because, according to biologists, philosophers of science continue to use the physical sciences especially Physics as a model for all of the sciences. The points raised by biologists are summarized in the table below and are as follows:

Understanding Organisms: One approach to understanding a phenomenon is to reduce it to its fundamental aspects, and, by understanding each component, you can gain some appreciation of the overall process. This approach, often referred to as reductionism, is useful, especially in the physical sciences, where, for example, knowledge of the behaviour of individual atoms allows you to predict the dynamics of an reaction system. However, the hierarchical organization of biological systems makes it impossible to understand all aspects of even a single organism by studying each of its components. Furthermore, there are certain biological processes, like Natural Selection, which cannot be predicted based on only a knowledge of Physics and Chemistry. In other words, the entire range of material phenomena are to be found in biological systems, whereas Physics and Chemistry only deal with a subset of these phenomena.

History: There are many disciplines, besides History itself, where unique historical events play a critical role. Astronomy and Geology, for example, are often concerned with individual historical events. In Biology, however, we study not only historical events but also the organisms which have been either directly or indirectly shaped by those events. A good case in point is the effect of the extinction of the dinosaurs on subsequent mammalian diversification. This historical aspect of biology is compounded by the fact that the DNA within each organism is in fact an historical record of the ancestor-descendant relationships of that particular individual.

PRINCIPLES

Principles that should be included in the formation of a philosophy for the biological sciences.

- That a full understanding of organisms cannot be secured through the theories of Physics and Chemistry alone.
- That the historical nature of organisms must be fully considered, in particular their possession of an historically acquired genetic programme.
- That individuals at most hierarchical levels, from the cell up, are unique and form populations, the variance of which is one of their major characteristics.
- That there are two biologies, functional biology, which asks proximate questions, and evolutionary biology, which asks ultimate questions.
- That the history of biology has been dominated by the establishment of concepts and by their maturation, modification, and - occasionally - their rejection.
- That the patterned complexity of living systems is hierarchically organized and that higher levels in the hierarchy are characterized by the emergence of novelties.
- That observation and comparison are methods in biological research that are fully as scientific and heuristic as the experiment.
- That an insistence on the autonomy of biology does not mean an endorsement of vitalism, orthogenesis, or any other theory that is in conflict with the laws of chemistry or physics.

FEATURES

Uniqueness

One of the things that enables research in the physical sciences to be so efficient and precise is the fact that there is so little variability in many of the entities studied. For example, all atoms of a particular isotope of carbon behave in exactly the same way, and this means that an organic chemist can readily predict the outcome of a particular reaction. Contrast this situation with that of a biologist, who, regardless of his or her field must deal with the fact that the subjects being investigated are not all the same, but instead differ to some degree because they have different genotypes. Even studies at the biochemical level must take into account the possible existence of more than one protein variant in a given system. The variance that is observed in physical systems is treated as either an error in measurement or as the result of some random "noise" factor, but in biological research the observed variance is a reflection of a fundamental aspect of living systems.

Approaches to Biology

The tendency to look at some aspects of biology as being somehow less "scientific" than the physical sciences is not restricted to philosophers of science who use the physical sciences as their model; the same attitude can be found within biology because there are two main ways in which biologists can approach their research. In studying a particular phenomenon, you can ask either proximate or ultimate questions. The proximate aspects of a phenomenon are usually related to the question "How...?", while the ultimate issues are usually addressed by "Why...?". For example, it is well known that male frogs call during the mating season in order to attract females. You could study this phenomenon by describing the vocalization mechanism of the males, the frequencies of the sounds produced, and the auditory apparatus of the females. Each of these is basically a functional, physiological question, but there is the other approach to the same question which is to determine the significance of what is happening. One simple explanation is that these calls are the only way in which the sexes can find each other in the dark. However, an increasing amount of research shows that these calls are critical to the process of mate selection and subsequent mating success.

Addressing this issue requires that we determine the evolutionary processes associated with the mating system - the fitness consequences of mating with a particular male, the correlation, if any, between male calling frequency and fitness, etc.

Obviously, studying this aspect of the phenomenon is not as clear cut as the physiological questions, but it is still a legitimate scientific inquiry. In fact, those who deal with proximate questions in biology often find that the more they learn about their systems, the more they must concern themselves with the ultimate, evolutionary issues.

Concepts in Biology

The model of the scientific method that is derived from the physical sciences leaves one with the impression that the goal of science is to generate "laws" (e. g., the statements of Newton and Kepler on general and planetary motion, respectively). Laws in this sense are statements of fact that have been demonstrated to fit all known cases.

Biologists have occasionally suffered from a desire to emulate the physical sciences by establishing laws, but the historical component and intrinsic variability of biological systems make such universal statements impossible. Biological science advances by developing general concepts which are used to guide our approach to particular phenomena.

Natural Selection is an example of a concept, and, while some have discussed it from the perspective of a law, it is merely a formal generalization about the interactions among the environment, organisms, and the genotypes of those organisms in terms of the impact of these interactions on genotypic frequencies.

The formal generalizations of biology always include exceptions that "prove the rule" and result in the modification and refinement of the concepts over time.

Hierarchy

Students in Biology are well acquainted with the listing of the biological hierarchy that runs from molecules and cells to ecosystems and the biosphere, but few ever stop to think about the ramifications of this hierarchy for the study of biological systems. The existence of this structure in biological systems means that we must deal with the fact of emergent properties at each level. The concept of emergence is the idea that the entire system may exhibit properties that are not deducible from knowledge of the individual components of the system. This idea is often summarized by the phrase "the whole is greater than the sum of the parts". The existence of emergent properties in living systems is what limits the usefulness of the reductionist approach to biology. The recognition of the hierarchical structure of life on this planet has caused some to suggest that major areas of biological investigation should operate formally with this structure in mind.

Observation and Comparison

The introductory textbook description of the scientific method has scientists operating by making observations, formulating hypotheses, and conducting experiments to test their hypotheses. This is an accurate description of how to study common, contemporary phenomena, but how, for example, do you go about scientifically studying the extinction of the dinosaurs? The notion of the laboratory experiment as the scientific method is so ingrained that even biologists who study proximate questions in existing organisms tend to discount the efforts of those who conduct evolutionary and/ or ecological research. However, evolutionary biologists can - and do - formulate hypotheses, but only some of these hypotheses are testable through controlled laboratory or field experiments. In many instances, evolutionary hypotheses can be tested only by comparing populations or species under different sets of conditions, or, in the case of past events, looking for evidence related to corollaries of the main hypothesis. For example, if an asteroid impact caused the extinction of the dinosaurs at the end of the Cretaceous, then there should be several geological and paleontological lines of evidence which would support this scenario.

Biology as an Autonomous Science

Whenever people argue that there is an intrinsic difference between living and non-living systems, they leave themselves open to the charge that they are advocating either vitalism or orthogenesis.

Vitalism is the discredited notion that what makes living systems different is their possession of some "vital force" that when removed from the system just leaves you with a mass of organic molecules. Orthogenesis is a related concept which holds that the evolutionary process is somehow goal-directed to produce progressively higher levels of perfection and complexity.

The application of this concept to evolution has a history. As you have seen, there is no need to postulate the existence of some metaphysical force to explain the difference between living and non-living systems. The reason why Biology differs from the physical sciences is because of the characteristics of living systems, which are, among others:

- The importance of history in organic evolution;
- The possession of a structured, inheritable genetic programme;
- The hierarchical structure of living systems, and the existence of emergent properties at almost every level;
- The fact that certain processes (e. g., Natural Selection) only occur in living systems.

CONCEPTUAL DIFFERENCES IN BIOLOGY

- The importance of historical narrative as an explanatory device.
- The prevalence of indeterminacy owing to the high frequency of stochastic processes, unknown factors, the presence of constraints, the interaction of multiple causes.

- The importance of quality (structure, form, function) in the properties and actions of objects, and a correlated reduction in the importance of purely quantitative differences.
- Presence of an historical constituent in the inherited programme; hence legitimacy of "why" questions; capacity for the storage of historical information.

METHODOLOGICAL DIFFERENCES IN BIOLOGY

- The importance of observation in addition to experiment.
- The frequency of independent multiple solutions to the same problem.

OTHER AUTONOMOUS ASPECTS OF BIOLOGY

- All biological phenomena have two sets of causations, those controlled by the historically accumulated information of the genetic programme (evolutionary or ultimate causations), and those controlled by the properties of the interacting system (proximate causations). The study of the historical components of each system is as legitimate a concern of biological science as the study of proximate causations.
- The outcome of biological processes is usually affected simultaneously by multiple causations, owing to the complexity of the systems interacting with complex biotic and physical environments
- Many properties of systems cannot be explained by a study of their isolated components.

BOTANY

DEFINITION

The science which treats of the structure of plants, the functions of their parts, their places of growth, their classification, and the terms which are employed in their description and denomination.

Botany is the Scientific Study of Plants

"Plants," to most people, means a wide range of living organisms from the smallest bacteria to the largest living things - the giant sequoia trees. By this definition plants include: algae, fungi, lichens, mosses, ferns, conifers and flowering plants. Today scientists believe bacteria, algae and fungi are in their own distinct kingdoms, but most general botany courses, and most Botany Departments at colleges and universities, still teach about these groups.

Because the Field is so Broad

There are many kinds of plant biologists and many different opportunities available. Botanists interested in ecology study interactions of plants with other organisms and the environment. Other field botanists search to find new species or do experiments to discover how plants grow under different conditions. Some botanists study the structure of plants. They may work in the field, concentrating on the pattern of the whole plant. Others use microscopes to study the most detailed fine structure of individual cells. Many botanists do experiments to determine how plants convert simple chemical compounds into more complex chemicals. They may even study how genetic information in DNA controls plant development. Botanists study processes that occur on a time scale ranging from fractions of a second in individual cells to those that unfold over eons of evolutionary time.

Results of Botanical Research

Increase and improve our supply of medicines, foods, fibers, building materials, and other plant products. Conservationists use botanical knowledge to help manage parks, forests, range lands, and wilderness areas. Public health and environmental protection professionals depend on their understanding of plant science to help solve pollution problems.

BOTANY AND SOCIETY

Explosive Growth of Human Population

Is changing the earth dramatically. Only by understanding how human activities affect our environment can we predict global climatic changes. Scientific studies of these changes and their effect on natural ecosystems and crop production are crucial to the future of our society

Plant Tissue Culture

Botanists can grow entire plants from single cells. This has exciting potential in biotechnology, horticulture, forestry, and plant pathology. For example, the stately American chestnut was once a widespread tree in our Eastern forests. Today it has virtually disappeared because of a disease-producing fungus that causes chestnut blight. The American chestnut recently has been grown in plant tissue culture. If we can develop a blight-resistant strain of American chestnut, we will be able to propagate disease-resistant trees very quickly. These trees could then be planted in our forests and the American chestnut would once again be one of our most important hardwood species.

Plants are Chemical Factories

Many of the chemicals that they produce are useful to humans. Besides food, plants provide raw materials for paper, building materials, solvents and adhesives, fabrics, medicines, and many other products. Botanists study the chemicals produced by different plants to find new uses for them. For example, we use some plant chemicals to treat certain types of cancer.

Earth's Biological Diversity

The kinds of organisms that populate the earth, is decreasing. As humans change the environment for their own purposes, plants and animals living in these areas become increasingly endangered. Plant taxonomists and plant ecologists work to identify and understand new plant species, especially in such biologically rich areas as tropical rain forests. Plants of the rain forests are important in their own right, but they could be major new resources for people as well. Perhaps a plant as yet undiscovered will become an important food crop. There are probably many undiscovered plants that produce useful drugs to cure or treat human diseases. Biological diversity also provides an important source of new genes to improve the plants we now use. As techniques of genetic engineering improve, so will our ability to improve our domestic plants.

ZOOLOGY

DEFINITION

Zoology is a branch of biology that focuses on the study of animals. Within this branch, people may also specialize and study certain forms of animals. For example a person working in zoology might study fish biology and work as an *ichthyologist*. Alternately, a zoologist could specialize in the study of mammals and be called a *mammalogist*.

The discipline of zoology dates to the Ancient Greeks. In fact our primary system of classifying animals is largely based on Aristotle's work, though he made numerous classification errors. Early zoologists who followed Aristotle include many unknown collectors of animals who attempted to understand animals, or who were merely fascinated by the animal kingdom.

Modern zoology arrived with the invention of the microscope, but it would be a mistake to leave out the extremely important contributions of Charles Darwin. With Darwin's theory of evolution, understanding the relationship between humans and animals increased and further spurred interest in animals because humans were thought by some to have descended from them. As Darwin's theory gained acceptance, humans became part of the animal kingdom in a way that was both inclusive and humbling.

Zoologists that followed Darwin often studied animals in

relationship to humans. Knowledge of the possible relationships of animals changed some classifications, and studies in zoology continue to refine animal classifications. The more zoologists learn about animals, the more diverse and complex the field of zoology becomes.

Since specializations within zoology are so diverse, it's somewhat difficult to describe exactly what a zoologist does. This can vary a great deal. Most zoology students in Bachelor of Science programs study biology, chemistry, ecology, microbiology, cell biology, and other fields that will help them to specialize.

OVERVIEW

Zoology, the scientific study of animal life, builds on centuries of human enquiry into the animal world. It helps us to understand more about the natural world and the animal inhabitants of varied and changing environments. It is a subject of immense richness and diversity, and zoologists make a significant input to wider questions such as evolution, natural history and conservation.

Zoology has many branches, including the life and habits of animals, the diversity of animals, the systematic study of the vertebrates and invertebrates and their classification into numerous major and minor groups. More specialized aspects of Zoology include the study of animal structure (morphology and anatomy), function (comparative physiology), reproduction and development (embryology), parasites, the integration of body systems (endocrinology and neurobiology) and inherited characteristics (genetics and evolution).

Zoology is the study of animals. Among Muslim and specifically Andalusian writers and practitioners on zoology, there were two types of zoological studies: literary and practical, (related either to agriculture or veterinary medicine). These eventually merged in some ways, with both contributing to the scientific study of animals. Islamic learning inherited three traditions that fused into what we call zoology today. One was the pre-Islamic Arab tradition of nomadism and breeding of horses, camels, sheep and goats, which with the spread of Islam, came in contact with the Indian-Persian and Greek traditions of animal study.

In classical and Medieval times, writers and artists produced bestiaries – a bestiary is a zoo in a book – in which exotic animals were described. Many rulers kept gardens in which exotic animals were raised, such as nightingales and peacocks, and rare animals might feature as royal gifts. Falcons and other animals used for hunting were especially popular, and there were many guides on the art of falconine. Other fields related to zoology were the study of domesticated animais and their care, breeding (reproduction) and veterinary medicine. Sheep, cattle, and especially horses were important, but so were fowl, such as chickens, ducks, geese, and doves.

The most famous Muslim writer on animals is al-Jahiz, a literary figure in Abbasid Baghdad. He was able to draw on the works being translated in the House of Wisdom, and was known to rent bookshops in order to read what they contained. His most famous work is *Kitab al-Hayawan,* or *Book of the Animals,* which built upon the work of Aristotle's *Generation of Animals,* as well as including stories about animals, verses from the Qur'an and Hadith concerning animals, poetry and proverbs.

Zoology is an integral component of many related areas of animal biology including the study of interactions between animals and the relationships between animals and their environment (e.g. animal ecology and ecophysiology).

Advances in knowledge have resulted not only through use of traditional zoological methods but increasingly from approaches that employ the most up-to-date cellular, immunological and molecular techniques. Many current projects make use of molecular tools to investigate zoological problems. These include applications of molecular biology to track key events in developing embryos, use of the latest techniques to assess differential gene expression resulting from a particular treatment (e.g. change in temperature) and investigation of the relationships between groups of animals (e.g. molecular taxonomy).

Given the richness and diversity of animal life, studying

Zoology can seem a daunting task. For example, there are more species of beetles on earth than there are plant species, and beetles comprise just one of 26 orders of insects! At Dundee we tackle the problem of animal diversity by adopting a strong evolutionary approach. This approach recognizes that the diversity of animal structure and function is based on relatively few basic designs that had evolved by the period, 500 million years ago. We have built considerable flexibility into our degree programme, such that zoologists can opt either for a more environmentally oriented or a more molecular approach - to suit their interests.

The field of zoology is a large one, with numerous specialists and numerous disciplines attached to it. Zoology scientists might study all animals, and branch out into ecological studies, or they may evaluate the chemistry of certain animals. Some zoologists devote their work to the study of one animal only, while other zoology scientists evaluate the lives of long extinct animal populations in the field called *pale zoology*.

A pale zoologist might study with paleontologists, pale botanists, and may include physical anthropology in their studies. Anthropologists study both cultural and physical anthropology since they principally study interactions between animals and people.

One interesting branch of zoology is *crypto zoology,* which evaluates and attempts to classify animals only rumored to exist, like the Loch Ness monster or the Yeti. Crypto zoologists might also do field studies if an animal thought previously extinct is re-discovered.

Zoology is certainly an important field, enhancing our understanding of the world in which we live. For the zoologist, there are numerous working opportunities, though some may not be particularly lucrative financially.

Zoologists may contribute their studies to animal behaviorists, work in zoos, study animals in the wild, participate in archaeological digs, apply their knowledge to improve raising of animals for food, be part of cloning experiments, or work primarily in labs analyzing the cell biology of animals. This large disciple, covering a variety of sub fields, also may act as accessory to many related branches of science.

GOALS OF TEACHING BIOLOGY

INTRODUCTION

- Students will learn and retain a broad base of knowledge in the discipline of Biology in order to prepare for a wide variety of post-graduate opportunities; including jobs in academia or industry, medical, dental or other professional schools, or graduate schools in various disciplines of biology or education.
- Students develop critical thinking and analysis skills.
- Students learn practical skills in biology.
- Students improve writing and presentation skills in biology.
- Students receive good academic and career advice.
- Students gain experience with computer use as it pertains to biology.
- Students motivated to perform better.
- Students will be successful in gaining employment on Biology fields or in being admitted to graduate or Professional schools.

GOALS

Equal Access to Learning

University is committed to equity in policy and practice, the University continues to strive for full inclusion of all students in our academic community and within our classrooms. Consistent with University policy, all teaching staff underscore their commitment to making all students feel welcome in BI course classrooms, laboratories, and in learning groups. We affirm that all students have the right to feel accepted in all course environments and to participate in an academic programme free of intimidation, intolerance, or disrespect. Further, we stress that all students are responsible for welcoming other students into courses and for helping maintain a positive environment free of any discriminating actions.

Synergy with University Science Learning

OSU is implementing a new University-level strategic plan that stresses the creation of a dynamic and vibrant learning environment with students actively engaged in relevant and integrated educational experiences. Also established are outcomes for science courses within the baccalaureate core (emphasis on critical thinking, understandings of fundamental concepts, historical perspectives, interrelationships between disciplines, the nature of science, and understanding of relationships between science and society. The Biology Programme continues to actively seek to match University and College goals.

Support for all Participants

Biology Programme serves a wide variety of participants, including undergraduate students from all colleges, teachers (graduate students and faculty) from a variety of life science departments, support staff, and advisors.

Critical Analysis of Literature

To develop critical thinking skills, graduate courses principally utilize primary scientific literature. Using primary articles, students are taught how to evaluate and critically analyse - research problems, the methods employed to dissect them, and how conclusions are derived.

Communication Skills

Enhancing presentation skills (written and oral) is an important component to the graduate training programme. Through our Departmental seminar series (all students are required to present their research yearly), a grant-writing course, and the written Preliminary Exam students' guided in developing effective communication skills.

TEACHING GOALS

To support the development of students as informed, socially responsible members of society.

- Guide critical evaluation of information.
- Share an awareness of current events and issues in biology.
- Emphasize connections between the study of biology and other areas of human activity.
- Emphasize individual and collective responsibility for preserving biodiversity and the integrity of ecosystems.
- Encourage participation in community activities and service learning related to biology.

To Offer a High Quality Undergraduate Major Programme That Provides Both a Broad Foundation in Biological Sciences and an Opportunity for Specialized Training

Maintain a faculty committed first and foremost to high quality teaching and learning:

- That encourages the use of technology and innovative or alternative pedagogy.
- That engages student in research experiences both as part of course laboratories and independent projects.

Build a sufficient core of tenured and tenure-track faculty

- That responds to changing needs of the Department, the discipline, and the community.
- To replace faculty lost through retirements or resignations.
- To achieve an 80/20 ratio of full-time to part-time faculty sufficient to effect the Department's programme, provide student advising and mentoring, and participate in governance.

Address deficiencies or weakness in the core curriculum and concentration curricula identified through outcomes assessment by designing or redesigning courses and to encourage new course offerings as fields and faculty expertise grows and changes.

Work diligently to find ways to address the critical immediate space and equipment needs and to actualize the new science building which will house the Biological Sciences Department to provide laboratories, equipment, and ancillary facilities to further the teaching of state-of-the art biology.

Encourage group study and peer-teaching and learning by providing formalized space for these activities in the new biology facility.

Continue to expand opportunities and acquire resources for undergraduate research in biology and interdisciplinary science including workload credit for faculty who supervise student research.

Encourage academic enrichment opportunities for students such as service learning, internships, cooperative education, summer programs, and study at Moss Landing Marine Laboratories.

To Provide Substantial Support in the Preparation and Evaluation of Pre-health Professional Students and Secondary School Science Educators

Maintain current information on health professional school and credential requirements.

Continue to participate in the evaluation of health professional school applicants through faculty participation as members of pre-health professional interview committees and to seek clerical support for the process.

Continue to participate in the evaluation of single subject credential applicants.

Provide training in pre-health professional advising and single subject evaluation for faculty not currently involved in the processes to more evenly distribute the workload associated with these activities.

Work with the new Natural Sciences and Mathematics (NSM) Director for Student Services to develop college-wide support for pre-health professional and single subject students, faculty advisors, and the evaluation process.

Continue to provide faculty advisors for pre-health professional clubs and work with the clubs to coordinate activities that overlap club interests.

Continue to facilitate internships in health and educational settings for career exploration.

To Provide Training for Students Pursuing a Minor in Biological Sciences or The Issues in Natural Resources Management Certificate

- Continue to discuss course work requirements for the minor to determine if the requirements can be further broadened to make it more attractive to students in a greater number of majors.
- Evaluate the viability of the Certificate in Issues in Natural Resource Management and explore alternative ways to achieve the objectives of the certificate.

To Offer a High Quality Graduate Programme that Provides Advanced Academic and Research Training in Biology

- Encourage and support faculty participation in teaching and mentoring at the graduate level by means of
  - Clarifying the RTP document to acknowledge that activities involved in mentoring graduate students in a primary research environment (e.g., training on and offsite, taking graduate students to conferences, facilitating the advancement of their careers) are valued equally with primary faculty research that leads to peer reviewed publications.
  - Giving assigned time credit to faculty who are mentoring graduate students and having the assigned time adjusted for the number of students mentored.
  - Providing faculty who supervise graduate students with appropriate primary research

resources (e.g., space, equipment, safety measures, infrastructure support).

- Encourage and support student participation in graduate level research by means of
  - Providing adequate space for graduate student research, including space in the new biology facility
  - Seeking to expand the level of funding available to support graduate students.
  - Strengthening relationships with industry, government, and other academic institutions to provide research and career opportunities for graduate students and to inform our preparation of them for their careers.
  - Acknowledging their contribution to the department by assigning mailbox and photo space to graduate students upon their acceptance by a major advisor.
- Strengthen the curriculum of the graduate programme by
  - Implementing the new concentration in Molecular and Cellular Biology and moving towards the establishment of an MS in Molecular and Cellular Biology.
  - Enhancing the curriculum in the Biological Conservation Concentration.
  - Maintaining the currency of the curriculum through continued contacts with the community.
- Continue to provide the opportunity to obtain experience in college-level biology teaching through the Graduate Teaching Associate Programme.
- Improve graduate student advising by
  - Obtaining permanent assigned time for the Graduate Programme coordinator
  - Exploring the idea of having an entry orientation session for graduate students.
- Soliciting comments from graduate student alumni to learn more about the strengths and deficiencies in the Graduate Programme.

- Providing opportunity for feedback and evaluation from current graduate students,
- Revisiting the Graduate Programme admission and requirements process.
- Supporting interdisciplinary research within the Deparment and College.
- Developing a mandatory academic advising requirement for graduate students.

To Recruit and Retain Majors Particularly those from Diverse Backgrounds and Groups Underrepresented in The Biological Sciences

- Work with University outreach to explore recruitment activities at area high schools and community colleges.
- Expand articulation endeavors with community colleges.
- Design and implement an additional Department web page and other materials promoting the benefits of majoring in Biological Sciences at CSUS.
- Explore establishment of undergraduate scholarships for gifted high school students and community college transfer students.
- Continue to support the Science Educational Equity (SEE) Programme.
- Explore ways to successfully implement the requirement for mandatory advising in Biological Sciences.
- Work with College and University programs in retention efforts to foster a sense of community in the College including the development of appropriate space for student activities and academic advising in the College.
- Develop a list of student services resources and work with Student Services offices to streamline and coordinate services.
- Ensure the participation of tenured and tenure track faculty in lower division major and General

Education courses and the coordination of these courses by full-time faculty.

- Continue to participate in freshman learning communities and freshman and transfer orientation and "Freshman Welcome Day" activities.
- Explore participating in the General Education Freshman Seminar the development of upper division GE learning communities, and the development of biology-oriented skills seminars for majors.
- Continue to support student groups such as the Pre-Health Professional Student Organization, Field Biology Group, American Medical Association Student Association, Student Association of Laboratory Scientists, andMulticultural Organization of Science Students.
- Continue to participate in the Science Olympiad and Academic Talent Search.

To Provide High Quality Academic Advising

- Recognize and value the contribution of faculty in providing student advising.
- Provide training for new faculty on academic advising.
- Explore ways to successfully implement the requirement for mandatory advising in Biological Sciences.

To Provide High Quality Career Advising

- Facilitate internships by expanding partnerships with public and private agencies in the Sacramento region.
- Continue to pursue an active relationship with the campus Cooperative Education staff to expand opportunities for students to participate in Cooperative Education programs related to biology.
- Encourage students to attend the two seminar series in the Department and interact with professionals in the community who present seminars.

- Maintain a list of alumni who work as professionals in the Sacramento region.
- Continue to support an annual career fair/forum.
- Continue to support student organizations including: PPSO, SALS,
- Maintain contacts with the regional workforce.
- Continue to offer service learning in some of our courses.
- Facilitate interaction of our students and faculty with the University Career Centre.

To Provide Training in Biology for Non-Biology Majors

- Continue to work cooperatively with those departments that require Biological Sciences courses in their academic programs to ensure that course content and scheduling is appropriate.
- Continue partnership efforts with the M.S. in Physical Therapy including providing courses as a service to the programme, supervising Masters student research, and service on programme committees, as requested.
- Offer and maintain currency and coordination of existing General Education courses.
- Continue to participate in freshman learning communities.
- Explore participating in upper division GE learning communities.

To Increase Public Understanding of Biology Through Community Outreach

- Continue to provide Biological Sciences facilities tours and off-site educational presentations for K-12 students and community groups.
- Continue to participate in CSUS outreach activities and the Science Olympiad.
- Continue to participate in the Centre for Mathematics and Science Education (i.e., SCATS).
- Continue to provide opportunities for students to engage in service learning.

- Continue to work toward the development of a Centre for Regional Environmental Science and Technology (CREST).
- Continue to provide interviews for print, radio and television media.
- Continue to provide expertise for the general public regarding organisms.

To Document and Preserve a Record of The Local Biotic Diversity To Serve As A Teaching, Research, And Community Resource

- Preserve for purposes of teaching, research and community outreach museum and living collections of representative biotic diversity.
- Maintain space and technical support staff sufficient for effective curation of those collections.
- Continue to honour the intent of the C.M. Goethe bequest through the activities of the Department Goethe Committee which manages the C.M. Goethe Arboretum and Goethe grant sponsored research in Biological Survey and Genetics.
- Foster faculty and student research studies that further the study of plant and animal diversity.

To Advance The Development and Practice of Biology Through Research and Scholarly Activity in Biology and Science Pedagogy

- Obtain adequate resources and facilities to support faculty in supervising and mentoring undergraduate and graduate student research and in individual faculty research.
- Expand collaborations with public and private agencies in support of student and faculty research.
- Obtain assigned time for faculty research and grant writing.
- Obtain institutional and system-wide travel funds for faculty to attend professional meetings.
- Encourage faculty to attend teaching, technology, and assessment workshops.

To Promote Professional Development and Productivity of Faculty

- Recognize and value the unique contributions and strengths of each faculty member in furthering the mission of the Department in their own way.
- Continue to recognize that, while faculty are evaluated in four areas in the RTP process, that yearly the emphasis on particular areas will vary during the course of a career.
- Continue to support junior faculty in the RTP process and assist them in defining yearly goals via Faculty Professional Development Committees established for each new tenure-track faculty member.
- Recognize and support faculty mentoring of student research on par with independent research and publication in the RTP process.
- Recognize and support faculty conducting independent research, including research in the area of science pedagogy.
- Recognize and support faculty providing outstanding service to the University through faculty leadership on committees and in University governance and involvement in student support services and advising activities.
- Recognize and support faculty providing outstanding community service through such activities as involvement in service learning, service on community boards in a professional capacity, and playing leadership roles in professional societies.

BIOLOGY IN BLOOM TAXONOMY

INTRODUCTION

At the present time it is sufficient to state that instructional objectives are concrete statements of the goals toward which instruction is directed. They play an important role in the process of learning and instruction.

When developing instructional objectives, providing

instruction, and evaluating student performance, it is important to keep in mind that there are different levels or outcomes of learning. Distinguishing among different levels and outcomes of learning is important. If teachers are unaware of different levels of learning, they are likely to focus on one level to the detriment of others. For example, a teacher may teach a vast amount of factual information but never get around to teaching students to apply and synthesize this information. Or a teacher may teach higher level thinking skills without realizing that these skills require the prior learning of basic skills that must be integrated into these higher order skills. n addition, it is not unusual to see a teacher who wants her students to learn higher order thinking skills give examinations that require only lower level skills. Under such circumstances, the students are likely to put their efforts into the lower order skills. Skills at different levels must be taught (and tested) in different ways; and therefore it is important for teachers and other instructional designers to take into account the different levels and outcomes of instruction.

Bloom's *Taxonomy of Educational Objectives* is the most renowned description of the levels of cognitive performance.

Bloom's Taxonomy is a wonderful reference model for all involved in teaching, training, learning, coaching - in the design, delivery and evaluation of these development methods. At its basic level (refresh your memory of the Bloom Taxonomy overview if helpful), the Taxonomy provides a simple, quick and easy checklist to start to plan any type of personal development. It helps to open up possibilities for all aspects of the subject or need concerned, and suggests a variety of the methods available for delivery of teaching and learning. As with any checklist, it ... helps to reduce the risks of overlooking some vital aspects of the development required

Clearly, Bloom's Taxonomy has stood the test of time. Due to its long history and popularity, it has been condensed, expanded, and reinterpreted in a variety of ways. Research findings have led to the discovery of a veritable smorgasbord of interpretations and applications falling on a continuum ranging from tight overviews to expanded explanations.

Nonetheless, one recent revision (designed by one of the co-editors of the original taxonomy along with a former Bloom student) merits particular attention

For the more precise original Bloom Taxonomy terminology and definitions see the more detailed domain structures beneath this at-a-glance model. It's helpful at this point to consider ... the 'conscious competence' learning stages model, which provides a useful perspective for all three domains, and the concept of developing competence by stages in sequence.

A search of the World Wide Web will yield clear evidence that Bloom's Taxonomy has been applied to a variety of situations. Current results include a broad spectrum of applications represented by articles and websites describing everything from corrosion training to medical preparation. In almost all circumstances when an instructor desires to move a group of students through a learning process utilizing an organized framework, Bloom's Taxonomy can prove helpful. Yet the educational setting remains the most often used application.

In 1956, Benjamin Bloom, a professor at the University of Chicago, shared his famous "Taxonomy of Educational Objectives". Bloom identified six levels of cognitive complexity that have been used over the past four decades to make sure that instruction stimulates and develops students' higher-order thinking skills.

BLOOM'S TAXONOMY THINKING SKILLS

When working with special needs students, it is helpful to recognize certain attributes about the kind of learning tasks we are giving children to do. We typically assign reading, followed by some discussion, and end up with some form of evaluation. Let me suggest a "model" that more closely reflects information about how we all organize information and ideas.

Many years ago, Dr. Benjamin Bloom proposed a theoretical ranking of the levels of thinking that people use. At the simple and basic level, Bloom suggested, people operate at a very "concrete" level of knowledge. Moving beyond that, people are able to "comprehend" what the facts are about and to some extent, they are able to manipulate those ideas by comparing or contrasting or even retelling events in their own words.

At the next level of complexity of thought, individuals are able to "apply" what they have learned from facts and comprehension. This level of thinking permits them to demonstrate knowledge, solve or apply what they know to new and related situations. Moving beyond "application," the next level of thinking allows people to "analyse" what they know. At this level, typically they can classify, categorize, discriminate or detect information.

The two highest levels of cognitive thought, according to Bloom, are synthesis and evaluation. In "synthesis," the individual is able to put ideas together, propose plans, form solutions, and create new information. In the "evaluation" stage, the thinker is able to make choices, select, evaluate and make judgments about information and situations.

BLOOM'S TAXONOMY IN TEACHING

We typically start very young children out with simple tasks of "naming" or telling. We ask them to tell us how old they are. They are taught to count and sing simple rhymes. These are very concrete forms of knowledge. We are not particularly interested in whether they truly "comprehend" the concept of counting up, as getting more, or counting down, as getting less. Many special needs students have considerable difficulty moving very far beyond this concrete level of processing information, and they typically run into great frustration when asked to carry out higher levels of thinking on academic tasks, such as "compare and contrast," or when they are asked to "classify" animals into the correct phylum or species. Their information base can be very concrete, and they are most successful in doing tasks that accommodate their way of handling information. For them, the true-false test, the matching tests, and the "fill-in-the-blank" tests are likely to be more "user friendly."

Generalizing is frequently a noticeable deficit in learning

disabled students, as well of in several other areas of special needs. While the average child without handicapping neurobehavioral difficulties is usually able to learn facts and generalize them to new situations, the special needs students must be taught explicitly how the "known" is related to the "new" situation. Thus, we are confronted squarely with the consequent failure of the whole language approach to the teaching of reading. Whole language is based on the assumption that children who are exposed frequently to good literature and some elements of phonics can generalize their day to day experiences in learning that is not sequentially organized and explicitly taught. The resulting leaps in numbers of older students entering special education for failure in reading skills is mute testimony to the poor fit between learner and curriculum.

Learning disabled students, and other students with limitations in their cognitive development or communication skills, need very carefully developed curriculum and appropriate testing. Lessons should be started at a very concrete level, and initial questions should be concrete and based on facts. Drill-type teaching is a very essential component that lays solid foundations of information on which future learning can be built. It is important here to urge balance in the use of drill – it should never be the sole basis for any form of learning! It is a tool to help when repetition is essential for reaching mastery.

After reaching a fair level of mastery in a limited set of facts, whether in phonics or beginning math, or any subject, students should be moved "up" the level of difficulty on Bloom's taxonomy wherever possible. Children should be asked, as often as possible, to retell information in their own words. Allow them to make comparisons on what is similar from one object to another. Help them to notice attributes that are different so they can contrast the differences. Show them how to estimate. Use many concrete examples that reinforce their strength, but always try to help them stretch their boundaries at the same time.

For some students, the skills required of them at the

"comprehension" level may be as complex as they are able to master. That does not mean you should ignore opportunities to demonstrate to them other ways that people use and apply information. For some children, you will notice that in academic areas, they are quite limited in moving beyond "comprehension" or "knowledge" kinds of thinking. However, you will be amazed to see how readily they can solve a problem with a toy, in a challenging situation or working with some artistic media. We are certainly fearfully and wonderfully made, and we must never impose our preconceived notions of how much our children can achieve.

When we test at the "comprehension" level, we should be moving beyond simple "multiple choice" questions and/or true-false information. Such facts can be useful if we are only seeking to create "talking heads" who have all the right words, but who lack understanding. Our responsibility is to teach and train up children in understanding, which God promises to those who ask. Thus, our testing should move the child along toward higher levels of thinking skills, such as asking them to extend what they have learned. Can they illustrate the concepts they have just learned either in art and/or in writing? We can ask them to explain how the lesson in "silent /e/" is different from the "short vowel" rules we have used. Or, we might have them explain how the causes of a particular event in history are different from the causes of an event many years before. This kind of testing will strengthen their thinking, and it will promote longer retention of what they learn.

At the next level, we find that we are reaching the place where activity and application make our use of information "real" to us. Edgar Dale in the 1950's studied what kinds of information people remember the most and for the longest period of time. He concluded that when students "do the real thing," "simulate" the real thing, or teach others what they have learned, the retention rate is about 90% of what was taught. You can see on Bloom's taxonomy that "application" is a higher order thinking skill than simple recall or telling. To apply, the student must truly have facts correct and be able to relate them to each other and to what they already know.

The complex working of the mind that allows this kind of "integration" to occur permits the learner to reach higher levels of accomplishment. Teaching parents should be asking the student to solve problems by using learned information, constructing projects or posters, writing plays or acting out mini-plays, making original portfolios or building models in order to help them with applying new learning. Testing should be less involved with pencil and paper tests with short answers, and more directed towards essays, hands-on projects or presentations, or having the student writing his or her own test, to see how well they can target key concepts. Outlining helps students with such thinking levels, as well as using graphic organizers, such as "spider webs," to lay out information in a manner that reflects the organization of the material in the mind.

The last three levels of higher level thinking are rather fluid, and there seems less of a simple discernible line among the thinking attributes here. Obviously, higher order thought demands higher difficulty levels of testing. At this point, many special education students with learning disabilities will have great difficulty carrying out assignments or assessments. These students will require more externally supplied supports, or scaffolding. The teacher will need to provide explicit explanations of the organization of the teaching materials or texts. Highlighting by the instructor assists students in paying attention to the appropriate content.

Students can generate flash cards to drill themselves on the materials. The use of the flash cards should not be limited, however, to simple "word" and "definition" usage. Where possible, the teacher/parent should be requiring students to manipulate the information in several ways that teach higher order thinking. For example, have the students organize the cards into categories of dates, places, important men, important women, and so on. Likewise, have them create a large-scale timeline and place the cards in the correct order. These activities stimulate higher order skills while forcing a review of basic knowledge and learning skills. Flash cards can also be used to help plan a writing activity. Unlike computer-based cut and paste activity, the manual activity increases the use of visual, auditory, kinesthetic and tactile learning that is so essential for special learners.

These are just a few of the ideas that can be implemented in working with Bloom's taxonomy of thinking skills. I hope you have acquired a basic perspective that will assist you in planning future instruction and assessment that more closely meets the individual needs of your special student. These principles work well for ALL students.

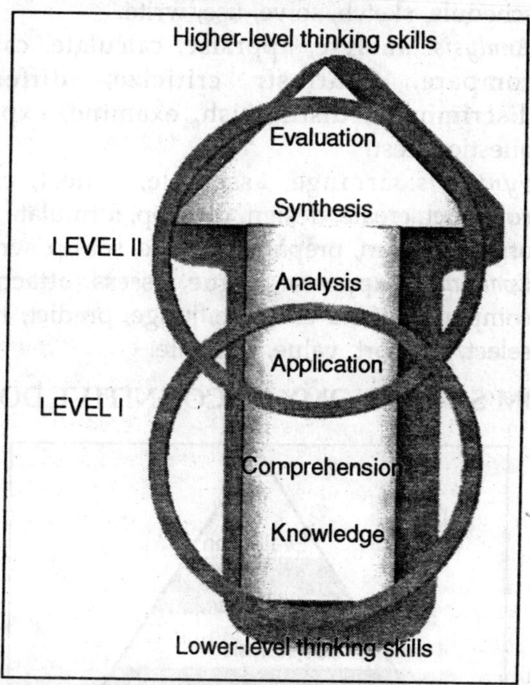

In 1956, Bloom headed a group of educational psychologists who developed a classification of levels of intellectual behaviour important in learning. Bloom found that over 95% of the test questions students encounter require them to think only at the lowest possible level...the recall of information. Bloom identified six levels within the cognitive domain, from the simple recall or recognition of facts, as the lowest level, through increasingly more complex and abstract mental levels, to the highest order which is classified as evaluation. Verb examples that represent intellectual activity on each level are listed here.

- *Knowledge:* arrange, define, duplicate, label, list, memorize, name, order, recognize, relate, recall, repeat, reproduce state.
- *Comprehension:* classify, describe, discuss, explain, express, identify, indicate, locate, recognize, report, restate, review, select, translate,
- *Application:* apply, choose, demonstrate, dramatize, employ, illustrate, interpret, operate, practice, schedule, sketch, solve, use, write.
- *Analysis:* analyse, appraise, calculate, categorize, compare, contrast, criticize, differentiate, discriminate, distinguish, examine, experiment, question, test.
- *Synthesis:* arrange, assemble, collect, compose, construct, create, design, develop, formulate, manage, organize, plan, prepare, propose, set up, write.
- *Evaluation:* appraise, argue, assess, attach, choose compare, defend estimate, judge, predict, rate, core, select, support, value, evaluate.

BLOOM'S TAXONOMY OF COGNITIVE DOMAIN

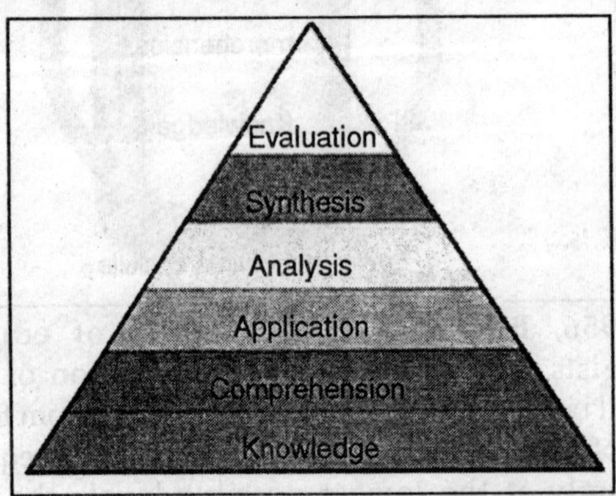

Bloom identified six levels within the cognitive domain, from the simple recall or recognition of facts, as the lowest level, through increasingly more complex and abstract mental levels, to the highest order, which is classified as evaluation. A description of the six levels as well as verb examples that represent intellectual activity are listed here.

KNOWLEDGE

Is defined as remembering of previously learned material. This may involve the recall of a wide range of material, from specific facts to complete theories, but all that is required is the bringing to mind of the appropriate information. Knowledge represents the lowest level of learning outcomes in the cognitive domain.

VERBS

Arrange, define, duplicate, label, list, memorize, name, order, recognize, relate, recall, repeat, reproduce state.

COMPREHENSION

Is defined as the ability to grasp the meaning of material. This may be shown by translating material from one form to another (words to numbers), by interpreting material (explaining or summarizing), and by estimating furture trends (predicting consequences or effects). These learning outcomes go one step beyond the simple remembering of material, and represent the lowest level of understanding.

VERBS

Classify, describe, discuss, explain, express, identify, indicate, locate, recognize, report, restate, review, select, translate.

APPLICATION

refers to the ability to use learned material in new and concrete situations. This may include the application of such things as rules, methods, concepts, principles, laws, and theories. Learning outcomes in this area require a higher level of understanding than those under comprehension.

Verbs

Apply, choose, demonstrate, dramatize, employ, illustrate,

interpret, operate, practice, schedule, sketch, solve, use, and write.

ANALYSIS

Refers to the ability to break down material into its component parts so that its organizational structure may be understood. This may include the identification of the parts, analysis of the relationships between parts, and recognition of the organizational principles involved. Learning outcomes here represent a higher intellectual level than comprehension and application because they require an understanding of both the content and the structural form of the material.

Verbs

Analyse, appraise, calculate, categorize, compare, contrast, criticize, differentiate, discriminate, distinguish, examine, experiment, question, test.

SYNTHESIS

Refers to the ability to put parts together to form a new whole. This may involve the production of a unique communication (theme or speech), a plan of operations (research proposal), or a set of abstract relations (scheme for classifying information). Learning outcomes in this area stress creative behaviors, with major emphasis on the formulation of new patterns or structures.

Verbs

Arrange, assemble, collect, compose, construct, create, design, develop, formulate, manage, organize, plan, prepare, propose, set up, write.

EVALUATION

Is concerned with the ability to judge the value of material (statement, novel, poem, research report) for a given purpose. The judgements are to be based on definite criteria. These may be internal criteria (organization) or external criteria (relevance to the purpose) and the student may determine the criteria or be given them. Learning outcomes in this area are highest in the cognitive hierarchy because they contain elements of all the other categories, plus conscious value judgments based on clearly defined criteria.

THE AFFECTIVE DOMAIN

The affective domain includes objectives which describe changes in interest, attitudes and values, and the development of appreciations and adequate adjustment. This domain has a pattern of development similar to the cognitive domain. At the lowest level, the child is merely aware of the fact that other people have particular attitudes and values. As children progress through personal experience, they slowly develop affective ideas which are uniquely their own. Again, it is felt that teaching should be directed towards this end rather than merely indoctrinating the child with the attitudes and values held by the teacher. Although some people would hold that there are some values which must be indoctrinated - respect for others' rights, honesty etc. - there is a school of thought which would seek to have these attitudes and values achieved by the child without this approach, through a process of development and clarification.

This domain relates to objectives concerned with interest, attitudes and values. The five levels of the affective domain from the simplest to the most complex are as follows:

- Receiving: Sensitivity to certain stimuli and a willingness to receive or attend to them.
- Responding: Involvement in a subject or activity or event to the extent of seeking it out, working with it or engaging in it.
- Valuing: Commitment to or conviction in certain goals, ideas or beliefs.
- Organisation: Organisation of values into a system, awareness of relevance of and relations between appropriate values and the establishment of dominant personal values.

Characterization by a Value Complex: Integration of beliefs, ideas and attitudes into a total philosophy of world view."

Category	*Example and Key Words*
Receiving Phenomena: Awareness, willingness to hear, selected attention.	*Examples:* Listen to others with respect. Listen for and remember the name of newly introduced people. *Key Words:* Asks, chooses, describes, follows, gives, holds, identifies, locates, names, points to, selects, sits, erects, replies, uses.
Responding to Phenomena: Active participation on the part of the learners. Attends and reacts to a particular phenomenon. Learning outcomes may emphasize compliance in responding, willingness to respond, or satisfaction in responding (motivation).	*Examples:* Participates in class discussions. Gives a presentation. Questions new ideals, concepts, models, etc. in order to fully understand them. Know the safety rules and practices them. *Key Words:* answers, assists, aids, complies, conforms, discusses, greets, helps, labels, performs, practices, presents, reads, recites, reports, selects, tells, writes.
Valuing: The worth or value a person attaches to a particular object, phenomenon, or behavior. This ranges from simple acceptance to the more complex state of commitment. Valuing is based on the internalization of a set of specified values, while clues to these values are expressed in the learneris overt behavior and are often identifiable.	*Examples:* Demonstrates belief in the democratic process. Is sensitive towards individual and cultural differences (value diversity). Shows the ability to solve problems. Proposes a plan to social improvement and follows through with commitment. Informs management on matters that one feels strongly about. *Key Words:* completes, demonstrates, differentiates, explains, follows, forms, initiates, invites, joins, justifies, proposes, reads, reports, selects, shares, studies, works.
Organization: Organizes values into priorities by contrasting different values, resolving conflicts between them, and creating an unique value system. The emphasis is on comparing, relating, and synthesizing values.	*Examples:* Recognizes the need for balance between freedom and responsible behavior. Accepts responsibility for one's behavior. Explains the role of systematic planning in solving problems. Accepts professional ethical standards. Creates a life plan in harmony with abilities, interests, and beliefs. Prioritizes time effectively to meet the needs of the organization, family and self. *Key Words:* adheres, alters, arranges, combines, compares, completes, defends, explains, formulates, generalizes, identifies, integrates, modifies, orders, organizes, prepares, relates, synthesizes.
Internalizing values (characterization): Has a value system that controls their behavior. The behavior is pervasive, consistent, predictable, and most importantly, characteristic of the learner. Instructional objectives are	*Examples:* Shows self-reliance when working independently. Cooperates in group activities (displays teamwork). Uses an objective approach in problem solving. Displays a professional commitment to ethical practice on a daily basis. Revises judgments and changes behavior in light of new evidence. Values people for what they are, not how they look. *Key Words:* acts, discriminates, displays, influences, listens, modifies, performs, practices, proposes, qualifies, questions, revises, serves, solves, verifies.

PSYCHOMOTOR DOMAIN TAXONOMY

INTRODUCTION

Simpson built this taxonomy on the work of Bloom and others:

- Perception: Sensory cues guide motor activity.
- Set - Mental, physical, and emotional dispositions that make one respond in a certain way to a situation.
- Guided Response: First attempts at a physical skill. Trial and error coupled with practice lead to better performance.
- Mechanism: The intermediate stage in learning a physical skill. Responses are habitual with a medium level of assurance and proficiency.
- Complex Overt Response: Complex movements are possible with a minimum of wasted effort and a high level of assurance they will be successful.
- Adaptation: Movements can be modified for special situations.
- Origination: New movements can be created for special situations.

The classification of educational objectives in the psychomotor domain:

Dave developed this taxonomy:

- *Imitation:* Observing and copying someone else.
- *Manipulation:* Guided via instruction to perform a skill.
- Precision: Accuracy, proportion and exactness exist in the skill performance without the presence of the original source.
- *Articulation:* Two or more skills combined, sequenced, and performed consistently.
- *Naturalization:* Two or more skills combined, sequenced, and performed consistently and with ease. The performance is automatic with little physical or mental exertion.

Harrow developed this taxonomy. It is organized

according to the degree of coordination including involuntary responses and learned capabilities:

- Reflex movements: Automatic reactions.
- Basic fundamental movement: Simple movements that can build to more complex sets of movements.
- Perceptual: Environmental cues that allow one to adjust movements.
- Physical activities: Things requiring endurance, strength, vigour, and agility.
- Skilled movements: Activities where a level of efficiency is achieved.
- Non-discursive communication: Body language.

The following list is a combination of the above taxonomies:

Psychomotor Domain		
Level	*Definition*	*Example*
1. Observing	Active mental attending of a physical event.	The learner watches a more experienced person. Other mental activity, such as reading may be a pert of the observation process.
2. Imitating	Attempted copying of a physical behavior.	The first steps in learning a skill. The learner is observed and given direction and feedback on performance. Movement is not automatic or smooth.
3. Practicing	Trying a specific physical activity over and over.	The skill is repeated over and over. The entire sequence is performed repeatedly. Movement is moving towards becoming automatic and smooth.
4. Adapting	Fine tuning. Making minor adjustments in the physical activity in order to perfect it.	The skill is perfected. A mentor or a coach is often needed to provide an outside perspective on how to improve or adjust as needed for the situation.

Reflex movements are actions elicited without learning in response to some stimuli.

Examples include: Flexion, extension, and stretch, postural adjustments.

Basic fundamental movement is inherent movement

patterns, which are formed by combining of reflex movements and are the basis for complex skilled movements.

Examples are: walking, running, pushing, twisting, gripping, grasping, manipulating.

Perceptual refers to interpretation of various stimuli that enable one to make adjustments to the environment. Visual, auditory, kinesthetic, or tactile discrimination. Suggests cognitive as well as psychomotor behaviour.

Examples include: coordinated movements such as jumping rope, punting, or catching.

Physical activities require endurance, strength, vigour, and agility which produces a sound, efficiently functioning body.

Examples are: all activities which require a) strenuous effort for long periods of time; b) muscular exertion; c) a quick, wide range of motion at the hip joints; and d) quick, precise movements.

Skilled movements are the result of the acquisition of a degree of efficiency when performing a complex task. Examples are: all skilled activities obvious in sports, recreation, and dance.

Non-discursive communication is communication through bodily movements ranging from facial expressions through sophisticated choreographic.

Examples include: body postures, gestures, and facial expressions efficiently executed in skilled dance movement and choreographic.

TEACHING AIMS

To deliver a range of education and training programmes that will empower public policy makers and public servants with the requisite knowledge, skills and capabilities to perform effectively within the changing context of governance and the new patterns of public service.

Increase both the quantity and the quality of the new generation of people practising public policy, policy analysis and management over the next decade.

Develop a high quality, fully integrated and staged

programme of accredited study and qualification in modern approaches to governance, public policy and management for senior policymakers and managers in the public, private and third sectors. This will build on and expand the Warwick MPA degree (the MBA for the public sector), as well as several inter-disciplinary programmes, including Postgraduate Diplomas in Local Government Management, Public Finance & Leadership, and Public Leadership & Management.

Improve the circuits of learning, exchange of experience and innovation between policymakers and managers from different levels of government, different sectors and different countries, through their participation in Warwick degrees and courses, and through an active Warwick alumni network.

Develop modern networked forms of learning ("combining high tech with high touch") to disseminate and distribute Warwick course modules and learning materials to students throughout the UK and world-wide (using web-board learning, computer conferencing, television, radio and digital interactive media).

Involve a number of University partners in the UK, Europe, the USA, Africa, Asia and Latin America in the design, development and delivery of these programmes. We envisage an integrated international programme with opportunities for cross-national exchanges, and for students to study in more than one country as part of their course.

Unit II

Lesson and Unit Planning

LESSON PLANNING

INTRODUCTION

Is special skill that is learned in much the same way as other skills. It is one thing to surf the Net to retrieve lesson plans from other sites and adapt them to your needs. It is quite another thing to have the skill to develop your own lesson plans. When you are able to create your own lesson plans, it means you have taken a giant step toward "owning" the content you teach and the methods you use, and that is a good thing. Acquiring this skill is far more valuable than being able to use lesson plans developed by others. It takes thinking and practice to hone this skill, and it won't happen overnight, but it is a skill that will help to define you as a teacher. Knowing "how to" is far more important than knowing "about" when it comes to lesson plans, and is one of the important markers along the way to becoming a professional teacher. It is also in keeping with a central theme of this site that you should learn to plan lessons in more than one way. The corollary is, of course, that there is no one "best way" to plan lessons. Regardless of the form or template, there are fundamental components of all lesson plans that you should learn to write, revise, and improve. The old adage, "Practice doesn't make perfect; perfect practice makes perfect" is at the core of learning this skill. Trust me on this.

Planning is an important part of any sphere of activity be it administration, economics, war or games. So why is planning necessary—the answer is obvious. Without a plan everything will go haywire and the end result is not what you want. Hence in order to achieve your goals, you have to plan your strategy. This is applicable even more while acquiring study skills. In order to benefit completely, lesson plans are absolutely necessary. The first and foremost part of the plan should be to work towards a definite goal. When a goal is set, the level of performance is enhanced and the ability to motivate yourself acts as an energetic vitalize. You are able to identify what you want to do, and what skills you have to acquire in order to achieve that. In the process of learning more about the skills that are required, you can evaluate yourself, identify your strengths and weakness and learn to improve upon previous performances. The Study skills lesson plans should be drawn up to cater to the difficulty level of all students, remembering that the range of difference in abilities is sometimes astounding. There are students with handicaps and disorders, slow learners and quick ones; any lesson plan should try to take this fact into account.

The study skills lesson plans should be so structured that it is dynamic and capable of being altered to suit the student's growing and changing needs. This helps to make the students more focused in their approach, as they are continually involved in the process of change. After all the students are the ultimate beneficiaries. This however does not mean that the content can be ignored. There should be adequate coverage of any topic so that a certain degree of mastery is indicated.

So, you have taken care of the dynamic levels and the content, but there can be no let up. All this becomes redundant if the study skills lesson plans do not allow you to keep track of the student's progress. This is often referred to as formative evaluation. Monitoring does not merely imply collecting information from the students about their progress. It goes way beyond that. It helps you to identify the lacuna in the lesson plans and allows you to make changes. If the plans have not met their objectives, obviously they would need restructuring. A more difficult situation to combat is the one that is normally encountered in a set of students with different abilities. Can a lesson plan be modified to cater to the fast learner and the slow learners at the same time? This is an eternal problem that teachers face. There is no straight answer –you have to tackle it as you encounter it.

Something that all study skills lesson plans should incorporate is time and room for practice, for it is practice, which hones the skills. Not only is the quantity of practice important, but also the quality. Last but not least, conceptual learning should be an inherent part of any lesson plan. Since there is no straight way for practicing this sort of learning, tackling problems in more than one way does help to some extent. Whatever study skills lesson plans are drawn up, remember there is no end to it. All plans have only beginnings, for human beings are unique, and it is this uniqueness, which is conceptually infinite. Whatever plan we draw up will be inadequate, but we do require a basic framework from which to operate.

This is among the most popular pages on the ADPRIMA web site, and for good reason. Good lesson plans do not ensure students will learn what is intended, but they certainly contribute to it. Think of a lesson plan as a way of communicating, and without doubt, effective communication skills are fundamental to all teaching. Lesson plans also help new or inexperienced teachers organize content, materials, and methods. When you are learning the craft of teaching, organizing your subject-matter content via lesson plans is fundamental. Like most skills, you'll get better at it the more you do it and think of ways of improving your planning and teaching based on feedback from your students, their parents, and other teachers. Developing your own lesson plans also helps you "own" the subject matter content you are teaching, and that is central to everything good teachers do.

It's simple; effective lesson plans communicate, ineffective ones don't. Teachers create lesson plans to communicate their instructional activities regarding specific subject-matter. Almost all lesson plans developed by teachers contain student learning objectives, instructional procedures, the required materials, and some written description of how the students will be evaluated. Many experienced teachers often reduce lesson plans to a mental map or short outline. New teachers, however, usually find detailed lesson plans to be indispensable. Learn to write good lesson plans - it is a skill that will serve you well as a teacher. If you're really serious, become proficient in writing effective learning objectives. All lesson plans begin, or should begin with an objective. Toward that end, I have developed a self-instructional, interactive programme that teaches this important skill within the context of lesson planning.

OVERVIEW

There are many maxims in education, great words of wisdom, and sincere advice from countless sources. But, without question, it is true that the very best teachers, the most effective teachers, are good planners and thinkers. The success of professional teachers doesn't "just happen." The road to success for teachers requires commitment and practice, especially of those skills involved in planning lessons and learning activities, and in managing classroom behaviour. Planning lessons is a fundamental skill all teachers must develop and hone, although implementation of this skill in actual teaching can, and usually does, take some time. Being able to develop an effective lesson plan format is a core skill for all who teach. If you are serious about improving your skill in planning lessons, you should begin by first thinking carefully about what the lesson is supposed to accomplish. *There is no substitute for this.* In teaching students how to develop lesson plans, the following are mistakes I have observed that students make most often:

OBJECTIVES OF LESSON PLAN

- The objective of the lesson does not specify what the student will actually do that can be observed. Remember, an objective is a description of what a student does that forms the basis for making an inference about learning. Poorly written objectives lead to faulty inferences.

- The lesson assessment is disconnected from the behaviour indicated in the objective. An assessment in a lesson plan is simply a description of how the teacher will determine whether the objective has been accomplished. It must be based on the same behaviour that is incorporated in the objective. Anything else is flawed.
- The prerequisites are not specified or are inconsistent with what is actually required to succeed with the lesson. Prerequisites mean just that — a statement of what a student *needs to know or be able to do* to succeed and accomplish the lesson objective. It is not easy to determine what is required, but it is necessary. Some research indicates that as much as 70% of learning is dependent on students having the appropriate prerequisites.
- The materials specified in the lesson are extraneous to the actual described learning activities. This means keep the list of materials in line with what you actually plan to do. Overcalling with materials is not a virtue!
- The instruction in which the teacher will engage is not efficient for the level of intended student learning. Efficiency is a measure that means getting more done with the same amount of effort, or the same amount with less effort. With so much to be learned, it should be obvious that instructional efficiency is paramount.
- The student activities described in the lesson plan do not contribute in a direct and effective way to the lesson objective. Don't have your students engaged in activities just to keep them busy. Whatever you have your students do should contribute in a direct way to their accomplishing the lesson objective.

A lesson plan that contains one or more of these mistakes needs rethinking and revision. Below is a rationale and guide to help you develop effective lesson plans and avoid the six common mistakes.

FIRST, YOU MUST KNOW HOW TO PLAN

The purpose of a lesson plan is really quite simple; it is to communicate. But, you might ask, communicate to whom? The answer to this question, on a practical basis, is YOU! The lesson plans you develop are to guide you in organizing your material and yourself for the purpose of helping your students achieve intended learning outcomes. Whether a lesson plan fits a particular format is not as relevant as whether or not it actually describes what you want, and what you have determined is the best means to an end. If you write a lesson plan that can be interpreted or implemented in many different ways, it is probably not a very good plan. This leads one to conclude that a key principle in creating a lesson plan is specificity. It is sort of like saying, "almost any series of connecting roads will take you from Key West Florida to Anchorage Alaska, eventually." There is however, one and only one set of connecting roads that represents the shortest and best route. Best means that, for example, getting to Anchorage by using an unreliable car is a different problem than getting there using a brand new car. What process one uses to get to a destination depends on available resources and time.

PROCEDURE OF LESSON PLANNING

The effective teacher cannot create a single extra second of the day — any more than anyone can. But the effective teacher certainly controls the way time is used. Effective teachers systematically and carefully plan for productive use of instructional time.

One of the primary roles that you will perform as a teacher is that of designer and implementer of instruction. Teachers at every level prepare plans that aid in the organization and delivery of their daily lessons. These plans vary widely in the style and degree of specificity. Some instructors prefer to construct elaborate detailed and impeccably typed outlines; others rely on the briefest of notes handwritten on scratch pads or on the backs of discarded envelopes. Regardless of the format, all teachers need to make wise decisions about the strategies and methods they will employ to help students move systematically toward learner goals.

Teachers need more than a vague, or even a precise, notion of educational goals and objectives to be able to sequence these objectives or to be proficient in the skills and knowledge of a particular discipline. The effective teacher also needs to develop a plan to provide *direction* toward the attainment of the selected objectives. The more organized a teacher is, the more effective the teaching, and thus the learning, is. Writing daily lesson plans is a large part of being organized.

Several lesson plan outlines will be presented. You as a teacher will probably begin by choosing a desirable outline and sticking fairly close to it. Planning and classroom delivery innovations usually come once you are in the classroom with your own set of learners, have developed your own instructional resources, and have experimented with various strategies. Although fundamental lesson planning elements tend to remain unchanged, their basic formula is always modified to suit the individual teacher's lesson preparation or style of presentation.

The lesson plan is a dreaded part of instruction that most teachers detest. It nevertheless provides a guide for managing the learning environment and is essential if a substitute teacher is to be effective and efficient. Three stages of lesson planning follow:

Pre-Lesson Preparation

Goals
Content
Student entry level

Lesson Planning and Implementation

- Unit title
- Instructional goals
- Objectives
- Rationale
- Content
- Instructional procedures

- Evaluation procedures
- Materials

Post-Lesson Activities

Lesson planning involves much more than making arbitrary decisions about "what I'm going to teach today." Many activities precede the process of designing and implementing a lesson plan. Similarly, the job of systematic lesson planning is not complete until after the instructor has assessed both the learner's attainment of the anticipated outcomes and effectiveness of the lesson in leading learners to these outcomes.

One final word. Even teachers who develop highly structured and detailed plans rarely adhere to them in lock-step fashion. Such rigidity would probably hinder, rather than help, the teaching-learning process. The elements of your lesson plan should be thought of as *guiding principles* to be applied as aids, but not blueprints, to systematic instruction. Precise preparation must allow for flexible delivery. During actual classroom interaction, the instructor needs to make adaptations and to add artistry to each lesson plan and classroom delivery.

LESSON PLANNING FOR BEGINNERS

Start and End

Visualize how you would like your ideal lesson to start.....

Maybe the children are lining up outside your classroom. They are quiet or talking calmly. Perhaps you have the odd word with them about their appearance, a little "ça va?", a personal bit of banter in English here and there.

The class are now in the room having taken out their books. They are calmly standing behind their table. You wait for total silence and greet them with a "Bonjour tout le monde!"

Well, it's probably possible for you to have that start to most lessons if you work at it. These routines don't just happen, however. You need to work at them each day until you have the start to the lesson you would like. Children have to learn routines and you have to practise them until they get them right. Be insistent, persevere, try not to accept second best. When they are standing in front of you use eye contact, make sure the class know you are looking at them, maybe with a smile, maybe severely.

In the real world, of course, it doesn't always work that way, so you could help the process along with a trick or two. With younger classes why not tell the class that you are going to count down from 20 to zero and that they must have all their books out by the time you get to zero? Or why not have the class recite or sing the alphabet as they come in and they have to have all their books ready by the time they get to Z? When it comes to the class sitting down, why not occasionally break the routine by saying that they can sit down when they hear the first letter of their name?

These patterns exploit the behaviourist dimension of learning. Children like habits, they know what to do, and they feel safe with them, as do you.

The mood of a class when it arrives will be partly dependent on the previous lesson. If they have been very quiet for an hour they may need to be noisier now. If they have been allowed to be too noisy in the previous lesson this could carry on to your lesson.

What if you get latecomers? In most cases make little fuss. Perhaps you have taught them to say "Excusez-moi, je suis en retard". In certain cases you may need to make a big fuss, show great disapproval. In this way the rest of the class know that you will not accept lateness and that they may be embarrassed in public if they are late. If a whole class is very late for no good reason you may need to have the class back at break or lunchtime to make your point

Ends of lessons need a tidy routine as well. I try to end with a "Rangez vos affaires". Then I ask classes to stand with a "Levez-vous". To ensure an orderly departure I would let the class out in rows or boys first, then girls (or vice versa). Even that last trick makes the class listen to whether you are going to say "Les garçons" or "les filles" first. They will let you know if you are favouring one group over the other! Make sure you leave enough time for your end routine. It's very easy to be rushed at the end. Give yourself and your class plenty of time to write down any homework.

Planning a Sequence of Lessons

You will hopefully have a well-organized scheme of work in your department. In my experience it is difficult to plan every lesson too far in advance because you have to adapt to the pace and the needs of the class in front of you and they are all different. I do my detailed lesson planning a week ahead. I hope to get my Sunday mornings back one day!

Over a sequence of lessons try to mix up the skills you are going to practice. Allow for some reading, listening, speaking and writing. Remember that students become good at what you practice. If you do lots of oral work they will get better at oral work. If you do lots of grammar, they get good at grammar, and so on. Think about when you have your lessons with the class. You may be wise to plan for a greater amount of "passive" work like listening, gap-filling, dictate, reading work in the afternoons. They are tired, you are tired, and may find it hard to get a class going for oral work. Conversely, morning lessons may be better for a larger diet of oral work (pair work, group work, question and answer, games, repetition). There is no doubt that feeling the mood of a class and a degree of flexibility and important attributes of a classroom teacher.

Plan for revision from one lesson to the next. This is vital. Your start to the lesson might be a quick recap of a grammar point or some vocal from the previous lesson. Don't just revise from the previous lesson, go back over various things you have done in the last few lessons. Remember that many children's memories are nowhere as good as yours. The idea of "little and often" is a key one for language teachers.

Planning Individual Lessons

Plan for variation within a lesson. In a one-hour session

you might include four, five or more different tasks. Try to put the oral work nearer the start of the lesson. Put the quieter activities nearer the end. Work in bursts of, say, 10 minutes. The attention span of youngsters is often quite short. Why not set short time targets to create a slight sense of urgency.

Make sure each task follows on logically from the previous one and that you are constantly reinforcing the main learning points. You may only be working on one or two key points in a whole lesson. Be prepared to repeat tasks in different ways. You might do a task from a worksheet or the board orally and then get the class to do the same task in writing. This leads to a quick transition, reinforces previous learning and practises more than one skill.

Be crystal clear with your instructions. Use English where you need to. Don't use a questioning intonation when you give an instruction. Children are quite happy to be told what to do firmly and politely.

Try to ensure tidy transitions from one task to the next. This is a tough one. When you stop one task there is a natural release of tension and children tend to start talking off the subject at that point. You may actually want a bit of that, because it acts as a pause for breath before the next task. On the whole, however, it wastes valuable time and you have to work at transitions just like you have to work at starts and ends.

Why not tell the class why it's important to have a quick transition? Let them into your thinking a bit; make them part of the process. If you have a reward system, why not tell them that the first three to finish will get a merit/stamp/house points etc?

Try to mix up your "interaction styles" with the class. Don't talk too much to them, they will probably get bored and learn less. Elicit responses, ask for hands up, sometimes say that you are going to just choose students to answer. (That's a controversial one since we don't want to make students uncomfortable with language learning, we don't want them scared, yet we do need to ensure they are concentrating. If you use this technique sparingly it can work well. The class come to attention and you just need to ensure that you don't throw an impossibly hard question to a student.)

Use pair work when you are confident the class will do it usefully. Use games when you are confident the class will not abuse the situation. Your lesson does not need to be fun. It's great and it's motivational when you are having fun, but the main aim is to work!

Use the computers. Many children who are not very comfortable doing language learning will be more at ease and learn more with a screen in front of them. Technology is great for us language teachers, use it a good deal, but remember that language learning is primarily about communicating with people so do not over rely on computers.

When you start teaching you will need to write out your lesson plan in some detail, preparing exactly which questions you are going to ask, how you are going to drill an item, how you are going to mix, say, group repetition with individual oral work. This takes time and care. With more experience these skills will become second nature and your preparation will be less time-consuming, allowing you to focus on other areas of your professional life.

Seating Plans

Many teachers find it useful to have a seating plan which can later be adjusted depending on the behaviour of individual students. We sit our younger classes in a boy-girl pattern mainly, to be honest, to keep potentially chatty friends apart (boys tend to hang around with boys, girls with girls). It may also be the case that the different leaning styles of boys and girls complement each other.

Why not change totally your seating plan every now and again? If children always work with the same partner they will always hear the same accent, the same errors, always be in the comfort zone, maybe not do enough work. I find that occasionally saying "Now go and work with someone you do not know very well" gives a freshness to lessons and gets students to put in a bit more effort.

To learn names you could either draw your seating plan

out, or get the children to make name plates which they put on their desk for the first few lessons. Some teachers take a photo of the class for their planner. As you walk around the class in the early days try to learn names by looking at exercise books. Hand out exercise books yourself getting students to put up their hand. It all helps to learn names quickly.

Correcting

In class oral work you need to find a balance. Tend to allow you brightest student to answer first to give a good model. If someone makes an error, usually correct them with a positive tone. Go to other students, then return to the student who made the error so that they have a chance to do it well without your help. Make the whole idea of pronouncing accurately fun. Try to get children to enjoy making the funny sounds. Use backward repetition. E.g. A student says "natashion" instead of"natation". Get the whole class to say "on", then "ion", then "sion", then "ation", then "tation", then "atation", then the whole word. Then get the individual to say the word. Speak English with an amusing French accent. Why not get students to do the same, along with shrugging shoulders and flailing arms?

When correcting written errors in an exercise book, it is wise to make sure students write on alternate lines so that your correction are clear to them. If there is a common pattern to their errors, for example, always missing adjective agreements, then highlight this with numbers or asterisks. Comment on it at the end of their work and ask them to focus on this next time.

Marking

How much marking should you do? Much depends on the nature of the work you have set. If it is easy to mark with ticks, then you ought to some in class time. It is a well-structured task, children learn from it (probably more than when you hand them back their book with some red or green ink on it) and it saves you time. On the other hand, your students need to know that you are going to spend time looking carefully at their work, making sure it is neat and careful, giving them personal feedback and advice. The exercise book is your quiet and confidential way of communicating with your students and they usually value highly what you write to them. Words of praise in the exercise book go a long way. Equally, if you know that the work is not up to scratch then be prepared to cross it out or give a very low mark. You will probably find that the next piece is much better and that the student is back on track.

With weaker students do not correct every error as this is dispiriting and confusing. Focus on the key teaching point you want to get home. With clever students be particularly fussy, they need to be stretched and need to know that you expect perfection.

Target Language

Language teachers talk a lot about this and it is fair to say that opinions vary! I'll put this as simply as I can: children need to hear lots of the target language to allow their brains to exploit their natural language learning capability. But children also need to develop a relationship with you, the teacher, and they need to understand what they have to do in a lesson. So, my rule would be use the target language most of the time, maybe in chunks of ten minutes or so, then "release tension" with some English. Try not to constantly "echo", by which I mean use a bit of French then instantly translate it into English. Why should a child bother to listen to the French if they know you are going to translate it?

Why not occasionally check meaning with a "Comment dit-on en angles?". Whatever you do, don't lose the class by speaking too much of the target language for them. Students often report that that they lose interest when the teacher doesn't use English enough. Match your use of target language to the needs of the class, but try to use as much target language as you can. Don't get lazy about it.

Ultimately the amount of the target language used will depend on the quality of the lesson planning. A well-planned lesson with good visual support will allow you to use lots of the target language with nearly every class. Use mime, gesture, flashcards, pictures, PowerPoint, OHP, written words on the board – whatever it takes.

Learning Styles

Without getting into the whole area of multiple intelligence and learning styles, let's just say that different students do learn in different ways. Language learning is demanding on the ears and eyes, but you can mix up your planning to include body movement (Simon Says works with all ages!). Why not get classes to chant verb paradigms while pointing in different directions for different persons of the verb? Why not get students to spell out words in the air with their fingers? Get them to move around the class looking for words you have stuck up? Get then to come up and use the board. Let them be the teacher sometimes. Let them jump up and down while singing the alphabet to an American marines marching song. You know the one! Even using a computer allows a fidgety child to be busy with their hands and probably suits the so-called kinaesthetic learner.

Mathematical children may enjoy number games and code breaking vocab games. Musical children may enjoy singing. Artistic children may like making posters or drawing on the board.

Teaching Grammar

Giving grammar rules is important. Most children like to know how the language works and many are good at applying the rules they have learned. Do this with notes, presentations and examples. Give them oral and written drills to practice.

However, the kind of internalization of grammar rules (which allows learners to use the language creatively and without having to stop and think about the rule) can only be developed if you give students lots of input in the target language and lots of practice. I sometimes say to my classes that if they keep their eyes and ears open during lessons nature will take its course and they will make progress. I tell students why I am doing things in a certain way so that understand how they are learning. They are often interested in ideas to do with child language acquisition and second language learning.

So make sure you incorporate all sorts of opportunities to practise grammatical structures: drills (repetition, question-answer, answer-question, structured written questions, gap fill, multi-choice etc). Don't just do three or four examples; make sure students hear lots of examples and hopefully some of the practice will stick.

Get students to work out rules for themselves following an oral introduction. This is, ideally, better than just giving the rule before practising it. Don't dismiss the idea, though, of just giving a rule – this has the merit of clarity.

Short oral grammar drills make good starts to lessons: "Je vous donne une phrase au présent, transformez la phrases au passé composé". Give a couple of examples, then do some with the whole class. Maybe they could then try some with a partner.

Tips

Don't spend ages making your own resources when there is so much good published material and free material on the internet. Do be careful, however, that the published material suits the learners in front of you. If you think your course book is poorly suited to your students' abilities, then tell someone.

Expect high standards. If you want your students to present work neatly insist on it and tale marks off if they do not reach the standard you have set.

If you want your class to be silent when writing or listening, try to insist on it. You are the boss! If students start to call out questions rather than putting up a hand, try to cut this out early in the year and it will pay dividends later.

If pairs or groups of students are too noisy you can threaten them with being separated. In the end, you may need to separate them. If a parent says "Well, why didn't you separate them?" you need a good answer!

If a student is persistently disruptive or disrespectful use the support networks in your school sooner rather than later. In the end, though, you do need to win the class's respect. Don't let your classroom become a battleground between you and them. Work on individual students rather than criticizing the whole group. If your lesson is poorly planned or at the wrong level you will suffer the consequences.

Use lots of praise, but not necessarily in public. A quiet word in the ear will be more effective and will go a long way to winning a child's confidence.

If you have a bad lesson try not to brood too long over it. Your class won't worry about it nearly as much as you. Your lesson is one small part of their day. You can start afresh the next day.

IMPORTANCE OF LESSON PLAN

A lesson plan is a plan for learning. As is true in most activities, the quality of planning affects the quality of results. Successful executives and professional people know the price of excellence is careful preparation. A lawyer spends hours planning a case before appearing in court. A minister does not ad-lib a sermon, but plans days or weeks in advance. In anticipation of the big game, the coach spends hours planning the plays and watching the team execute them. Should we attempt such a complicated process as learning with less attention than is given to other important activities? The answer is obvious: of course not. The effective instructor devotes much time and energy in carefully planning and preparing each lesson, whether the lesson encompasses one or several periods of instruction.

To ensure the greatest probability of learning, we must carefully select and arrange activities that will produce the desired learning outcomes in our students. Only through careful planning can we be certain we include all necessary information and have our lesson plan properly organized to achieve the lesson objective.

The complete cycle of lesson planning includes the following steps as shown below:

Determining the objective, researching the topic as defined

by the objective, selecting the appropriate instructional method, identifying a usable lesson planning format, deciding how to organize the lesson, establishing a strategy statement, choosing appropriate support material, preparing the introduction and conclusion of the lesson, and preparing a final outline.

Determining the Objective

Often begin our lesson planning with an objective or objectives clearly in mind. At other times, the objective may be shaped by the research and additional planning we do. In other words, although the first step of the lesson planning process is to determine the objective, our objective may not fully evolve until after we have completed other steps of the process.

Objectives need to be student-centered. We should not state them in terms of what we want to teach, but rather in terms of what we want our students to learn. For instance, the objective of a lesson on developing a lesson plan might be for each student to know the eight steps of effective lesson planning as listed in this chapter.

Teaching Lesson at Higher Level

We might want each student to comprehend the eight steps appropriate to effective lesson planning or even to be able to apply the eight steps of lesson planning. But whatever the level, the student-centered objective should guide our subsequent planning. Without a clear objective, we won't know if we, or more importantly, our students ever get there.

Researching the Topic

After writing or determining an instructional objective, we are ready to decide on the main points of the lesson and gather materials about the lesson topic. Normally we do not collect a mass of research materials and then develop an objective to match the findings. Not only is this approach inefficient, but it is also likely to be ineffective. It may well ignore the specific needs of the students and the Air Force.

The objective should determine the research needed. On the other hand, research may justify a decision to modify an objective or rearrange main points for greater accuracy or clarity.

Appropriateness and usefulness are two important criteria for selecting relevant material. To be appropriate, information should relate to the lesson objective and have a high possibility for student retention. To be useful, it should aid both the instructor and the students in the teaching-learning process. If the instructor selects material solely on the basis of its interest, a lesson may be filled with interesting information of little learning value. On the other hand, dry, uninteresting facts—even though very important—may also defeat the instructor's purpose. Students are more likely to grasp and retain facts and concepts enriched with interesting support material and arranged in a way to enhance learning.

With the objective clearly in mind, we are now ready to gather actual material or do research on the subject. The sources for this material are our own experiences, the experience of others we gain through conversation and interviews, and written or observed material. Instructors concerned with teaching a good lesson will often draw from all of these sources.

The first step in researching a lesson topic is to see what we ourselves know about the subject. Our personal knowledge may suggest a tentative organization, but more importantly, it will point to gaps in our knowledge needing further research.

The second step in the research process is to draw on the experience of others. The most fruitful source is the expert who may help us clarify our thinking, provide facts and testimony, and suggest sources for further research.

Library and Internet

Libraries and the internet provide an abundance of sources such as books, newspapers, magazine articles, scholarly journals, abstracts, subject files, and microfilms. Quantity is no problem; quality is more difficult. We must always concern ourselves with the accuracy and relevance of the material we select. For example, using an article from 1950 to discuss atomic physics today might well lead to inaccurate, irrelevant conclusions.

The next step in the research process is to evaluate the material gathered. We will probably find we have enough material for several lessons. We must now combine some ideas, eliminate others, and perhaps expand on what we found in the research materials. We will also want to give special attention to the types of support material we have selected (definitions, examples, comparisons, statistics, and testimony). Later in this chapter we will discuss types of support material in detail.

Sometimes we have an organizational pattern in mind before we start. If not, as we gather our material, we will probably see the ideas begin to form into some type of pattern. Later in this chapter, we will discuss ways of organizing the lesson.

During the research phase, the instructor is likely to find material students should read to prepare for a given class session. If we keep this possibility in mind when we begin our research, we can prepare a suggested student reading list and save time in selecting student references. When deciding on supplementary reading for the students, choose interesting and informative materials that reinforce or support the lesson objectives.

Selecting Instructional Methods

After deciding exactly what to teach, the instructor determines how best to teach it and what instructional method to use. When related to instruction, "method" refers to a combination of techniques or skills used by the instructor to engage students in meaningful learning experiences.

Philosophy Underlying Selection

We should choose a teaching method suited to the student's needs as a learner. In making the selection, we consider the ways people learn—by doing, discussing, listening, observing, and participating. We should select the instructional method most effective for guiding students toward desired learning outcomes. Our role is to select the method and the techniques that will result in a meaningful learning experience.

Selection Process

No one method is suitable for all teaching situations, because no single method is sufficiently flexible to meet the needs of students in every learning situation. In general, the nature of a learning outcome suggests the type of activity most helpful to students in achieving that outcome.

If, for example, we want students to gain skill in performing a certain task, one of the activities should be practice in performing the task. If the desired outcome is knowledge, students should observe, listen, and/or read so they can relate what they are learning to their own experience. If students must learn to apply a principle, the instructor should ask them to solve problems or perform tasks requiring an application of that principle.

The instructional approach we choose for one learning outcome may be different from the approaches we select for other outcomes in the same lesson. Our primary concern is to plan and select the most appropriate approach for students to achieve each outcome.

Lesson Planning Format

Good lesson planning is essential for any systematic approach to instruction. Although many instructors become discouraged with the time required for good lesson planning, a well written and properly used lesson plan can be a very worthwhile teaching aid.

Experienced instructor's use written lesson plans for a variety of purposes. They can be checkpoints to ensure well-planned learning experiences. They can serve as teaching guides during lessons and as references for other instructors who may teach for us in emergencies. They can also serve as convenient records of an instructor's planning techniques and methods of teaching. One of the most practical functions of lesson plans is they serve as step-by-step guides for instructors in developing teaching and learning activities.

WRITING INSTRUCTIONAL OBJECTS

Instructional objectives may also be called performance objectives, behavioral objectives, or simply objectives. All of these terms are used interchangeably. Objectives are specific, outcome based, measurable, and describe the learner's behaviour after instruction.

The purpose of instructional objectives and performance outcomes is to define the type of learning that will occur at the conclusion of instruction and how learning will be assessed. Both objectives and performance outcomes should be written as precisely as possible in order to best determine whether they have been achieved. In order to write accurate instructional objectives, a designer should be cognizant of the different learning domains as well as different formats for writing them. Here, we outline the three most prominent formats: the Mager format, the ABCD format, and the Gagné and Briggs format.

THE MANAGER FORMAT

A Critical Tool in the Development of Effective Instruction (1997), Mager outlines three important characteristics to include in all instructional objectives. They are:

- *Performance:* An objective always states what a learner is expected to be able to do and/or produce to be considered competent.
- *Conditions:* An objective describes the important conditions (if any) under which the performance is to occur.
- *Criterion:* An objective describes the criteria of acceptable performance; that is, it says how well someone would have to perform to be considered competent.

Ultimately, the Mager format includes the learner's actions, the learning conditions, and the criteria for assessing the learner's performance.

The following are examples of the Mager format:

Given a list of thirty five chemical elements (condition), the learner must be able to recall and write the valences (performance) of at least thirty (criterion).

Given a meter scale (condition), the learner is to be able to identify the value indicated by the position of the pointer (performance) as accurately as the construction of the meter will allow (criterion).

THE GAGNÉ AND BRIGGS FORMAT

The Gagné and Briggs format for writing instructional objectives consists of five components. They are:

Situation
Learned Capability
Object
Action
Tools and Other Constraints

The components of the Gagné and Briggs format match Mager's condition, performance, and criterion, only to add the **object**, or content, of the learning activity as well as any tools **used**. Here are some examples of objectives according to Gagné & Briggs:

Given a battery, light bulb, socket, and pieces of wire (situation), demonstrate (learned capability) the making of an electronic circuit (object) by connecting wires (action) to battery and socket (tools) and testing the lighting of the bulb (action).

In response to a question (situation), the learner will state (learned capability) orally (action) three technological trends that will affect the future capabilities of navies (object). The answer is to be completed in three minutes (constraints/tools).

THE ABCD FORMAT

The name of the ABCD format for writing instructional objectives is simply a mneumonic for:

- Audience
- Behaviour
- Condition
- Degree

These are the four components that comprise the instructional objective. Notice again that it is similar to Mager's format, yet includes an additional element for identifying the target audience. Below are examples of the ABCD format:

Given all the basic shapes - cone, cylinder, cube, and sphere (condition), each second-semester geometry student (audience) will identify (behaviour) orally each shape (degree).

Using tape recorded readings of the tryout sessions for the school play (condition), students in the drama class (audience) will select (behaviour) the proper voice for each character as indicated in the drama text (degree).

CLASSIFICATION OF OBJECTIVES

Teachers should classify objectives because the type of objectives attempted dictate the selection of instructional methods, media and evaluation used in the lesson. Objectives may be classified according to the primary learning outcomes that take place. These learning outcomes are classified into one of three domains (categories): cognitive, psychomotor or affective. Let's take a closer look at these categories to see how they differ.

COGNITIVE DOMAIN

The Cognitive Domain receives the most attention in instructional programs and includes objectives related to information or knowledge. Benjamin Bloom and his colleagues (1956) developed a widely accepted taxonomy, referred to as Bloom's Taxonomy (method of classification on differing levels of higher order thinking) for cognitive objectives. This taxonomy has been adapted by Anderson and Krathwohl (2001) for relevance in 21st century learning and remains the most significant model used. Presented here is the revised taxonomy, known as the Revised Bloom's Taxonomy, as well as links for more reading. Six levels of learning are in the classification. The lowest level is remembering. The remembering level is followed by five increasingly difficult levels of mental abilities: understanding, applying, analysing, evaluating and creating.

BLOOM'S TAXONOMY

Remembering

Objectives written on the remembering level (the lowest cogitive level) requires the student to recall or recognize specific information. Below are verbs appropriate for objectives written at the remembering level.

- Define fill in the blank identify label list.
- Locate match memorize name recall.
- Spell state tell underline state.

Understanding

Objectives written on the understanding level, although a higher level of mental ability than remembering, requires the lowest level of understanding from the student. Below are verbs appropriate for objectives written at the understanding level.

- Convert describe explain interpret paraphrase.
- Put in order restate retell in your words rewrite summarize.
- Trace translate.

Applying

Objectives written on the applying level require the learner to implement (use) the information. Below are verbs appropriate for objectives written at the applying level.

- Apply compute conclude construct demonstrate.
- Determine draw find out give an example illustrate.
- Make operate show solve state a rule or principle use.

Analysing

Objectives written on the analysing level require the learner to break the information into component parts and describe the relationship. Below are verbs appropriate for objectives written at the analysing level.

- Analyse categorize classify compare contrast.
- Debate deduct determine the factors diagnose diagram.

- Differentiate dissect distinguish examine infer.
- Specify.

Evaluating

Objectives written on the evaluating level require the student to make a judgment about materials or methods . Below are verbs appropriate for objectives written at the evaluating level.

- Appraise choose compare conclude decide.
- Defend evaluate give your opinion judge justify.
- Prioritize rank rate select support.
- Value.

Creating

Objectives written on the creating level require the student to generate new ideas, products and ways of viewing things. Below are verbs appropriate for objectives written at the creating level.

- Change combine compose construct create.
- Design find an unusual way formulate generate invent.
- Originate plan predict pretend produce.
- Rearrange reconstruct reorganize revise suggest.
- Suppose visualize write.

PSYCHOMOTOR DOMAIN

The Psychomotor Domain includes objectives that require basic motor skills and/or physical movement such as construct, kick or ski.

AFFECTIVE DOMAIN

The Affective Domain includes objectives pertaining to attitudes, appreciations, values and emotions.

PREPARATION AND USE OF UNIT PLAN

PREPARING UNIT PLAN

In this topic we will study, how to prepare Unit Plan. It is a general overview that highlights the key points of creating a unit plan. Below is a list of the steps involved in developing a lesson plan as well as a description of what each component should be.

Step 1: The first thing to consider, obviously, is what you want to teach. This should be developed based upon your state (or school) standards. You also need to be aware of what grade level you are developing the lesson plan for (and keep that in mind of course), and also record a time estimate for your lesson plan to help in time budgeting. Once you have your topic, you can begin determining how you want to teach the topic. If you didn't use the state standards to help in developing your topic, refer to them now to see what specific standards your lesson plan can fulfill. Having your lesson plan correctly aligned with state standards helps to prove its worthiness and necessity. It also helps in assuring that your students are being taught what your state requires. If you are able to correlate your lesson plan with standards, record links to those standards in your lesson plan.

Step 2: To make sure your lesson plan will teach exactly what you want it to; you need to develop clear and specific objectives. Please note that objectives should not be activities that will be used in the lesson plan. They should instead be the learning outcomes of those activities. As an example, if you wanted to teach your class how to add 2 + 3, your objective may be that "the students will know how to add 2 + 3" or more specifically "the students will demonstrate how to add 2 + 3."

Objectives should also be directly measurable (we'll get to this in assessment / evaluation). In other words, make sure you will be able to tell whether these objectives were met or not. You can certainly have more than one objective for a lesson plan.

To make objectives more meaningful, you may want to include both broad and narrow objectives. The broad objectives would be more like goals and include the overall goal of the lesson plan, i.e. to gain familiarity with adding two numbers together. The specific objectives would be more like the one listed above, i.e. "the students will demonstrate how to add the numbers 2 and 3 together."

Step 3: You would probably find out exactly what materials you are going to use later, but they should be shown early in your lesson plan. This way if someone else were going to use your lesson plan, they would know in advance what materials are required. Be specific here to make sure the teacher will have everything they need. For the addition lesson, you should make sure you have 10 or so unifix cubes per student, paper, and pencils.

Step 4: You may also want to write an Anticipatory Set, which would be a way to lead into the lesson plan and develop the students' interest in learning what is about to be taught. A good example deals with a lesson on fractions. The teacher could start by asking the students how they would divide up a pizza to make sure each of their 5 friends got an equal amount of pizza, and tell them that they can do this if they know how to work with fractions.

Step 5: Now you need to write the step-by-step procedures that will be performed to reach the objectives. These don't have to involve every little thing the teacher will say and do, but they should list the relevant actions the teacher needs to perform.

For the adding 2 + 3 lesson, you may have procedures such as these:

- The teacher will give each child 2 cubes.
- The teacher will ask the students to write down, how many cubes they have on paper.
- The students should then write a + sign below the number 2, like this:
  2 +
- The teacher will then pass out 3 more cubes to each student.
- The students will be asked to write down how many cubes they were just given. They should write this number below the number 2 that they just wrote, so that it looks like this:
  2 +3
- Students should now draw a line under their 3.
- Now the students should count how many cubes they

have together and write this number just below the 3, like this:

$$2 + 3 = 5$$

- Ask students how many cubes they had to start, how many they were given to add to that, and how many they had total after the teacher gave them the 3 cubes.

Step 6: After the procedures have been completed, you may want to provide time for independent practice. For the example of above, students could be given time to add different numbers of cubes together that a partner would provide them with.

Step 7: Just before moving on to the assessment phase you should have some sort of closure for the lesson plan. A good idea for this is to return to your anticipatory set, i.e. ask students how they would divide up that pizza now that they know how to work with fractions.

Step 8: Now you want to write your assessment / evaluation. Many lesson plans don't necessarily need an assessment, but most should have some sort of evaluation of whether or not the objectives were reached. The key in developing your assessment is to make sure that the assessment specifically measures whether the objectives were reached or not. Thus, there should be a direct correlation between the objectives and the assessments. Assuming the objective were to be able to add two single digit numbers together, an example would be to have students approach the teacher and add two single digit numbers on paper using cubes as a guide.

Step 9: Adaptations should also be made for students with learning disabilities and extensions for others. Examples would be adding 1 cube to 1 cube for students with learning disabilities and adding 9 cubes to 13 cubes for gifted students. This is best done with specific adaptations for specific students, to take into account their individual differences.

Step 10: It's also a good idea to include a "Connections" section, which shows how the lesson plan could be integrated with other subjects. An example would be to have students paint 2 apples, then 3 more apples below them, etc. to integrate

Art into the lesson plan. A better integration would involve creating 2 or 3 different types of textures on those apples, assuming texture was being studied in art class. Putting a lot of work into this can develop complete thematic units that would integrate related topics into many different subjects. This repetition of topics in different subjects can be extremely helpful in ensuring retention of the material.

TEACHING AIDS

FLASH CARDS, PICTURES, CHARTS, MODELS, BLACKBOARD SKETCHES

A teaching aid is something a classroom teacher uses in her class to help students improve reading and other skills, reinforce a skill, or to make learning fun. Teaching aids can be used in any of the core classes.

TYPES OF TEACHING AIDS

Chart

A chart is something that shows a group of facts in the form of a diagram, table, or a graph. Teachers can use small alphabet charts on student desks to aid in learning the alphabet. Charts can be large enough to mount on a wall. Wall charts can be used for whole group lessons; the teacher can write an outline or word definitions on the wall chart.

Flash Cards

A flash card is part of a set of cards that has numbers, letters, pictures or words on it. They are commonly used for drilling students on facts. Flash cards may also be used to enhance student memory. Try playing a memory game with the facts on the cards. This is a great and fun way to help students memorize. Most teachers use flash cards in their English lessons when they have to introduce new vocabulary. Using flash cards our students will be able to understand the new vocabulary without any kind of translation. Anyway, we have to take into account that there are lexical fields that cannot be illustrated through flash cards. In this article, I'm going to suggest some activities with flash cards that can be applied to any kind of vocabulary and almost any age and level. To start with, we will always choose comprehension activities. This means that the students are not required to say the new words, just to understand them. After this stage, it is good to introduce activities, which require repetitive production.

Then they will be ready to develop tasks in which they have to speak without models. Finally we will have to introduce interaction activities, which involve contextual zed use of the language. Saying hello: Very young children enjoy saying hello to the animals, the people and even the objects. We can put the flash cards in different places of the classroom and greet them alternatively. When the students have mastered the main vocabulary, we can make errors like saying 'Hello kangaroo, how are you?' when we are speaking to the monkey.

The Chain

We put all the flash-cards in different places. We choose one student and we say one word, for example 'donkey'. The student has to find the corresponding flash-card. It doesn't matter if they don't know the vocabulary yet. They can try luck. If one student fails, we choose another one, and so on until someone finds the donkey. Then we say another word, for example 'monkey', and we go on until the student fails. Then we choose another student and we start the chain again 'donkey, monkey,...'. The idea of the chain is that when one student finds out the meaning of a word, the others will try to remember it. You will see that in twenty minutes all your students will have mastered all the vocabulary.

Point To

The teacher says 'point to the donkey, point to the kangaroo, ...' and the students have to perform the actions. When you see that the students are getting tired of this boring activity, you can transform it into a memory game: say 'point to... the monkey, the elephant, the snake and the hippo' and they have to make it in the right order. If you speak very quickly they will find it funny. We turn all the cards upside down (on the floor or on a table).

Then we choose one student and we ask 'where is the donkey?' and the students uncovers one card. If s/he gets right, we ask again 'where is the elephant?', and so on until s/he fails. Then we turn all the cards upside down, we choose another student and we start the chain again.

We put all the flash-cards in different places of the classroom. Then we ask two students to stand up. Then we say one word, for example 'giraffe' and both students will try to take it in first place. We go on with the other words. At the end, the student that has taken more flash-cards is the winner.

Flip Charts

Flip charts are useful for teaching large groups at one time. A flip chart is a large group of papers that are attached at the top so that the papers can be flipped over one at a time to show a new page of paper. Flip charts are often placed on an easel, which allows the teacher to easily move it. A teacher can use a flip chart when she is showing different parts of a lesson, stages in the process of something, steps of something, or the progress of a story as it unfolds. Flip charts are very versatile and can be used for all classes.

Maps

Maps are something teachers can use for various projects or lessons. A map is something to use when a teacher is describing where a city, state, country, or continent is located. Teachers can show students different types of terrain, the population of a specific state or country, or the amount of precipitation in various areas. Maps are great for social studies and science and give students a great understanding of spatial relations.

Calendar

A calendar is a chart that shows dates in each month of the year. Teachers can use calendars for teaching days of the month and the months to her class. Using a calendar that is in a different language is also a unique way to teach days of the month in that particular foreign language.

Newspapers

Many teachers may not know that a newspaper is a great teaching aid. Newspapers can be used for any of the core classes.

Teachers can use them to teach about people, places and things in language arts.

Newspapers can be used for math activities, such as clipping coupons and doing basic math.

A teacher can use a newspaper for finding parts of speech, teaching about life skills, or to keep kids current on news events.

Graphs

Graphs are a wonderful teacher's aid and can be used for any subject. Teachers can make their own graphs and use them to compare population growth in social studies, numbers or ratios of objects in math class, or even use them for charting student growth. Teachers can make their own graphs using computer programs or can choose to go the old-fashioned way and use graph paper.

Surveys

These are another great teaching aid. Teachers can make their own survey to pass out to the class. On that survey, the teacher may ask the students to answer yes, no, multiple choice, or short answer questions regarding a recent teaching unit, the overall performance of the teacher or the school in general. Surveys are a great way for a teacher to get feedback and use that feedback to improve teaching skills or change future lessons for more success

EVALUATION

Evaluation is the process of determining the value or worth of collected data. Evaluation must be conducted in terms of the general goals of the discipline.

Types of Evaluation

Norm-referenced standards is a level of achievement relative to a clearly defined subgroup, such as all women or women your age. It means that you report how well a performance compares with that of others (people of the same age, gender, or class). Norm-referenced standards are designed to rank order individuals from best to worst and are usually expressed in percentile ranks. Criterion-referenced standards is one in that one compares an individual's result against the a specific, predetermined level of achievement (standard) to determine mastery. Criterion-referenced standards are a minimum proficiency or pass-fail standard.

Examples: Divers license test standards

Red Cross lifesaving and first aid certification standards

A measure of VO2 max on someone who had a hard attack. A physician may be interested in whether the patient can achieve a VO2 max of 25. A physical educator might establish a grading scale for a knowledge test which 70% of the questions must be answered correctly to pass the test.

Formative and Evaluative Evaluation

Formative: Formative evaluations are initial or intermediate evaluations. Formative evaluation provides information about the progress of the participant each day throughout a learning unit. Formative evaluation involves breaking a learning unit down into smaller parts to enable both the physical educator and the participants to identify the precise of a task or performance that are in error and need correcting. Formative evaluations should occur throughout the instructional, training or research process.

Summative: A final, comprehensive judgment conducted near the end of an instruction or training programme. For example the final grade.

RECAPITULATION

DEFINITION

Recapitulation is not only an important part of teaching

but an essential element in every area of education.

For example: Repeating these central basic facts regarding the birth of Jesus, which took place around early October during the Feast of Tabernacles, is necessary, because man has attempted to garland the incarnation of the Son of God with much fantasy.

Jesus Christ was born in Bethlehem, outside what we would catagorise as a one star hotel, where the animals were housed - nothing emotional or sentimental about that.

Was He not wrapped in lovely cosy 'swaddling clothes'? Well yes, but Dr Luke makes it clear that He was swathed in medical bandages.

There was no doctor or nurse standing by - no midwife present, to take and wash the newly born Jesus and present Him to Mary.

Did angels really appear? Yes - but to shepherds in fields about a mile away. These shepherds were like nighwatchmen. They were not highly regarded by society, and not trusted to be reliable witnesses in a court of law, yet God announced the birth of his Son to shepherd boys, in the same way as today we place a notice in the newspaper.

Jesus came to save people from their sins. Many people would like God to deal firstly with their difficult situations, serious problems, or sicknesses and pains - or even circumstances around our troubled world.

Jesus came primarily to deal with sin, and as sin is dealt with thoroughly and adequately, many of the other urgent matters will gradually disappear, but always remembering that the perplexities which cause unrest and distress globally, will only be satisfactorily resolved when the risen living Jesus returns.

That too is a fact, which not only requires to be taught, but needs repeating and repeating.

There is a highly apposite parallel at end of Jesus Christ's physical life on earth.

When the women made their way to anoint the crucified body of Jesus Christ the situation was not as they expected to find it.

Life is seldom the way we thought it was going to be.

The stone sealing the door of the grave had been moved, and there was no dead Jesus inside. How would you have reacted? While they are puzzled, perplexed, and wondering what on earth has happened, two angels appear. What would your response be now?

They are challenged with - Why do you look for the living among the dead? This is the cemetery. He is not here. He has risen. Do you not remember that Jesus told you He would be delivered into the hands of sinful men, be crucified, and be raised three days later?

Two of these have already happened. Could you not believe for the third?

Then they remembered Jesus' words. All kinds of confusion and bewilderment arise when we forget the words of Jesus. They had seen Him taken down from the cross and laid in that tomb.

Common sense says dead men don't rise. Not so on this occasion. They were so wrong. Circumstances had changed.

They expected things to be as they had always been, and God can have a difficult job changing us from our expectations and opening us up to what He is doing and saying.

But God does not become angry with us if we do not get everything right first time round, provided we are willing to learn. We all need reminders of the words of Jesus, and can need reminding often.

It is when we forget, ignore or reject His Word - individually or nationally - that things tend to go terribly wrong.

Definition

Recapitulation is a technique used to heal emotional charges. On a deeper level, it is used to reclaim energy and return it to self. Carlos Castaneda first introduced recapitulation into mass consciousness in his book, *The Toltec Path of Recapitulation: Healing Your Past to Free Your Soul,* Victor Sanchez speaks about learning procedures from the people, who he calls the 'surviving', similar to the process of recapitulation. One purpose of recapitulation is to eliminate emotional charges. Emotional charges cause one to misperceive the world around them and make it impossible to perceive the Nagual with clarity. For example, if a young girl is relentlessly teased about her curly hair by her father, she may become emotionally charged. Later, when she is a adult, whenever someone compliments her, particularly her hair, she becomes angry. She may not know why compliments cause her to get angry as she doesn't remember how her father used to tease her as a young child. What is worse is that she misperceives another person's good intent, i.e. giving her a compliment, as teasing her about her looks. This misperception causes upset both in her life and other people in it.

The average person is full of emotional charges, many that they are not aware of as they were suppressed as painful memories during childhood. This causes the average person to misperceive the world and the people in it. Systematic recapitulation discharges emotions and frees one up to perceive the world clearly. Recapitulation releases negative emotions that are trapped in one's subconscious freeing up their life. Many people have a habitually negative emotional state, or are moody for reasons they do not know why. More times than not, the reason lies in the suppressed emotional charges that lie in their subconscious.

On a deeper level, recapitulation is used to reclaim one's energy. Everywhere one has lived they leave an energetic piece of themselves. In every person you interact with you live energetic cords or filaments that, unless reclaimed back to self drain you of your vital energy. This is particularly true of sexual encounters. Through the consistent use of recapitulation you restore the vital energy necessary to progress on a spiritual path. Most do not realise how much energy is required to break free of the Dream of the Planet.

Unit III

Microteaching

DEFINITION

Microteaching is so called since it is analogous to putting the teacher under a microscope so to say while he is teaching so that all faults in teaching methodology are brought into perspective for the observers to give a constructive feedback. It eliminates some of the complexities of learning to teach in the classroom situation such as the pressure of length of the lecture, the scope and content of the matter to be conveyed, the need to teach for a relatively long duration of time (usually an hour) and the need to face large numbers of students, some of whom are hostile temperamentally.

Microteaching also provides skilled supervision with an opportunity to get a constructive feedback. To go back to the analogy of the swimmer, while classroom teaching is like learning to swim at the deeper end of the pool, microteaching is an opportunity to practice at the shallower and less risky side.

Microteaching was developed in the early and mid 1960's by Dwight Allen and his colleagues at the Stanford Teacher Education Programme. The Stanford model emphasized a teach, review and reflect, re-teach approach, using actual school students as authentic audiences. The model has been adapted for college and university teaching where it has been used most often for graduate teaching assistants. It often offers a concentrated, focused form of peer feedback and discussion. A very similar model called Instructional Skills Workshop (ISW) was developed during the early 1970s by British

Columbia's Education Ministry as a training support programme for all college and institute faculty in British Columbia and has now spread throughout Canada, the US and internationally. While there are significant differences between the two models, they both share some commonalities and were designed to enhance teaching and promote open collegial discussion about teaching performance.

A micro lesson is an opportunity to present a sample "snapshot" of what/how you teach and to get some feedback from colleagues about how it was received. It is a chance to try teaching strategies that you may not use regularly. This is a good, safe time to experiment with something new to you or to get feedback on a technique you've been trying but are not sure about its effectiveness.

The components of the microteaching cycle are shown. The Microteaching cycle starts with planning. In order to reduce the complexities involved in teaching, the student teacher is asked to plan a "microlesson" i.e a short lesson for 5-10 minutes which he will teach in front of a "microclass" i.e a group consisting 3-4 students, a supervisor and peers if necessary. There is scope for projection of model teaching skills if required to help the teacher prepare for his session. The student teacher is asked to teach concentrating one or few of the teaching skills enumerated earlier. His teaching is evaluated by the students, peers and the supervisor using cheekists to help them. Video recording can be done if facilities permit. At the- end of the 5 or 10 minutes session as planned, the teacher is given a feedback on the deficiencies noticed in his teaching methodology. Feedback can be aided by playing back the video recording. Using the feedback to help himself, the teacher is asked to replan his lesson keeping the comments in view and reteach immediately the same lesson to another group. Such repeated cycles of teaching, feedback and reteaching help the teacher to improve his teaching skills one at a time. Several such sequences can be planned at the departmental level. Colleagues and postgraduate students can act as peer evaluators for this purpose. It is important, however, that the cycle is used purely for helping the teacher and not as a tool for making a value judgement of his teaching capacity by his superiors.

ADVANTAGES OF MICROTEACHING

Microteaching has several advantages. It focuses on sharpening and developing specific teaching skills and eliminating errors. It enables understanding of behaviors important in classroom teaching. It increases the confidence of the learner teacher. It is a vehicle of continuous training applicable at all stages not only to teachers at the beginning of their career but also for more senior teachers. It enables projection of model instructional skills. It provides expert supervision and a constructive feedback and above all if provides for repeated practice without adverse consequences to the teacher or his students.

Life is not a bed of roses; and we usually confront as many problems in our daily life. Problem is not a problem itself however we convert it to a difficult one by dealing with trivial issues or sometimes ignoring the significant ones. Our attitude to such problems compels us to face more complicated issues in even small problems.

In our daily life, the busy schedule tends us to invite more problems and we get caught in situation by one way or another. If these problems are not attended properly; these tend to tease you on every step. They say if you are not a part of solution than you are a part of problem; however the significance lies in the solution of the problem, no matter what procedure one adopts to acquire the solution .In every day life, we are confronted with many problems. Some of them continue to persist if left unsolved.

PURPOSE OF MICRO TEACHING

The purpose of microteaching is to give you confidence, support, and feedback by letting you try out with a small group of colleagues a short sample of the kind of teaching you are currently doing or which you are preparing yourself for. The microteaching will be organized as follows:

- You need to prepare a short teaching episode (between 10 and 15 minutes) drawn from the kind of teaching you are involved in or want to develop. It can be an extract from a session you have actually taught, something you are going to be teaching, or just something you want to try out.
- We normally organize the microteaching in small groups of 5-7, each with a facilitator. Members of the group take it in turn to give their teaching episode, with the other group members in the role of 'student' or 'observer'.
- The microteaching will take place in a 'classroom' setting but you will be able to re-arrange the room, as appropriate to the kind of teaching methods involved.
- AV equipment will be available – including OHP, whiteboard, flip chart, PC + projector.
- If appropriate, you can prepare a handout (e.g. a task or problem sheet, case study, or vignette) for your microteaching session or otherwise, you will need to make sufficient copies yourself and bring them to the session.
- Those involved give one another constructive feedback on their teaching. The person who has 'performed' should be the first to comment, giving their own self-evaluative views and, if they wish, identifying particular areas for others to comment on.
- A digital video recording of the microteaching will be made. You will have the opportunity for a one-to-one review of your microteaching video with a course tutor. The recording is regarded as the property of the person whose teaching is recorded. A copy will be provided for each participant as soon as possible after the event.

PREPARATION OF MICRO TEACHING

- To prepare a short lesson for a small group of learner.
- Your lesson can be excerpted from the beginning,

middle or end of one course lesson and you will be able to explain this in setting up your lesson and as part of your application or instruction form.

- You have several decisions to make concerning the preparation of your micro lessons:

  Topic: Choose a teaching topic that you are comfortable with in order to focus on a particular teaching method or element.

Or, preparing material that you especially would like to make sure your students understand by the end of your next class.

  Lesson objectives: Think about and be able to articulate what you want your students to learn from your lesson (e.g., facts, concepts, skills, and/ or values) and how your teaching methodology might work to fulfill your objectives.

  What you want feedback on. You can specify to the group what you would like them to focus on. For example, you may wish to have overall, general feedback or perhaps you might wish for the group to simply attend to a specific issue, such as how you use questions or reinforcement with students

  – Not only plan out how to treat the subject matter, but also give some thought to how you are going to present yourself, manage the class, and involve the students.
  – Striving to create as natural a classroom setting as possible.
  – While one person takes his or her turn as teacher, everyone else plays the roles of students. It is the job of these pretend pupils to ask and answer questions realistically. It is the job of the pretend teacher to involve his or her "class" actively in this way.

A timer is used to keep to the strictly enforced time limit.

- Don't be offended if you are cut off; it will be necessary to keep to the time limit so that everyone might participate fully.

OBSERVATION

- When you are in the role of students, you should combine the role of student and observer.
- Do not feel like you must role play specific student behaviors, but do feel free to ask questions and comment as a learner in the classroom environment.
- Try to focus on what is happening during the micro lesson.
- The best way to give feedback is to identify a small number of things the person can improve, so think about what is best to focus on for each micro-teacher.

PURPOSE OF MICROTEACHING

The purpose of microteaching is to give you confidence, support, and feedback by letting you try out with a small group of colleagues a short sample of the kind of teaching you are currently doing or which you are preparing yourself for.

The microteaching will be organized as follows:

- You need to prepare a short teaching episode (between 10 and 15 minutes) drawn from the kind of teaching you are involved in or want to develop. It can be an extract from a session you have actually taught, something you are going to be teaching, or just something you want to try out.
- We normally organize the microteaching in small groups of 5-7, each with a facilitator. Members of the group take it in turn to give their teaching episode, with the other group members in the role of 'student' or 'observer'.
- The microteaching will take place in a 'classroom' setting but you will be able to re-arrange the room, as appropriate to the kind of teaching methods involved.
- AV equipment will be available — including OHP, whiteboard, flip chart, PC + projector.
- If appropriate, you can prepare a handout and bring them to the session.
- Those involved give one another constructive

feedback on their teaching. The person who has 'performed' should be the first to comment, giving their own self-evaluative views and, if they wish, identifying particular areas for others to comment on.

- A digital video recording of the microteaching will be made. You will have the opportunity for a one-to-one review of your microteaching video with a course tutor. The recording is regarded as the property of the person whose teaching is recorded. A copy will be provided for each participant as soon as possible after the event.

MICRO-TEACHING TECHNIQUE

This is a laboratory training procedure geared towards simplification of the complexities of regular teaching-learning process. It is also miniature teaching scaled down in terms of class size, time, task or content and skill. However, in practice, microteaching follows a teach-critique-ret each procedure, which involves the following:

The supervisor demonstrates the skill to be practiced. This may be live demonstration of the skill or a video presentation of the skill, which has been prerecorded for the purpose.

The group members select a topic(s) from a list and prepare the lesson of five to ten minutes, in which they will practice the particular skill that was demonstrated

The teacher trainee then has the opportunity to practice and evaluate his use of the skills. Practice takes the form of a ten-minute microteaching session in which five to ten pupils are involved. When real students are used, the other trainee teachers act as observers and evaluators. When the trainee are used a pupils they play the role of the pupils at the same time observe and evaluate the lesson objectively together with the supervisor.

QUESTIONING

- QUESTIONING is a basic tool for rebellion. It breaks open the stagnant hardened shells of the present, and opens up the options that might be explored.

- QUESTIONING reveals the profound uncertainty that is imbedded deep in all reality beyond the facades of confidence and sureness. It takes this uncertainty towards growth and new possibilities.
- QUESTIONING can change your entire life. It can uncover hidden powers and stifled dreams inside of you ... things you may have denied for many years.
- QUESTIONING can change institutions and entire cultures. It can empower people to create strategies for change.
- ASKING A QUESTION that leads to a strategy for action is a powerful contribution to resolving any problem.
- ASKING QUESTIONS that open up more options can lead to many unexpected solutions.
- ASKING QUESTIONS that help adversaries shift from their stuck positions on an issue can lead to acts of healing and reconciliation.
- ASKING QUESTIONS that are unaskable in our culture at the moment can lead to the transformation of our culture and its institutions.
- ASKING QUESTIONS and listening for the strategies and ideas embedded in people's own answers can be the greatest service a social change worker can give to a particular issue.

TYPES OF QUESTIONING

Open and Closed Questions

A closed question usually receives a single word or very short, factual answer. For example, "Are you thirsty?" The answer is "Yes" or "No"; "Where do you live?" The answer is generally the name of your town or your address.

Open questions elicit longer answers. They usually begin with what, why, how. An open question asks the respondent for his or her knowledge, opinion or feelings. "Tell me" and "describe" can also be used in the same way as open questions.

Here are some examples:

- What happened at the meeting?
- Why did he react that way?
- How was the party?
- Tell me what happened next.
- Describe the circumstances in more detail.

Open Questions Are Good For

- Developing an open conversation: "What did you get up to on vacation?"
- Finding our more detail: "What else do we need to do to make this a success?"
- Finding out the other person's opinion or issues: "What do you think about those changes?"

Closed Questions are Good For

- Testing your understanding, or the other person's: "So, if I get this qualification, I will get a raise?"
- Concluding a discussion or making a decision: "Now we know the facts, are we all agreed this is the right course of action?"
- Frame setting: "Are you happy with the service from your bank?"

A misplaced closed question, on the other hand, can kill the conversation and lead to awkward silences, so are best avoided when a conversation is in full flow.

Funnel Questions

This technique involves starting with general questions, and then homing in on a point in each answer, and asking more and more detail at each level. It's often used by detectives taking a statement from a witness:

"How many people were involved in the fight?"

"About ten."

"Were they kids or adults?"

"Mostly kids."

"What sort of ages were they?"

"About fourteen or fifteen."

"Were any of them wearing anything distinctive?"

"Yes, several of them had red baseball caps on."

"Can you remember if there was a logo on any of the caps?"

"Now you come to mention it, yes, I remember seeing a big letter N."

Using this technique, the detective has helped the witness re-live the scene and gradually focus on a useful detail. Perhaps he'll be able to identify young men wearing a hat like this from CCTV footage. It is unlikely he would have got this information if he's simply asked an open question such as "Are there any details you can give me about what you saw?"

Tip: When using funnel questioning, start with closed questions. As you progress through the tunnel, start using more open questions.

Funnel Questions are Good For

Finding out more detail about a specific point: "Tell me more about Option 2." Gaining the interest or increasing the confidence of the person you're speaking with: "Have you used the IT Helpdesk?", "Did they solve your problem?", "What was the attitude of the person who took your call?"

Probing Questions

Asking probing questions is another strategy for finding out more detail. Sometimes it's as simple as asking your respondent for an example, to help you understand a statement they have made. At other times, you need additional information for clarification, "When do you need this report by, and do you want to see a draft before I give you my final version?", or to investigate whether there is proof for what has been said, "How do you know that the new database can't be used by the sales force?"

An effective way of probing is to use the 5 Whys method, which can help you quickly get to the root of a problem.

Tip: Use questions that include the word "exactly" to probe further: "What exactly do you mean by fast-track?", "Who, exactly, wanted this report?"

Probing Questions are Good For

Gaining clarification to ensure you have the whole story and that you understand it thoroughly; and

Drawing information out of people who are trying to avoid telling you something.

Leading Questions

Leading questions try to lead the respondent to your way of thinking. They can do this in several ways:

- With an assumption: "How late do you think that the project will deliver?". This assumes that the project will certainly not be completed on time.
- By adding a personal appeal to agree at the end: "Lori's very efficient, don't you think?" or "Option 2 is better, isn't it?"
- Phrasing the question so that the "easiest" response is "yes" (our natural tendency to prefer to say "yes" than "no" plays an important part in the phrasing of referendum questions): "Shall we all approve Option 2?" is more likely to get a positive response than "Do you want to approve option 2 or not?". A good way of doing this is to make it personal. For example, "Would you like me to go ahead with Option 2?" rather than "Shall I choose Option 2?".
- Giving people a choice between two options, both of which you would be happy with, rather than the choice of one option or not doing anything at all. Strictly speaking, the choice of "neither" is still available when you ask "Which would you prefer of A or B", but most people will be caught up in deciding between your two preferences.

Leading Questions Are Good For

Getting the answer you want but leaving the other person feeling that they have had a choice.

Closing a sale: "If that answers all of your questions, shall we agree a price?"

Tip: Use leading questions with care. If you use them in a self-serving way or one that harms the interests of the other person, then they can, quite rightly, be seen as manipulative and dishonest.

Rhetorical Questions

Rhetorical questions aren't really questions at all, in that they don't expect an answer. They're really just statements phrased in question form: "Isn't John's design work so creative?"

People use rhetorical questions because they are engaging for the listener - as they are drawn into agreeing rather than feeling that they are being "told" something like "John is a very creative designer".

Tip: Rhetorical questions are even more powerful if you use a string of them. "Isn't that a great display? Don't you love the way the text picks up the colors in the photographs? Doesn't it use space really well? Wouldn't you love to have a display like that for our products?"

Rhetorical Questions Are Good For

Engaging the listener

Using Questioning Techniques

You have probably used all of these questioning techniques before in your everyday life, at work and at home. But by consciously applying the appropriate kind of questioning, you can gain the information, response or outcome that you want even more effectively.

Questions are a powerful way of:

Learning: Ask open and closed questions, and use probing questioning.

Relationship building: People generally respond positively if you ask about what they do or enquire about their opinions. If you do this in an affirmative way "Tell me what you like best about working here", you will help to build and maintain an open dialogue.

Managing and coaching: Here, rhetorical and leading questions are useful too. They can help get people to reflect and to commit to courses of action that you've suggested: "Wouldn't it be great to gain some further qualifications?"

Avoiding misunderstandings: Use probing questions to seek clarification, particularly when the consequences are significant. And to make sure you avoid jumping to conclusions, the The Ladder of Inference tool can help too.

Diffusing a heated situation: You can calm an angry customer or colleague by using funnel questions to get them to go into more detail about their grievance. This will not only distract them from their emotions, but will often help you to identify a small practical thing that you can do, which is often enough to make them feel that they have "won" something, and no longer need to be angry.

Persuading people: No one likes to be lectured, but asking a series of open questions will help others to embrace the reasons behind your point of view. "What do you think about bringing the sales force in for half a day to have their laptops upgraded?"

EFFECTIVE USE OF QUESTIONING

Questioning can.....

- Arouse curiosity
- Stimulate interest in the topic
- Clarify concepts
- Emphasize key points
- Enhance problem-solving ability
- Encourage students to think at higher cognitive levels
- Motivate student to search for new information
- ascertain students' knowledge level to aid in modifying instruction

Bloom's Taxonomy

The types of questions and the manner in which questions are asked have a direct impact on the effectiveness of the questioning.

Bloom's Taxonomy of Thinking Skills	
Knowledge	Students are required to recall the information learned and repeat it to the teacher. Example: *What are the major causes of fistula?*
Comprehension	Students must explain topics, review items, and discuss issues; this includes translation, interpretation, extrapolation, and focuses on the meaning and intent of the material. Example: *What study would you order to confirm the diagnosis of myocardial infarction in a patient with a left bundle branch block?*
Application	Students must use an abstraction (principle, theory, etc.) brought from other experiences. It requires that students apply previously learned knowledge and skills to new situations and necessitates the use of abstractions in specific situations. Example: *A 35-year-old woman presents to your office with a 1-month history of polyarthritis, rash, pleuritic pain, and low grade fever. What is the most likely diagnosis?*
Analysis	Students must break down material into its component parts and then use a systematic process to reach a logical conclusion. Example: *How would you distinguish between polymyositis and viral myositis in a 42-year-old man with weakness and a rash?*
Synthesis	Students must hypothesize, predict, and use the available information to arrive at a generalization—putting together elements or parts from many sources to constitute a new pattern or structure. Example: *If the blood culture were negative of the patient with echocardiographic valvular vegetations, how would you proceed with the antibiotic treatment?*
Evaluation	Students must use specific criteria to assess situations or to justify previous responses. Example: *Explain your rationale for using combination drug therapy instead of mono therapy to treat a patient with pulmonary tuberculosis.*

TECHNIQUES OF EFFECTIVE QUESTIONING

Establish an Appropriate Environment

Only certain questions should be posed in front of the patient; bedside questions should focus principally on knowledge and recall and to a lesser extent on comprehension.

Create a Climate Conducive to Learning

A happy facial expression, nod, or verbal acknowledgement of a correct response encourages other students to participate in the discussion.

Pose questions in a non-threatening way and receive answers in a supportive fashion.

A harsh tone, especially when used to interrupt a response

from the student, can be devastating for both the student and his or her peers.

Prepare the Students for the Questioning Session and Discussion

Explain to students the format, expectations, and how this knowledge will help them.

Use Both Pre-planned and Emerging Questions

Pre-planned questions are those incorporated into the educational plan prospectively that are asked during the teaching session to introduce new concepts, focus the discussion on certain items, steer the discussion in specific directions, or identify student knowledge level on the topic.

Emerging questions derive from the discussion itself and the specific answers given to previous questions. Think quickly and act decisively to phrase these questions accurately and pose them at appropriate times in the discussion.

Use an Appropriate Variety and Mix of Questions

One good strategy is to start with convergent questions and then continue with divergent questions, perhaps asking questions in hierarchical sequence and building from the recall of facts to higher levels of thinking and problem-solving. If a question requiring a higher level thinking skill stymies the student, go down to a question requiring a lower-level thinking skills and then work up the hierarchy.

Avoid Trick Questions and Those that Require only a YES or NO Response

Trick questions should be avoided, as they frustrate students and tend to encourage frivolous responses. YES or NO questions encourage students to respond without fully understanding or thinking through the issue. When used, such questions should be followed by other questions to determine the thinking process of the student.

Phrase the Questions Carefully, Concisely, and Clearly

Improper phrasing and the use of multiple questions

related to the same topic may result in unintentional cueing and inability to accurately assess student understanding.

Address Questions to the Group, versus the Individual

Pose the question to the entire group and wait before identifying a student to respond. The wait time encourages all students to think about the response, as they do not know who is going to be called upon to answer the question. Select students at random to answer questions, as it tends to keep everyone attentive and involved.

Select both Volunteers and Non-volunteers to Answer Questions

Adapt Questions to the Needs of the Learners

Assess the students' needs and tailor questions to maximize the number of correct answers while moving toward more and more difficult questions. Remember, no two groups of students will be alike or at the same level.

Use Sufficient Wait Time

The teacher can significantly enhance the analytic and problem-solving skills of students by allowing sufficient wait times before responding, both after posing a question and after the answer is given. This allows everyone to think about not only the question but also the response provided by the student. Three to five seconds in most cases; longer in some, maybe up to 10 seconds for higher-order questions.

Respond to Answers Given by Students

Listen carefully to the answers given by students; do not interrupt students while they are responding to questions unless they are straying far off course, are totally unfocused, or are being disruptive. Acknowledge correct answers and provide positive reinforcement. Do not use sarcasm, reprimands, accusations, and personal attacks. Repeat answers only when the other students have not heard the answers; other repeats waste time. Keep questioning until the learning objectives for the session have been achieved; this may be the best opportunity to teach a particular concept. Handle incomplete answers by reinforcing what is correct and then asking probing questions.

Types of Probing Questions:	
Extension	Require students to elaborate on the response given to an earlier question. Such questions indicate to the learner that the original response was in the right direction but was not adequate.
Clarification	Useful when the student's response is unclear or incomplete.
Justification	Require the learner to provide rationale for the previously-given response. Useful in providing insights into thinking and reasoning processes of students and revealing errors in these processes.
Prompting	Useful when students do not respond to the original question
Redirection	Used to elicit a variety of opinions during problem-solving sessions or discussions.

Use Questions to Identify Learning Objectives for Follow-up Self-study

Pose questions towards the end of the teaching session to identify specific areas for additional learning opportunities that students can pursue on their own time.

BLACKBOARD

When you evaluate the performance of a protocol, you need information on internal state changes of your protocol, maybe even from protocols that you use. You could monitor these changes using e.g. vector files from within you protocol and remove these monitors once you are done. Another way is to use a blackboard. The state changes are published on it, and the monitors subscribe to these values. This allows other researchers to tap your protocol for performance evaluation, while imposing nearly no runtime penalty when the information is not needed.

Maybe even more importantly, the blackboard allows you to exchange information between layers, without passing pointers to the modules around. Some items might not only be interesting for the layer they are created/changed in. The physical layer for example can sense whether a channel is busy or not. If the MAC protocol is based on carrier sense it needs the information the physical layer has. The *Blackboard* is a module where the corresponding information can be published and then is accessible for any module interested in it.

The *Basic Module* provides everything necessary to interact with the blackboard. It is derived from *Modifiable* - a pure virtual base class that allows the blackboard to inform your module of changes - and contains a pointer named *bb* to the blackboard module.

The majority of the teaching on this course will be delivered *using* software called

Blackboard. Blackboard is one of many Virtual Learning Environments used to teach over the internet. It can be used to present study information online either to complement

traditional face-to-face classes, or as a main method of teaching. This document will

introduce you to *Blackboard* and how to use it during the course.

Section One demonstrates how to log into *Blackboard,* and describes the *Blackboard*

student homepage. Section Two introduces the Delve Deeper distance learning pages.

In order to use *Blackboard,* you will need a Newcastle University log-in and password.

These will be posted out to you before the beginning of your course.

There are several formatting conventions used in this document.

Please take note of the formatting styles:

- Buttons and drop-down lists will be indicated in italics.
- Locations on the screen are indicated in *italic*

REINFORCEMENT

The principle of reinforcement is a psychological concept based on the idea that the consequences of an action will influence future behaviour. Rewarding behaviour is considered reinforcement, because it teaches the subject that the behaviour is desired, and encourages the subject to repeat it. Punishing a behaviour, on the other hand, teaches the subject that the behaviour is not desired, and should not be repeated.

There are actually two types of reinforcement: positive reinforcement and negative reinforcement. Positive reinforcement refers to introducing a new stimulus to the subject's environment in order to reward desired behaviour. For example, a child might be given a balloon after behaving well at the dentist, or a rat might learn to press a bar for a treat. Positive reinforcement associates a pleasant outcome with the desired outcome. Negative reinforcement, on the other hand, involves removing an unpleasant stimulus from the environment. For example, a mouse entering a cage with an electrified floor would quickly learn to press a button if the current was stopped every time the button was pressed. Negative reinforcement is used in escape and avoidance conditioning. In escape conditioning, the subject learns to quickly remove him or herself from a situation where the negative stimulus exists, much as people evacuate a building with a screaming fire alarm. Avoidance conditioning involves learning to avoid the potentially unpleasant situation altogether, and the most classic example of avoidance conditioning is eating when you expect to be hungry, to avoid the unpleasant sensation of hunger.

Likewise, punishment is divided into positive and negative aspects. In a positive punishment situation, something unpleasant is introduced the environment, such as a spanking for a misbehaving child. Negative punishment removes a pleasant thing from the environment, much as a parent might take ice cream away from a screaming child.

MACRO TEACHING

Macros are Programs that Generate Programs

Mention macros to most programmers, perhaps even you, and the first image that comes to mind is string substitution -

you use a macro to glue together a few parameters in a new way, maybe with a bit of compile-time decision making thrown in. And because of the typical (in languages other than Lisp) disparity between the macro language and the programming language, the difficulty of writing a macro increases much faster than its complexity.

Lisp macros are Lisp programs that generate other Lisp programs. The generated Lisp code has a fully-parenthesized notation, as does the macro that generates the code. In the simplest case, a macro substitutes forms within a template, clearly establishing a visual correspondence between the generating code and the generated code. Complex macros can use the full power of the Lisp language to generate code according to the macro parameters; often a template form is wrapped in code that constructs appropriate sub-forms, but even this approach is just a typical use pattern and not a requirement (or restriction) of the Lisp macro facility.

In the following sections, we'll examine the mechanism by which the Lisp system translates code generated by a macro, then we'll see several increasingly sophisticated examples of macros.

SKILLS OF DEMONSTRATIONS

DEFINITION OF DEMONSTRATION

We can define demonstration as "a skilled performance of a task or technique showing precisely how it should and could be done on the job". It's a time old way of teaching, and one based on common sense. It's one area of teaching and learning where common sense, research and theory converge.

For many learning purposes, the terms demonstration and modeling are functionally equivalent, with demonstration being the more common sense term, while modeling is derived more from research in learning, primarily by Albert Bandura and Social Learning Theory. Other similar terms include vicarious learning, and observational learning.

The work of Bandura has shown that not only does observational learning affect skill acquisition, but that it affects the probabilities that already learned skills will be demonstrated or used in real life.

TYPES OF DEMONSTRATIONS

Formal Demonstrations

Formal demonstrations are for mature presentations that can be communicated effectively in front of a large audience using projection technology. After a formal demonstration has been conducted, presenters are encouraged to schedule a follow-up informal demonstration for participants interested in a more interactive setting.

Follow-up informal demonstrations are dependent on available space and time. Formal demonstrations will be scheduled into 40-minute blocks of time.

Informal Demonstrations

Informal demonstrations are appropriate for work that is very new, in a prototype stage, or otherwise not as fully developed as a formal demonstration. Informal demonstrations can also be used by presenters who feel that their work may be more effectively presented to a small audience. Informal demonstrations are presented to a small number of people without the benefit of projection technology. Significant audience interaction is possible with informal demonstrations, and hands-on experience with the systems is encouraged. Informal demonstrations will be scheduled into 30-minute blocks of time. Informal demonstrations are not reviewed. Those persons interested in presenting an informal demonstration may sign up at the conference and they will be assigned a time slot. Informal demonstrations are dependent on available space and time. No audio-visual or computing support is provided for informal demonstrations.

ACHIEVING CLOSURE

Achieving *Closure* is the positive feeling you get when you finish a task. Lack of *closure* results in the panicked feeling that you get when you still have a million things to do, and this stress may entice you to give up. Dividing a task into manageable goals, listing them, and checking them off your list as you complete them helps you obtain *closure*. For example, suppose your chemistry professor assigns three chapters of reading. If your goal is to read all three chapters, you may feel discouraged if you don't complete the reading at one time.

A more effective way to complete the assignment involves dividing the assignment into smaller goals. To do so, you think of each chapter as a separate goal, or you subdivide the chapters into sections. You experience more success by completing each section or chapter. Even if you fail to complete all three chapters in one sitting, your progress results in feelings of accomplishment.

Unfinished business also results in a lack of *closure* and procrastination. You may have several tasks with the same deadline.

Although changing from one task to another serves as a break, changing tasks too often wastes time. Each time you switch, you lose momentum.

You may be unable to change gears fast enough or find yourself out of the mood for study. You may find yourself thinking about the old project when you should be concentrating on the new one. In addition, when you return to the first task, you lose time. This happens because you have to review where you were and what steps are still left to be finished.

Often you solve this problem by determining how much time you have to work. If the time available is short (that is, an hour or less), you need to work on only one task.

You alternate tasks when you have more time. Completing one task or a large portion of a task contributes to the feeling of *closure*.

Sometimes, when working on a long-term project, other tasks take precedence before you can complete it. If this occurs, take time to write a few notes before moving to the new task. The clarity of your thinking or the status of your progress may seem fresh at the time, but you'll forget what you were doing after awhile. Your notes could include the goal of the task, how far along you are toward its completion, and a list of questions to be answered or objectives to be reached. You need to store references, papers, and other materials for the task together.

This provides the organization you need when you return to it. Finally, update your daily "To Do" list at the end rather than at the beginning of the day. This gives you a sense of accomplishment for the day's activities and prepares you for a quick start the next day.

Unit IV

Method of Teaching Biology

TEACHING METHODS

As any good teacher knows, all students do not learn in the same way. In addition, it is common for a class of students to be at a variety of levels in any particular subject. Teachers need to use different teaching methods in order to reach all students effectively. A variety of teaching strategies, a knowledge of student levels, and an implementation of which strategies are best for particular students can help teachers to know which teaching methods will be most effective for their class.

The first step to choosing a teaching method is to assess the students. This assessment can be formal or informal. Formal assessments include standardized tests, tests from the textbook or curriculum being used, or teacher-created tests. These assessments can give you an idea of the previous instruction that the students have received as well as their academic level. The students in your class may have undergone various teaching methods and quality of instruction in previous years.

Informal instruction is, as the name suggests, much less formal. Good teachers know their students. If you have been teaching a particular group of students for some time, you probably already know quite a bit about their interests, ability levels, and learning styles. If the group of students is new to you, you can make a point of asking them, individually or in a group, about their interests and academic strengths. Depending on the age of the children, they may also be able to write about this, or answer some form of questionnaire about their hobbies, interests, previous instruction, strengths, and weaknesses. Students generally enjoy talking about themselves and having their teacher get to know them well, as it makes them feel special, as well as directing you in choosing your teaching methods.

Once you have assessed your students, you need to plan for different teaching methods. Direct instruction is the most common form of instruction. This is the lecturing method of teaching.

Many teachers use this teaching method almost exclusively, as it is considered the simplest, and you can cover large amounts of material in a short period of time. However, this is not the most effective teaching method to reach all students, especially younger ones, who often need a more engaging, hands-on strategy in order to learn effectively. In addition, it is hard for teachers to tailor instruction to students at different levels.

Inquiry-based learning is a teaching method which is rapidly gaining popularity in the United States. Based on the scientific method, this teaching method can be used for virtually all subjects.

Using inquiry-based learning takes a lot of time, energy, and planning, but it is often very effective. Students practice problem solving and critical thinking skills to arrive at a conclusion. This teaching method is extremely student-centered and student-directed, and can be modified for students at any level, reaching them where they are. Teachers will generally need to start by modeling the process to the students.

Cooperative learning is another teaching method that is considered highly effective when done correctly. With cooperative learning, students are put in small groups to work together. They are usually not grouped by ability, but put in a group with children at a variety of levels. The students are then given tasks to accomplish together. Teachers may need to monitor these groups carefully, to make sure they are staying on task and that all students are participating. This form of instruction also lends itself well to differentiation, because the teacher can assign specific tasks to children at different ability levels.

One more common teaching method is to teach information processing strategies. While it is often advisable to have students really understand the teaching methods and not just memorize facts, there are some cases when facts need to be memorized. Facts and concepts may also need to be grouped or organized in order to facilitate better understanding.

Lecture
STRENGTHS:
- Presents factual material in direct, logical manner.
- Contains experience which inspires.
- Stimulates thinking to open discussion.
- Useful for large groups.
LIMITATIONS:
- Experts are not always good teachers.
- Audience is passive.
- Learning is difficult to gauge.
- Communication in one way.
PREPARATION:
- Needs clear introduction and summary.
- Needs time and content limit to be effective.
- Should include examples, anecdotes.

Lecture With Discussion
STRENGTHS:
- Involves audience at least after the lecture.
- Audience can question, clarify & challenge.
LIMITATIONS:
- Time may limit discussion period.
- Quality is limited to quality of questions and discussion.
PREPARATION:
- requires that questions be prepared prior to discussion.

Panel of Experts
STRENGTHS: - Allows experts to present different opinions. - Can provoke better discussion than a one person discussion. - Frequent change of speaker keeps attention from lagging. *LIMITATIONS:* - Experts may not be good speakers. - Personalities may overshadow content. - Subject may not be in logical order. *PREPARATION:* - Facilitator coordinates focus of panel, introduces and summarizes. - Briefs panel.

Brainstorming
STRENGTHS: - Listening exercise that allows creative thinking for new ideas. - Encourages full participation because all ideas equally recorded. - Draws on group's knowledge and experience. - Spirit of congeniality is created. - One idea can spark off other other ideas. *LIMITATIONS:* - Can be unfocused. - Needs to be limited to 5 - 7 minutes. - People may have difficulty getting away from known reality. - If not facilitated well, criticism and evaluation may occur. *PREPARATION:* - Facilitator selects issue. - Must have some ideas if group needs to be stimulated.

Videotapes
STRENGTHS:
- Entertaining way of teaching content and raising issues.
- Keep group's attention.
- Looks professional.
- Stimulates discussion.
LIMITATIONS:
- Can raise too many issues to have a focused discussion.
- Discussion may not have full participation.
- Only as effective as following discussion.
PREPARATION:
- Need to set up equipment.
- Effective only if facilitator prepares questions to discuss after the show.

Class Discussion
STRENGTHS:
- Pools ideas and experiences from group.
- Effective after a presentation, film or experience that needs to be analyzed.
- Allows everyone to participate in an active process.
LIMITATIONS:
- Not practical with more that 20 people.
- Few people can dominate.
- Others may not participate.
- Is time consuming.
- Can get off the track.
PREPARATION:
- Requires careful planning by facilitator to guide discussion.
- Requires question outline.

Small Group Discussion
STRENGTHS: - Allows participation of everyone. - People often more comfortable in small groups. - Can reach group consensus. *LIMITATIONS:* - Needs careful thought as to purpose of group. - Groups may get side tracked. *PREPARATION:* - Needs to prepare specific tasks or questions for group to answer.

Case Studies
STRENGTHS: - Develops analytic and problem solving skills. - Allows for exploration of solutions for complex issues. - Allows student to apply new knowledge and skills. *LIMITATIONS:* - People may not see relevance to own situation. - Insufficient information can lead to inappropriate results. *PREPARATION:* - Case must be clearly defined in some cases. - Case study must be prepared.

Role Playing
STRENGTHS: - Introduces problem situation dramatically. - Provides opportunity for people to assume roles of others and thus appreciate another point of view. - Allows for exploration of solutions. - Provides opportunity to practice skills. *LIMITATIONS:* - People may be too self-conscious. - Not appropriate for large groups. - People may feel threatened. *PREPARATION:* - Trainer has to define problem situation and roles clearly. - Trainer must give very clear instructions.

Report-Back Sessions
STRENGTHS:
- Allows for large group discussion of role plays, case studies, and small group exercise.
- Gives people a chance to reflect on experience.
- Each group takes responsibility for its operation.
LIMITATIONS:
- Can be repetitive if each small group says the same thing.
PREPARATION:
- Trainer has to prepare questions for groups to discuss.

Worksheets/Surveys
STRENGTHS:
- Allows people to thing for themselves without being influences by others.
- Individual thoughts can then be shared in large group.
LIMITATIONS:
- Can be used only for short period of time.
PREPARATION:
- Facilitator has to prepare handouts.

Index Card Exercise
STRENGTHS:
- Opportunity to explore difficult and complex issues.
LIMITATIONS:
- People may not do exercise.
PREPARATION:
- Facilitator must prepare questions.

Guest Speaker
STRENGTHS:
- Personalizes topic.
- Breaks down audience's stereotypes.
LIMITATIONS:
- May not be a good speaker.
PREPARATION:
- Contact speakers and coordinate.
- Introduce speaker appropriately.

Values Clarification Exercise
STRENGTHS:
- Opportunity to explore values and beliefs.
- Allows people to discuss values in a safe environment.
- Gives structure to discussion.
LIMITATION:
- People may not be honest.
- People may be too self-conscious.
PREPARATION:
- Facilitator must carefully prepare exercise.
- Must give clear instructions.
- Facilitator must prepare discussion questions.

SELECTION OF TEACHING METHOD

Teaching methods come in many forms: lecture, class discussion, small group discussion, and videotapes are among just a few types of teaching methods. A well-rounded class should be exposed to multiple teaching methods, not just one. Different students learn better in different ways – there are visual learners, tactile learners, and auditory learners. Also, different subjects and topics are often more understandable when taught in different ways. Here are the strengths and limitations of some of the most common teaching methods:

TEACHING METHOD 1 – LECTURE

Lecture is, perhaps, the most common form of teaching method. Both auditory learners and visual learners can benefit from a lecture – auditory learners natural do best when they have something to listen to, and visual learners can watch gestures and facial expression and take good notes. Tactile learners, on the other hand, may become bored and disinterested. They need something a bit more involving.

Positive aspects of lectures are that they are very useful when teaching large groups and they present factual material in a logical way.

Problems are that the audience is passive and the road of

communication is only one way. It is hard to tell how much the students are learning, as well.

TEACHING METHOD 2– CLASS DISCUSSION

A class discussion is an excellent teaching method – the road to communication is a two-way street, and teachers can really gauge how much their students are learning. A class discussion is a great way to end a lecture – then you get the best of both worlds. And students are more likely to retain the information given in the lecture if they have to use it immediately. Class discussions are a very positive form of teaching methods because you can get ideas from the entire groups 20 brains are better than one. Also, a class discussion can analyse the lecture or even a film or whatever. Everyone can participate in a class discussion.

The problem with a class discussion as a teaching method is that not everyone will participate some students may feel uncomfortable sharing their thoughts in such a large group. Also, the discussion can get way off track. Also, a class discussion takes much more time than a lecture, and therefore although the students may be retaining more information, they may be learning less all together. Also, a class discussion is very difficult with more than 20 people. Another small problem is that with class discussion, students may get confused as to which information is true that is presented and which may be false.

TEACHING METHOD 3– SMALL GROUP DISCUSSION

A small group discussion can be a better teaching method than a class discussion, especially in larger classes. Everyone gets a chance to participate if they are put into a smaller group a smaller group is less intimidating. Also, it is more likely that a small group can reach a consensus.

Of course, just as with class discussions, small group discussions can get side-tracked, and it can be harder for a teacher to gauge whether the group is actually talking about the subject at hand or last night's episode of whatever.

TEACHING METHOD 4 – VIDEOTAPES

Videotapes can show a lot more important visual stimuli than just a teacher with a chalkboard. When talking about a certain animal or a culture, etc., students may understand it better if they can actually see it. Also, videotapes can be very interesting for students – they can grab the attention of students. Videotapes can also stimulate discussion.

Of course, as with other teaching methods, there are also problems with videotapes. Videotapes can raise too many issues. It can be hard to find a video that focuses on the exact subject that you want to present. You have to worry about finding all of the equipment and making sure that it works – if you have trouble with the equipment, valuable time is lost. Also, some students view videotapes as a chance to slack off – they may not feel that they have to learn anything from a video, nor will they likely take notes.

INDUCTIVE METHOD OF TEACHING

Inductive reasoning works the other way, moving from specific observations to broader generalizations and theories. Informally, we sometimes call this a "bottom up" approach. In inductive reasoning, we begin with specific observations and measures, begin to detect patterns and regularities, formulate some tentative hypotheses that we can explore, and finally end up developing some general conclusions or theories.

These two methods of reasoning have a very different "feel" to them when you're conducting research. Inductive reasoning, by its very nature, is more open-ended and exploratory, especially at the beginning. Deductive reasoning is more narrow in nature and is concerned with testing or confirming hypotheses. Even though a particular study may look like it's purely deductive (e.g., an experiment designed to test the hypothesized effects of some treatment on some outcome), most social research involves both inductive and deductive reasoning processes at some time in the project. In fact, it doesn't take a rocket scientist to see that we could assemble the two graphs above into a single circular one that continually cycles from theories down to observations and back up again to theories. Even in the most constrained experiment, the researchers may observe patterns in the data that lead them to develop new theories.

In the process of induction, you begin with some data, and then determine what general conclusion(s) can logically be derived from those data. In other words, you determine what theory or theories could explain the data. For example, you note that the probability of becoming schizophrenic is greatly increased if at least one parent is schizophrenic, and from that you conclude that schizophrenia may be inherited. That is certainly a reasonable hypothesis given the data. Note, however, that induction does not prove that the theory is correct. There are often alternative theories that are also supported by the data. For example, the behaviour of the schizophrenic parent may cause the child to be schizophrenic, not the genes. What is important in induction is that the theory does indeed offer a logical explanation of the data. To conclude that the parents have no effect on the schizophrenia of the children is not supportable given the data, and would not be a logical conclusion.

Deduction and induction by themselves are inadequate for a scientific approach. While deduction gives absolute proof, it never makes contact with the real world, there is no place for observation or experimentation, no way to test the validity of the premises. And, while induction is driven by observation, it never approaches actual proof of a theory. The development of the scientific method involved a gradual synthesis of these two logical approaches.

DEDUCTIVE METHOD OF TEACHING

Deductive reasoning works from the more general to the more specific. Sometimes this is informally called a "top-down" approach. We might begin with thinking up a *theory* about our topic of interest. We then narrow that down into more specific *hypotheses* that we can test. We narrow down even further when we collect *observations* to address the hypotheses. This ultimately leads us to be able to test the hypotheses with specific data — a *confirmation* (or not) of our original theories.

In the process of deduction, you begin with some statements, called 'premises', that are assumed to be true, you then determine what else would have to be true if the premises are true. For example, you can begin by assuming that God exists, and is good, and then determine what would logically follow from such an assumption. You can begin by assuming that if you think, then you must exist, and work from there.

In mathematics you can begin with some axioms and then determine what you can prove to be true given those axioms. With deduction you can provide absolute proof of your conclusions, given that your premises are correct. The premises themselves, however, remain unproven and unprovable, they must be accepted on face value, or by faith, or for the purpose of exploration.

SYNTHETIC METHOD

A type of method of "treating at, and working at, scientific cognitions", opposed to the analytic method. The synthetic method goes from principles to consequents, from the simple to the composite. Also called the progressive method.

A straightforward heuristic-oriented method for stream tearing is proposed in this work. It does not use the traditional methods of evolutionary process-cycle analysis. First, an edge (stream) weighted *spanning-tree* is constructed from the *process graph* using weights based on the 'in' and 'out' degrees of the process digraph vertices.

Second, a *directed acyclic graph* (*DAG*) is constructed such that it is the maximum edge (stream) acyclic sub-set of the process digraph. The *DAG* is constructed by adding ('put-back'), where possible, directed edges (streams) not already in the spanning-tree. A hierachial ordering based on the same preferential weighting system as the *spanning-tree* determines the sequence of the 'put-back' trials.

The remaining edges which cannot be 'put-back' into the *DAG* form a tear set. The weighting system used formed a *minimal cardinality* tear set in all of the examples tested. Prepartitioning of the network into strongly connected components is not required and a node computational order is easily derived. Further, the method is extended to produce tear sets which minimise another set of stream weights, in this case the variables per stream. While the scheme proposed in this paper is heuristic-oriented, most of its methods are contained in classical graph theory and are consequently easily reproduced with efficient algorithms.

A synthetic estimator is one of the simplest estimators for a small area, and it has several variants. In this paper, a ratio-synthetic estimator is proposed and compared with the existing synthetic estimator and it is observed that the gain due to stratification in the case of a synthetic estimator reduces proportional to the domain coverage.

HEURISTIC METHOD

The first heuristic suggests that we make it a habit to purposefully pause and notice things because we know that our automatic perception processes miss a great deal of what goes on around us. The importance of learning to perceive the world in a fresh way is clearly a part of the generally accepted theory of creative thinking. If creative thinking is the novel association of existing concepts in memory, then it follows naturally that it is useful to create a storehouse of concepts. When you pause and notice, you are not looking for anything in particular.

A rule of thumb, simplification, or educated guess that reduces or limits the search for solutions in domains that are difficult and poorly understood. Unlike algorithms, heuristics do not guarantee optimal, or even feasible, solutions and are often used with no theoretical guarantee.

Heuristic is the art and science of discovery and a rule of thumb, simplification, or educated guess that reduces or limits the search for solutions in domains that are difficult and poorly understood. Unlike algorithms, heuristics do not guarantee optimal, or even feasible, solutions and are often used with no theoretical guarantee. 2. (algorithm) approximation algorithm.. The word comes from the same Greek root as "eureka", meaning "to find". A heuristic is a way of directing your attention fruitfully.

The mathematician brought heuristics into popularity in the twentieth century in his book How to Solve It. He learned mathematical proofs as a student, but didn't know how mathematicians think of proofs, nor was this taught. How to Solve It is a collection of ideas about heuristics that he taught to math students: ways of looking at problems and casting about for solutions that often lead somewhere fruitful very quickly.

In computer science, a heuristic is an algorithm or procedure designed to solve a problem that ignores whether the solution is provably correct, but which usually produces a good solution or solves a simpler problem that contains or intersects with the solution of the more complex problem. A heuristic is not guaranteed always to solve the problem, but often solves it well enough for most uses, and often does so more quickly than a more complete solution would.

More formally, a *heuristic* is a function, defined on the nodes of a search tree, which serves as an estimate of the cost of the cheapest path from that node to the goal node.

Heuristics are used by informed search algorithms such as Greedy Best-first search and A* to choose the best node to explore. Greedy Best-first search will choose the node that has the lowest value for the heuristic function. A* will expand nodes that have the lowest value for, where is the (exact) cost of the path from the initial state to the current node. When h(n) is admissible - that is if never overestimates the costs of reaching the goal - A* is provably optimal.

The classical problem involving heuristics is the n-puzzle. Commonly used heuristics for this problem include counting the number of misplaced tiles and finding the sum of the distances between each block and its position in the goal configuration.

HEURISTIC PROBLEM SOLVING

Many heuristics are extremely clever, taking great advantage of the particular structure of the problem to be solved. A problem is a set of instances. Generally, we will look at heuristics for problems, though sometimes a particular instance is important enough to justify heuristics for itself. Furthermore, heuristics for an individual instance can often be generalized to a larger problem. But it is equally important to find general methods of creating heuristics.

These provide quick and dirty solutions to many problems. Although the solution quality may not be the best, often they work well enough. In this section, we will examine some general heuristic techniques. These are random, greedy and exchanging methods. The first two are *solution generation* methods, while the last is a *solution improvement* method. Again, I will illustrate these ideas with the traveling salesman problem, but these are very general heuristic techniques as illustrate in figure

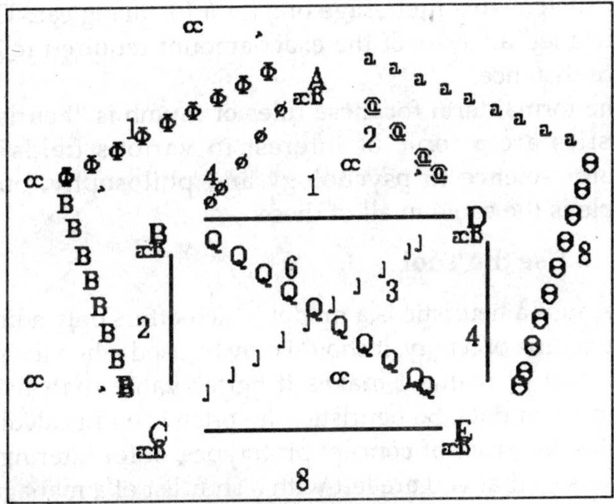

HEURISTIC METHOD

Most of us use "rules of thumb" in all sorts of areas of our daily lives. "When the needle on the fuel level indicator gets to the red, it shows that only 20 miles will be covered", for example, or "Software with a user interface that's anything other than grey or blue hardly ever gets through the user acceptance testing."

These rough rules, based on experience, are invaluable because they help us to make decisions without further detailed fact-finding: Drivers know they don't need to divert immediately to find a fuel station, and the software designer can save him or herself rework later by making the interface blue or grey in the first place.

But no one expects these rules to be 100% accurate: If the car ran out of fuel in 18 miles, the driver wouldn't be particularly surprised, and if testing showed that users actually liked an application that had a tasteful green interface, the developer might raise an eyebrow, but that would be all.

This is because rules of thumb are only used in situations where the risks associated with using a "good enough" approximation are acceptable. No one would use a rule of thumb such as this fuel usage one for a F1 racing car: They'd do a detailed analysis of the exact amount required to cover the race distance.

The formal term for these rules of thumb is "heuristics". Heuristics are a topic of interest in various fields from computer science to psychology and philosophy, but the principle is the same in all of these.

When to Use the Tool

Because a heuristic is a model which offers only a limited representation of reality, it should only be used when the speed or low cost of using it makes it better value than using a detailed set of data. So heuristics are often used in calculating estimates, for proof-of-concept prototypes, or for filtering a set of options so that you are left with a shortlist of a manageable size.

Constructing a Heuristic

Heuristics need to be formalized if they are to be most useful. This raises them above the level of "gut instinct", and it also means that they can be shared with other people.

When you find yourself using your experience to make a judgment, try to work out the rule of thumb that you've just invoked. If possible, add this to your procedure manual, or talk about it with a colleague so that your experience is validated and passed on.

A typical example in a car breakdown call centre might be, "25% of all reported breakdowns are caused by running out of fuel, so always start by asking the driver to check this before you schedule a mechanic."

In this case, using the heuristic allows a certain proportion of breakdowns to be "fixed" immediately, which means that the limited number of mechanics can focus on the real breakdowns.

Heuristics can also be created specifically to solve a problem. For example, creating a diagram or straw man showing a possible solution will help you identify where your basic idea doesn't work, or is lacking some important feature, so that you can refine it more easily.

Another heuristic approach is to take a solution to another problem, and adapt it to solve yours. TRIZ is a systematic and highly developed approach for doing this.

Heuristic Checklists

Whether heuristics are used to filter a large number of options down to a manageable number, or whether you want to make an early "go/no go" decision, you will usually need to draw up a checklist of heuristics, rather than simply use an individual rule of thumb.

For example, in the food industry, the following heuristics might help the product development team decide whether it's worth investing in taking a new pie to the test marketing stage:

- Does the pie look appetizing in its packaging?
- Can it be packaged so that it won't be damaged in transit?
- Can it be cooked in under 20 minutes, so that busy people will buy it?
- Is its shelf life at least 5 days from manufacture to "use by" date?
- Does it maintain its integrity when sliced (or will the pastry topping fall apart when being transferred to a plate)?

This type of list will have been developed based on experience of previous products, and from market research. Of course, there's no guarantee that a pie that meets all these criteria will prove to be a success: it might not taste as good as rival products, and so not attract repeat sales, or the mix of filling ingredients might make it too expensive. However, the heuristic checklist will help the development team quickly and cheaply weed out "non-starters".

Key Points

Heuristics or "rules of thumb" are models based on experience. When you use heuristic, it's important to remember that these models have their limitations, and so heuristics should not be applied in situations where there is a high degree of risk associated with making the wrong choice.

The term "heuristic methods" can be used to describe any problem solving or creativity technique that involves creating a basic model as a starting point for further experimentation or refinement. Heuristic methods are trial-and-error approaches.

DALTON PLAN

OVERVIEW

Its aim is to extend to pupils in secondary departments the opportunities for self -development, which have long been granted to children in the more modern primary schools. The classroom is to be a freer place than usual, the teacher taking the position of a friend and adviser rather than a taskmaster, and the students gathering in natural groups for the working out of problems, which have been suggested rather than assigned. Each room is to be a laboratory in one way or another, with its own library, maps and other apparatus easily accessible to the inquiring student. For certain studies it is suggested that weekly or monthly meetings are sufficient, at which times the teacher can receive reports from the pupil upon the progress of his work.

The practical difficulties seem to be two. In the first place, especial care must be exercised in the estimate of the work which the individual student is capable of doing without waste of time, and in the second place, teachers with sufficient imagination and personality are hard to find. But the search for the latter is worthwhile, and under ideal conditions it should be possible to furnish the students what they require. The ideal conditions include money for space and equipment. The crowded state of most American high schools would be an unfortunate obstacle to the perfecting of the scheme in this country. But the plan, where it does not involve a meaningless kind of freedom, has great educational value, and the means may in time be worked out.

The Dalton Plan is an educational concept inspired by the intellectual ferment at the turn of the nineteenth century, educational thinkers which began to cast a bold vision of a new progressive American approach to education. Helen Parkhurst caught the spirit of change and created the Dalton Plan, aiming to achieve a balance between each child's talents and the needs of the growing community. Specifically, she had these objectives: to tailor each student's programme to his or her needs, interests and abilities; to promote both independence and dependability; to enhance the student's social skills and sense of responsibility toward others. Developed a three-part plan that continues to be the structural foundation of a Dalton education—the House, the Assignment, and the Laboratory. Today, as in the early years, The Dalton School is committed to educating students in accordance with the Dalton Plan.

INTRODUCTION

Inspired by the intellectual ferment at the turn of the 19th century, educational thinkers began to cast a bold vision of a new progressive approach to education. Helen, the teacher who had actually taught the Gold medal winning glass-enclosed Montessori classroom at Panama, after splitting with Montessori, caught the spirit of change and created the Dalton Plan, aiming to achieve a balance between each child's talents and the needs of the growing American community.

Specifically, she had these objectives: to tailor each student's programme to his or her needs, interests and abilities; to promote both independence and dependability; to enhance the student's social skills and sense of responsibility toward others. Park Hurst developed a three-part plan that continues to be the structural foundation of a Dalton education—the House, the Assignment, and the Laboratory.

Inspired by the intellectual ferment at the turn of the nineteenth century, educational thinkers such as John Dewey began to cast a bold vision of a new progressive American approach to education.

Helen caught the spirit of change and created the Dalton Plan, aiming to achieve a balance between each child's talents and the needs of the growing community.

Specifically, she had these objectives: to tailor each student's programme to his or her needs, interests and abilities; to promote both independence and dependability; to enhance the student's social skills and sense of responsibility toward others.

Park Hurst developed a three-part plan that continues to be the structural foundation of a Dalton education—the House, the Assignment, and the Laboratory.

Today, The Dalton School educates students in accordance with some of the precepts of the Dalton Plan.

Inspired by the intellectual ferment at the turn of the nineteenth century, educational thinkers began to cast a bold vision of a new progressive American approach to education. Helen Park Hurst caught the spirit of change and created the Dalton Plan, aiming to achieve a balance between each child's talents and the needs of the growing community.

Specifically, she had these objectives: to tailor each student's programme to his or her needs, interests and abilities; to promote both independence and dependability; to enhance the student's social skills and sense of responsibility toward others.

Park developed a three-part plan that continues to be the structural foundation of a Dalton education—the House, the Assignment, and the Laboratory.

PRECEPTS OF DALTON PLAN

Today, The Dalton School educates students in accordance with some of the precepts of the Dalton Plan.

Freedom

"By 'freedom' we mean freedom to work without interruptions in order to pursue an interest and in order to develop concentration. As applied to an individual, it is understood to mean that he is to be free from those habits or conditions which enslave his life or impede his complete development."

Co-operation

"Instead of the usual grade rooms and grade teachers, we have subject laboratories and specialists; instead of confining the pupils of a single grade to one room, the pupils of four or five grades have access to as many laboratories and are permitted to go from subject laboratory to subject laboratory, mingling and living, within the school, while engaged in school pursuits, just as the community outside the school lives and works."

Budgeting Time

"Under a properly conducted scientific management system, each worker becomes his own efficiency engineer; he studies every factor that influences his production; and he acquires new habits and drops wasteful ones so as to increase his efficiency."

Co-operation

"It is the social experience accompanying the tasks, not the tasks themselves, which stimulate and further both these kinds of growth. Thus the Dalton Plan lays emphasis upon the importance of the child's living while he does his work, and in the manner in which he acts as a member of society, rather than upon the subjects of his curriculum. It is the sum total of these twin experiences which determine his character and his knowledge."

"It is culture acquired through individual development and through collective co-operation."

Budgeting Time

"The Dalton Plan permits pupils to budget their time and to spend it according to their needs."

"From the academic, or cultural point of view the pupil must be made free to continue without interruption his work upon any subject in which he is absorbed, because when interested he is mentally keener.

INSTRUCTIONAL TECHNOLOGY

DEFINITION

Instructional Technology: A self-correcting, systems approach that seeks to apply scientifically derived principles to the planning, design, creation, implementation, and evaluation of effective and efficient instruction.

Instructional Technologists apply research in learning theory, psychology, and emergent technologies to solve instructional and performance problems.

The Presidential Commission on Instructional Technology highlighted four performance areas:

- Design of instruction
- Production of instructional products and events
- Management of instructional settings and resources
- Evaluation of instructional programs

Design activities include analyzing the needs of learners and developing learning systems that are consistent with those needs.

Production involves creating learning materials that meet instructional needs. These materials take many forms, including but not limited to: print-based materials, audio and video tapes, computer-assisted instructional programs, Internet sites, multimedia presentations, interactive video programs, simulations, and games.

Management activities include media centre administration; learning centre design, project supervision and direction, and resource allocation. Evaluation of instruction involves assigning worth to instructional products, programs, or processes designed to solve performance problems or meet instructional needs.

Instructional needs or performance problems may exist in any organization or setting where people are expected to perform. For instance, relevant scenarios might include:

- Instructing limited-English proficient parents regarding child care or school readiness
- Training customers to use a product or employees to use new equipment
- Teaching school teachers or students to use computers
- Providing programs for homebound learners via distance education technologies

Every business, agency, institution, and school is concerned with performance; that is, about each individual's ability to contribute to the mission of the organization and society. Education and training are potent forces to enhance performance because they help assure that people will have the skills, abilities, and attitudes that they need to do their jobs. Workers in the field of Educational Technology use systematic processes to meet educational and training needs. As a result, Educational Technologists help people perform more effectively in rapidly changing technical and social environments.

HISTORY

A Brief History

1920's: Educational objectives, individualized instruction, self-paced, self-corrective workbooks, diagnostic placement tests, must careful design such instruction if its self-led as opposed to traditional, teacher led.

1930's: Objectives were written in terms of student behaviors and thus called "behavioral objectives", formative evaluation (evaluating instructional systems as they are administered) was recognized

1940's: Thousands of soldiers had to be trained quickly,

thousands of training films & instructors' manuals, military training drew well-funded research & development, instructional designers gained prestige (in addition to subject matter experts (SME) and media producer).

1950's: B.F. Skinner, programmed instruction (clear behavioral objectives, small frames of instruction, self-pacing, active learner response, immediate feedback), shifted focus from the teacher behaviour and the educational process to the learners' specific behaviors, task analysis became more important then ever before, Bloom's Taxonomy of Learning

1960's: Gagne & his analysis of learning objectives, criterion-referenced evaluation rather than norm-referenced, military used instructional systems development in standard training procedures

1970's: Needs assessment was first used to determine what the objectives of an instructional system should be rather than assuming a set of objectives, cognitive psychology began to really merge with instructional design

1980's: Personal computer (subverting gains in IT by "computerizing" instruction? or great potential?), instructional systems development by businesses

1990's and Beyond

- 1/ if technology is defined broadly then everyone is an instructional technologist
- 2/ large expenditures on technology while steadfastly keeping hold of teacher-centered traditional instruction (reluctance to move to student-centered learning).
- 3/ little effective research is done in IT because corporations, government and even academia pressure instructional technologists to produce (efficiently, inexpensively trained workers) rather than find answers to the field's questions.
- 4/ thorough needs analysis and evaluation (formative and summative) is avoided as taking too much time and money.
- 5/ lack of proper budget for IT projects and tools,

school districts locked into a structure of educating which is good at funding technology of industrial revolution (mass production, replaceable parts) but poor at accommodating modern technology (distance learning, individualized instruction, etc.)

- 6/ no real consensus between theories of learning (e.g. constructivism vs. behaviorism).
- 7/ education is not recognizing market & business' call for prepared workforce with technology skills and abilities.

PROGRAMMED INSTRUCTIONS

Programmed instruction, method of presenting new subject matter to students in a graded sequence of controlled steps. Students work through the programmed material by themselves at their own speed and after each step test their comprehension by answering an examination question or filling in a diagram. They are then immediately shown the correct answer or given additional information. Computers and other types of teaching machines are often used to present the material, although books may also be used.

Computer-assisted instruction, which both tests students' abilities and marks their progress, may supplement classroom activity or help students to develop ideas and skills independently. The first teaching machine was invented by Sydney L. Pressey, but it was not until the 1950s that practical methods of programming were developed. As programming technology developed, so did the range of teaching machines and other programmed instruction materials.

Programs have been devised for the teaching of spelling, reading, arithmetic, foreign languages, physics, psychology, and a number of other subjects. Some programs are linear in concept, allowing advancement only in a particular order as the correct answer is given. Others are branching, giving additional information at the appropriate level whether a correct or incorrect answer is given.

Although there has been considerable controversy regarding the merits of programmed instruction as the sole method of teaching, many educators agree that it can contribute to more efficient classroom procedure and supplement conventional teaching methods.

Teaching machines enable students to work individually, calling for active participation of the learner. In industry and the armed services, programmed instruction is often used to train personnel. Programmed instruction, method of presenting new subject matter to students in a graded sequence of controlled steps. Students work through the programmed material by themselves at their own speed and after each step test their comprehension by answering an examination question or filling in a diagram.

They are then immediately shown the correct answer or given additional information. Computers and other types of teaching machines are often used to present the material, although books may also be used. Computer-assisted instruction, which both tests students' abilities and marks their progress, may supplement classroom activity or help students to develop ideas and skills independently. Others are branching, giving additional information at the appropriate level whether a correct or incorrect answer is given.

Although there has been considerable controversy regarding the merits of programmed instruction as the sole method of teaching, many educators agree that it can contribute to more efficient classroom procedure and supplement conventional teaching methods. Teaching machines enable students to work individually, calling for active participation of the learner. In industry and the armed services, programmed instruction is often used to train personnel.

OVERVIEW

Operant conditioning has been used in developing programmed learning. According to Skinner, the purpose of programmed learning is to manage human learning under controlled conditions. Typically, a textbook or computer presents the material to be learned in a series of very small steps, called frames. Each frame contains some information and a statement with a blank that the student fills in. The student then uncovers the correct answer (by moving a paper down the page) before going on to the next frame.

Each frame introduces a new idea or reviews material covered earlier. The agreement between the uncovered answer and the student's own response reinforces correct responses, making it likely that they will occur again.

Moreover, shaping is employed, in that the frames start from the student's initial knowledge and in small steps proceed to the final knowledge. The student is therefore usually correct and continues to be reinforced, which keeps him or her at the task until completion.

The principles of programmed learning have been incorporated into a method of instruction that is usually called Personalized System of Instruction (PSI). PSI is a self-paced instruction format where each student works his or her way through the course material, which is broken down into small steps.

Each student must "master" the material in one unit through a quiz before moving on to the next unit. Because of active student participation, small steps, immediate feedback, and reinforcement, PSI can be very effective.

Currently, the principles of programmed learning are being applied to a form of education called computer assisted instruction (CAI). The computer can be used to present learning material and help students learn through a variety of techniques such as quizzes, simulations, explorations, and tests. Computer assisted instruction is effective in part ecause of the availability of immediate feedback.

Computer and Internet sites provide the opportunity for students to actively participate in research. There are currently a number of research opportunities on the Internet. A recent meta-analysis of the efficacy of computer assisted instruction showed it to be an effective educational technique. Programmed learning continues to be an effective way to implement in the classroom some of the basic principles of operant conditioning. Programmed instruction, method of presenting new subject matter to students in a graded sequence of controlled steps. Students work through the programmed material by themselves at their own speed and after each step test their comprehension by answering an examination question or filling in a diagram.

They are then immediately shown the correct answer or given additional information. Computers and other types of teaching machines are often used to present the material, although books may also be used. Computer-assisted instruction, which both tests students' abilities and marks their progress, may supplement classroom activity or help students to develop ideas and skills independently.

TYPES OF PROGRAMMED LEARNING

Originally introduced by behaviorist Skinner, programmed instruction is a system whereby the learner uses specially prepared books or equipment to learn without a teacher. It was intended to free teachers from burdensome drills and repetitive problem solving inherent in teaching basic academic subjects like spelling, arithmetic, and reading. Skinner based his ideas on the principle of operant conditioning, which theorized that learning takes place when a reinforcing stimulus is presented to reward a correct response.

In early programmed instruction, students punched answers to simple math problems into a type of keyboard. If the answer was correct, the machine would advance to another problem. Incorrect answers would not advance. Skinner believed such learning could, in fact, be superior to traditional teacher-based instruction because children were rewarded immediately and individually for correct answers rather than waiting for a teacher to correct written answers or respond verbally. Programmed instruction quickly became popular and spawned much educational research and commercial enterprise in the production of programmed instructional materials. It is considered the antecedent of modern computer-assisted learning.

Two types of programmed learning can be compared. Linear programming involves a simple step-by-step procedure. There is a single set of materials and students work from one problem to the next until the end of the programme. Branching programming is more complex. Students choose from multiple-choice answers and then are prompted to proceed to another page of the book depending on their answer. If a correct answer is given, students move on to another page with more information to learn and more questions to answer. An incorrect answer leads to comments on why the answer is incorrect and a direction to return to the original question to make another selection.

Just as the programming developed more complexity over the years, so did the teaching machines themselves. Early, simple machines were little more than electronic workbooks. Later machines allowed students to be instructed on more complex material that required more than one-word or one-number responses. In some, students could write their responses and move ahead by comparing their answers to acceptable answers. Programmed-learning books differ from traditional workbooks because they actually teach new information through this step-by-step stimulus-response method rather than simply offering practice material for already-learned skills.

Research has shown that programmed learning often is as successful, and sometimes more successful, than traditional teacher-based learning because it recognizes the different abilities and needs of individual children. Students who have mastered the material can move ahead more quickly, while those who need more practice are repeatedly exposed to the problems. Programmed learning also allows teachers more time to concentrate on more complex tasks. One criticism of programmed learning centers on the lack of student-teacher interaction. It has been shown that some students thrive more fully with the human motivation inherent in more traditional learning situations.

CONCEPT OF PROGRAMMED LEARNING

Programmed learning represents a highly individualized and systematic instructional strategy for classroom instructions as well as self-learning. It is now considered as one of the most important innovations in the field of education.

Susan Markle's View

"Programmed leaning is a method of designing a reproducible sequence of instructional events to produce a measurable and consistent effect on behaviour of each and every acceptable student."

Harold W. Bernard's View

"Programmed learning refers to the arrangement of instructional material in progressive sequences".

Michael J. Apter's View

"Programmed instruction is a method of instruction in which the information to be taught is broken down into small units which are to be presented to the student (usually in written form) in a carefully planned sequence. Each unit or 'frame' contains not only conformation but is also terminated with a question."

View of Smith and Moore

"Programmed instruction is the process of arranging the material to be leaned into a series of sequential steps. Usually it moves the student from a familiar background into a complex and net set of concepts, principles and understanding."

View of Espich and Williams

"Programmed instruction is a planned sequence of experiences leading to proficiency, in terms of response relationship that has proven to be effective".

Edgar Dale's View

"Programmed instruction is systematic, step by step, self-instructional programme aimed to ensure the learning of stated behaviour". In the light of the above definitions it can be concluded that programmed learning is a method of individualized instructions in which the student receives information relating to his won needs in progressive sequences but in small units.

CHARACTERISTICS OF PROGRAMMED LEARNING

- Individualized instructions.
- Logical sequence of material.
- Interaction between the learner and the programme.
- Immediate knowledge of results.
- Organized nature of knowledge.
- Learner's own speed.
- Constant evaluation.

PRINCIPLES OF PROGRAMMED LEARNING

Mandatory principles Obligatory principles

- Objective specification 1.Overt/active responding
- Empirical testing 2.Immediate feedback
- Self pacing 3.Small step size

FUNDAMENTAL PRINCIPLES OF PROGRAMMED LEARNING

- Principle of small steps
- Principle of active responding
- Principle of immediate confirmation
- Principle of self-pacing
- Principle of evaluation

STYLES OF PROGRAMMING

Prominent important conventional styles of programming are as under:

- Linear Programming
- Branching Programming
- Mathematics
- Computer-assisted instruction
- Learner-controlled instruction

Here we shall discuss the first two.

Linear or Extrinsic Style of Programming

The linear style of programming was developed by Skinner and his associates. This is also known as the Skinnerian style of programming. The techniques associated with this style of programming are based on the principle that the learner's original response should be gradually altered or shaped until he meets some standard of acceptable performance.

Basic Assumptions of Linear Programming

- Activeness
- Small units
- Immediate reinforcement
- Psychological arrangement of contents
- Freedom
- Hindrance by errors

Features or Advantages of Linear Style of Programming

- Linear arrangement
- Small steps
- Controlled responses
- Response is emphasized
- Structural responses
- Active responding
- Immediate feedback
- Prompting
- Self-pacing
- Minimum errors
- Simple mechanism
- Best suited in certain subject areas
- Discouraging cheating
- Skip-linear programme

Applications of Linear Programme

Linear programs have effectively been used in the following situations:

- Small children

- Slow learner
- Homogenous
- Hierarchical order
- Immediate feedback
- Inadequate initial behaviour
- Difficult material
- Specific terminology
- Less motivated teachers
- Remedial instruction and self-study
- Complete mastery

Limitations of Linear Style of Programming

- Lack of motivation
- No freedom of choice
- No development of discriminative power
- Encouraging guesswork
- Serial order learning
- Difficulty in finding background
- Not student centered
- No specified role of teacher
- Teacher-proof programme

Branching or Intrinsic Style of Programming

Branching programme may be produced for use on a teaching machine or in a book form. The book form is known as a 'scrambled text' because the pages do not follow in a normal sequence.

Assumptions of Branching Programme

- Needs of the learner
- Wholeness of the content
- Meaningful units
- Analysis of the task
- New material
- No hindrance by errors
- Remediation
- Multiple choice items

- Sufficient freedom
- Discrimination

Techniques in Branch Programming (types of branching)

Backward Branching

It is based on the principle of 'repeating the missed frames'. As shown in the diagram below the learner from frameNo.1 of the main stream goes to frame No. 2 of the main steam only if he makes a correct choice.

But if he makes a wrong choice, he is led to remedial frame wherein he is given some more help in understanding the concept and in solving the solution by a better logic. He will be then directed to the original frame No. 1 so that he can red it again and answer it correctly in the light of the remedial material he has received.

So the learner who has committed error goes through the same frame twice (once before the remedial material and once after the remedial material).

Forward Branching

In the forward branching, whether the learner makes a wrong choice or correct choice he will always be going to new pages, thus physically progressing from page to page.

Principles of Branching Programme

- Principle of exposition
- Principle of diagnosis
- Principle of remediation

Features or Characteristics or Advantages of Branching Programme

- Based on traditional tutorial method
- Individualized instruction
- Larger frame
- Multiple choice questions
- Freedom to choose path
- Alertness of learners

- Detection and correction of errors
- Development of discrimination and creativity
- Useful in concept learning
- Controlled material
- Psychological and social motivation
- Easier to develop frames
- Teaching and instruction
- Programmed text

Limitations of branching programme:

- Guessing
- Difficulty in multiple choice questions
- Difficulty in arranging the branching sequences
- Unfeasibility of infinite branching
- Not suitable for small children
- Inability to control the student
- Costly
- Emphasis on remediation
- No sequence of pages
- Suitable feedback
- Programmer's imagination

COMPUTER ASSISTED INSTRUCTIONS

DEFINITION

Computers can play an important role in the teaching/ learning process occurring in medical education. Computer-Assisted-Instruction (CAI) is an area of computer use most often designed for direct instruction, skill development, tutorial, and enrichment. Software programs are available or can be developed in formats for many subjects and skill areas. CAI has been used for practice in thinking skills, problem solving and decision making, and for doing research. Usually each programme is designed for a specific instructional purpose. CAI-type software programs can be used for many learning activities. The capability of the computer to interact with individual students and to provide immediate feedback makes it the key to computer assisted instruction.

TIPS

Media Selection

The effectiveness of course design depends upon the media selected to help communicate the content. Each medium has its own strengths and weaknesses. These must be kept in mind when matching the medium to the learning environment.

The challenge is to find ways to use media to enhance or enable student learning. What does it take to have a successful learning experience?

Observation Techniques

Making an observation involves the use of the five senses, singularly or in any combination. Observation is a fundamental scientific skill. It is obviously very important to the practice of medicine. Observational skills are just as essential for effective teaching. It is the initial method by which the instructor collects information to understand his/her world, comparing it to his/her cognitive, procedural, or affective knowledge base.

Teachers observe what students say or do and compare that to their knowledge base. These observations of students and resultant comparisons are very important, as they form the basis for the next instructional step - a continuation with no comment, the provision of positive or negative feedback, or a redirection of instruction to address an identified student need.

It is a particularly useful skill in individualized, laboratory, small group, and clinical instruction.

The appearance of the microcomputer revitalized the CAI movement. Because computers were now smaller and cheaper, and because they were beginning to find their way into the everyday lives of average individuals, they became more palatable to schools and districts almost overnight.

During this time, CAI began to differentiate itself from some of its failed Skinnerian predecessors by changing its role, presence, and the relative ease of delivering instructional content; however, it was still grounded in its behaviorist roots.

Additionally Venezky go on to claim that the resurgence of CAI in the early 1980s did little, if anything, to solve the underlying problems with previous instructional efforts; rather, the relative simplicity of producing and delivering content on these byte-sized technological wonders encouraged publishers to go back to the well and develop new programs without any clear improvements or additional research.

In the two decades that have passed since the rebirth of CAI, the landscape of computer-based instruction has changed surprisingly little.

The National Educational Technology Plan points to near ubiquitous presence of computers and internet access in schools today, yet acknowledges a significant lack of planning and preparation for teachers and schools to make full use of these advantages.

Even in the event that large-scale planning and teacher training lead to increased use of computers in the classroom, it is unlikely that such a change will manifest itself as CAI; in an age where such programs are referred to as "drill-and-kill" software, institutional memory of previous failures works to inoculate schools and districts from widespread adoption of anything resembling 20th century CAI initiatives.

Instead, schools will be more likely to exploit specific advantages of computers in an attempt to deliver instructional content based on modern educational theories and practice

DESIGNING A CAI

In designing a CAI lesson you have to take care about the following items as explained:

HUMANIZE – PERSONIFICATION

- Name and Refer to Computer
- Good for Young Children
- Nonthreatening
- One-on-One

USE LEARNER'S NAME

- Conversational Context

Familiarity

Reminder of Individual

USE BACKGROUND INFORMATION

Identify Relevant Information

- Career goals
- Current grade level
- Sibling or pet names
- Level of experience, title

Sources of Relevant Information

- User Questionnaire
- Employee Files, Progress Reports

ADD PREVIOUS RESPONSES

Reminders of Previous Answers

- LTM ——> STM.
- Lesson, Unit, Course Level.
- Illustrate incorrectness.
- Queue for a more appropriate response.
- Track initial response and introduce at a given point in a lesson.

USE RELEVANT EXAMPLES

Based on Lesson Content and Context

- Concrete objects, manipulatives.
- "Real-life" illustrations of concepts.
- Contextually applied examples, illustrations are more effective.

LEARNER CONTROL

Instructional Options

- Unrestricted.

- Advisement strategy.
- Limited.
- Transfers the responsibility for learning from designer to the student.

USE DIFFERENT PACING OPTIONS

Computer Controlled

- Timing display frames.
- Designer sets time-frames.
- Good example - increase reading speed.
- Base decisions on amount of information, student familiarity, environment, nature of the performance.

Pacing Considerations

Learner-Controlled

- Student dictates lesson speed.
- Good for differing student abilities.
- Not good in situations where automatic responses are needed (recall of rote facts).
- Good for introducing facts, and situations where accuracy is valued over speed.

Pacing Considerations

Combined Pacing

- Provides balance unless unusually long viewing periods are observed.
- Good for a varied student groups.
- Provides substantial interaction with lesson content.

EMPHASIZE PERFECT PRACTICES

Increases Learner Interaction

- Encourages conceptual bridge development.
- Serves to strengthen prior learning.
- Reinforces correct learning.

- Fosters skill acquisition.
- Shapes and guides correct response generation.

USE CRITERION-BASED QUESTIONS

Based on level, interaction, & objectives

- Questions should:
  - Clearly relate to lesson content.
  - Have precisely defined directions.
  - Indicate acceptable responses.
  - Use screen space appropriately.
- Question formats:
  - Choice selection, press enter.
  - Y/N, T/F, (single keystroke responses).
  - Cursor & mouse control.

Write Goals and Objectives

Frame the Story and Develop the Patient Scenario Storyboard or Script

- A storyboard provides sketches of frames or scenes, with accompanying information regarding dialog, setting, and or transitions. The strength of the storyboard lies in its ability to give a visual representation or overview of what the scene should look like (usually through cartoon or stick figure diagrams).
- The script is a paper version or outline of your video. It contains dialog characters, plot, and can be broken down into parts called, scenes or acts.
- Answer: Who, What, When, Where, How and Why?

Develop Critical Thinking Questions, Include

- Correct answer with rationale.
- Incorrect answers with rationale.

Include Copyright Statement

- The United States copyright law protects this

product. Copyright law protects computer software and duplication or distribution of copyrighted software violates the law.

Include Disclaimer

- Nursing is a constantly changing field. New research has increased nursing knowledge and changes in nursing practice occur daily. Although attempts have been made to consistently update and provide the newest and most current information, readers must be advised that errors may occur. The information contained in this scenario is a synopsis of ideas from the literature. The recommendations included in the scenario about the care of patients are opinions formed from this information. The author assumes no responsibility or liability. Before acting on any of these suggestions, the reader should obtain and review detailed current information about these different treatments and medications.

Remember the Following Tips

- Content (function) is more important than style (fashion).
- Beware of bells and whistles:
  - Design for the lowest common denominator - students often do not have the latest technology and may be connecting to the Internet with dial up connections rather than DSL or cable.
  - Large images and audio files may take a long time to load and may frustrate the end user.

CAI PROGRAMME

- Click here to save the self-extracting zip file to your desktop.
- Create a new folder on your desktop named "CAI Template."
- Double click on the saved file (cai.exe) to begin the self-extractor.

- Extract the files to the "CAI Template" folder.
- Copy the "CAI Template" folder.
- Rename the copied folder to represent the topic of your CAI; for example, "Acute Renal Failure CAI."
- Make a similar copy of the "CAI Template" folder for each new CAI (always preserving the CAI Template folder for future development).
- Open the index.htm file in the newly renamed folder using your preferred html editor.
- Replace the text in the index file as directed; save the file (using the same file name) after changes are made.
- Modify each file in the newly renamed folder using the html editor; save each file (using the same file name) after changes are made.
- Transfer the the newly renamed folder containing the modified files from the hard drive of your computer to your web page using a file transfer protocol (FTP) utility such as WS-FTP LE (free to educational users) or ask your IT department for assistance.
- Place a link to the newly renamed folder on a web page that introduces the CAI and gives the student instructions for completion - your first CAI is ready to go!

SPECIFICATION OF CAI PLAN

Front-end analysis, as the name implies, takes place right at the beginning of a project. It involves a series of analyses:

- *Problem*: is there a problem? What is it?
- *Needs*: is there a need for training or should some other solution be employed?
- *Audience*: what are the skills, knowledge, and attitudes (SKAs) of the target audience?
- *Job*: what tasks make up the job? Which are most important?

- *Task*: what does each task entail?
- *Content*: what information must I/should I impart?

In education, we're lucky because some of the front-end analysis is already done for us, so we can simplify or eliminate several steps. Specifically, unless you're serving on a curriculum committee, someone somewhere has already decided there's a problem, and that problem can best be solved by instruction, so there go analyses 1 & 2.

Also, we sometimes may be able to reduce or eliminate the task analysis step, which leaves us with just three of the six front-end analyses: Audience analysis, job analysis, and content analysis.

AMERICAN SYSTEMS operates within a quality system that provides repeatable and predictable processes and procedures for a fully articulated front end analysis. Front end analysis clarifies overall organizational requirements.

An AMERICAN SYSTEMS FEA serves several purposes—identifies performance goals and specific task objectives to meet those goals, provides insight into gaps between what people actually do or know and what they need to do or know, defines the traits and characteristics needed to perform at a desired level of competency, documents the work environment and work flow of which training is one component, and helps you understand the technical capabilities and constraints of the workplace.

FEATURES

Front End Analysis encompasses a variety of products that support new training introduction, problem resolution and financial assessments. Cape Henry Associates develops a variety of analysis products to meet the needs of the Programme Manager or Training Developer.

- For new systems introduction, Cape Henry conducts an in-depth Training Situation Analysis to determine if additional training is required for the system. Data collection methods may include review of engineering drawings or technical manuals and interview with Subject Matter Experts, among other methods. This phase of analysis also examines existing training facilities, the student population and the current training support staff requirements. This analysis forms a basis for estimating the scope of the Instructional Systems Design process.

- For legacy systems, Needs Assessment is the process used to address specific problems associated with operating and/or maintaining a system or equipment. This assessment is conducted to determine the root cause of a deficiency. If the root cause is identified as a training deficiency, a Training Programme Needs Assessment and Analysis is conducted. The final product of these assessments is a recommendation for a training solution which produces the desired occupational result.
- Where multiple training options are available, a Cost-Benefit or Business Case Analysis is performed. This analysis defines the potential training options, their associated costs, and the advantages and drawbacks associated with each of the options. A final recommendation is forwarded that provides the basis for a Programme Manager to make an informed, defensible decision.

Front-End Module

It depends who makes it and for whom. The module is made of several components and sub-assemblies, including structural front-end carrier, headlights, radiator, engine cooling fan systems, and energy absorption beam. It may also contain wiring harnesses and related electrical functions and can include the bumper fascia.

The major functions of the front-end components are to act as a body frame, taking in and cooling air, protecting the vehicle and its occupants in the event of a collision, properly illuminating the front of the vehicle as well as improved appearance and exterior styling.

By outsourcing front-end modules, automakers are able to reduce the number of operations on their assembly lines, simplify their supply chains, reduce modular weight and improve the ergonomic aspects of the assembly process. It can also help cut tooling costs and improve working capital. The most important potential benefit of modular construction is standardisation, allowing suppliers to offer standard solutions to different manufacturers and hence bring costs down. On the global stage, the main proponents of outsourcing front-end modules include the Volkswagen Group, Chrysler, Hyundai Kia, Nissan, Mercedes, BMW and Fiat.

"Our customers select us because we bring our global experience to the table," said Martin Schüler, president and CEO of HBPO. "In many cases HBPO is completely responsible for the design and the integration of functions in the FEM including the qualification and selection of suppliers. We reach the targets for weight and space while fulfilling the safety requirements.

This leads to a better performance of the car and to better insurance classifications which then results to higher sales." Headquartered in Lippstadt, Germany, HBPO GmbH was founded in 2004 as a joint venture between the three auto parts suppliers, Hella, Behr, and Plastic Omnium to combine their expertise to produce front-end modules. It is the successor to Hella-Behr Fahrzeugsysteme GmbH joint venture which had been established in 1999. Each partner is a leader in its respective field: Hella in lighting and electronics, Behr in air conditioning and engine cooling systems, and Plastic Omnium Auto Exterior in body parts and modules, impact absorption and pedestrian protection systems. HBPO employs 1,300 people at sites dotted around Europe, North America and Asia.

"We supply front end modules at Audi, BMW, and Chrysler and front-end carriers at Renault and PSA," said Martial Pata, vice president in charge of Faurecia's front-end module division. "We leverage over 15 years experience in this product and expertise in module architecture to propose solutions that fulfill a wide range of customer needs." Faurecia produces over 1 million front-end modules, 2 million engine ventilation systems, 3 million front-end carriers and 4 million bumper systems annually.

The other main suppliers of front-end modules include Calsonic Kansei, Decoma International, Denso, Hyundai Mobis, Peguform and Visteon. However, the market has consolidated over the past decade. In terms of further market consolidation, Norm Guschewski, director, business development, exterior modules, Decoma International, told us: "We believe anything can happen in this environment. Becoming a global front-end module supplier requires a significant investment in human capital, which many companies simply cannot invest in until a programme is awarded. This can be an inhibitor to many up-start module suppliers." Decoma International's front- and rear-end modules include front and rear fascias, cooling modules, energy absorbers, bumper beams, air dams, lighting, grille opening panels, grilles and complete module assemblies. The company globally supplies two million front end modules and 18 million fascias annually.

While the European market stabilises, the North American market for front-end modules continues to grow. Guschewski added: "The original North American Big Three have begun to recognise that the European and Asian OEMs have executed many of their car lines with a front-end module strategy, providing best-in-class fit and finish, with significant cost and weight savings. Our customers have completed their own internal benchmarking and are questioning their past decisions." Over the past few years, Decoma International's position in the North American front-end module market has strengthened due to its stronger ties with Chrysler. "Chrysler has been the most aggressive in its shift to an FEM strategy."

in terms of establishing compatibility between different vehicle brands and models to compensate for differences in height and direct energies towards zones of structure deformation of the car. Above all, it has taken on a whole new dimension following recently adopted standards of pedestrian protection. Indeed, the interest in front-end modules has increased partly due to the focus on vehicle safety issues and the need to comply with guidelines from the European Union for pedestrian safety. The first phase of the EU's stringent pedestrian protection rules took effect in October 2005. This first phase considers 'leg' and 'adult head' impact and measures injury criteria. In response, some automakers have added plastic energy absorbers to their vehicle's front bumpers. The second phase will progressively come into force starting in 2010. This will introduce criteria concerning 'upper leg' (hip impact) and 'child head' impact and will see more stringent 'leg' impact criteria.

For some time, engineers at SABIC Innovative Plastics have been pushing back the technical boundaries in the front-end module arena using its plastic innovations. "Pedestrian protection rules effectively require cars to be constructed with a 'soft' energy absorbent layer surrounding the 'hard' steel crash structure," said Derek Buckmaster, global market director, automotive exteriors, SABIC Innovative Plastics. "Plastics can enable automakers to help them meet these rules through providing the energy absorption capabilities not readily obtained with steel structures. SABIC offers unique CAE [computer aid design] simulation capabilities and testing facilities dedicated to pedestrian safety protection. Our engineers work side-by-side with OEM and tier one supplier engineering to ensure performance that meets predicted results."

SYMPOSIUM

DEFINITION

The Symposium is a Socratic dialogue by Plato. The Symposium is one of the most controversial of Plato's dialogues.

Some argue that it proves incontrovertibly that Socrates engaged in pederasty; and furthermore that denial of this is merely wishful thinking by those who cannot bear a speck on Socrates' reputation. Others claim equally stridently, that not only does it not prove any such thing, but that it is in fact artfully constructed to rebut just those kinds of calumnies propagated by Socrates political enemies. Arguably it could also be intended thus without being true, but that view has not been proffered much. It is necessary to be careful when judging the ancients to avoid modern standards. Male homosexuality among the aristocracy was perfectly acceptable in ancient Greece, and pederasty was institutionalised in Sparta at least. Just as in many other societies, some circles of the middle class were much less liberal in outlook.

It is also a notable dialogue of Socrates with one of his own teachers, the deeply and broadly learned courtesan Diotima. This is still another type of forum. By providing two or three speakers, each charged with the duty of presenting a different point of view, the symposium consciously attempts to direct audience attention to various approaches toward the problem under consideration. In this it leaves less to chance than does the informal discussion or the panel discussion. It is to be preferred to the single-speaker forum unless the single expert can make a brilliant presentation. Naturally its success will also depend upon the competence of the symposium members.

A possible disadvantage of the symposium is inherent in dividing the lecture time between two or three individuals. No one of them can give anything but a cursory treatment of his phase of the subject. Thus the symposium may lose in depth while it gains in comprehensiveness. This tendency to lack detailed treatment may be balanced by spreading the symposium over several meetings, all dealing with the same general subject.

Participation by the audience is usually more limited in the symposium than it is in the single-speaker forum or dialogue, but the general technique, i. e., the duties of the moderator, the speakers, and the audience, are the same as in the single-speaker forum.

SETTING OF SYMPOSIUM

From the very start of the dialogue, the reader's nose is rubbed in the fact that this is no ordinary Socratic dialogue. The cultural elite of Athens is celebrating Agathon having won the prize for his first tragedy. Our first view of Socrates as he is about to join the second day of revels in the artists honour, has him washed and primped up and "even" wearing shoes! Such celebrations are the occasion of getting drunk, speaking with excessive liberty, and sometimes even the truth.

DISCUSSION

The beginning of the discussion is dominated by very lightharted banter and ribbing between all present, but as the evening progresses talk turns to the deep subject of Eros. Socratic irony notwithstanding, Plato is not known for using much hilarity in his dialogues. But now even Eros is subjected by most, including Socrates.

A challenge is presented, and Phaedrus, Pausanias, Eryximachus, Aristophanes, Agathon all make speeches of praise pursuant to the challenge. All that remains is for Socrates to give his.

First Socrates wants to interrogate Agathon in his usual manner. This he does, arguing somewhat flippantly that Eros is not beautiful. Though the argument is superficially lightheartedly constructed, some have argued that this is just Plato palming the card, and that it is actually the genuine view Socrates has of Eros.

Then comes the buildup to the final climax. Socrates speaks. He actually recounts a story! In his youth he associated much with the wise courtesan Diotima, who initiated the young Socrates into the Art of Love. As Socrates tells the story, Diotima revealed to Socrates that all lusts stem from the will to eternity and immortality through creation of things, and even the begetting of children, as this is the only victory over death.

The thoroughly soused Alcibiades saunters in shouting and making a scene. He is wearing garlands of violets, ivy and ribbons. Enquiring if the feast will allow him to join even in his excessively drunk state, he makes deprecating humour about it.

All gladly ask him to join, though Socrates makes a witty remark about what a jealous boy he is, not wanting Socrates to sit next to any other beautiful boy.

Since Alcibiades is new to the party but has not yet

participated in the challenge, they ask his proffer. But he in turn mocks Socrates, making the biting and somewhat indescreet remark that Socrates will not allow gods or men praised, unless it be Socrates himself. Intimating both in context of the party and of the dialogue itself, that Socrates did not indeed think much of gods. Even in a drinkathon this is too much for Socrates. He snaps: "Can't you hold your tongue?"

Eryximachus defuses the situation by suggesting that Alcibiades indeed praise Socrates.

Though he claims to do so, he wants to do so by simile. Oddly enough he launches into a mock-attack on Socrates, under the guise of being an unrequited lover of him. That though Socrates seeks the company of pretty boys, he never consummates a relationship with any of them. He tells how he himself tried to seduce Socrates, wrestling with him at the gym and so forth; nothing, zilch.

And then comes the climax of the whole dialogue. After a longwinded account of both their (but principally Socrates') wartime bravery, deprecating his own, but flattering Socrates'; Alcibiades makes the claim that Socrates' only interest in hanging out with young and sexy prepubescent boys is so he can prevent any other elder tutors having the chance of making love to them and instead make them love all the good and virtuous things.

After a bit of light byplay, the dialogue fades away, as a huge crowd of revellers enter, and in the general hubbub, no-one is able to hold sustained and focused conversation anymore.

CONCLUSIONS

The less controversial salient point of the dialogue is the insight we get both to Socrates' wartime relationship with Alcibiades and of Diotima tutoring Socrates in the purpose of sex among other things. These are confirmed elsewhere, but here they are expressed as coming from Socrates' and Alcibiades' own mouth, whatever we might think of the reliability of Plato in reporting those speeches.

What then of the more controversial question of Socrates' sexual inclinations. The only fair judgment, even if it appears to be equivocal, is to say that the Symposium definitely does offer ammunition to both those who say that Socrates did like boys, and also to those who deny it. Eros is in the eye of the beholder.

WORKSHOP

DEFINITION

Workshops bring together the key people in a project, in a facilitated group session, to accomplish certain objectives. Workshop attendees may be from the business community (users) as well as from the technical community, or they may be from outside of the enterprise; the point is to bring together all of the people who have the requisite knowledge to address an identified issue. Serial interviewing and the potential for misinterpretation of important information is avoided.

The workshop technique can be used for any situation which requires something more than a simple meeting or round table discussion, such as quick turnaround of information, multiple sources of information, and overcoming political or personal roadblocks to project success.

BENEFITS

There are many qualitative and quantitative benefits of employing the workshop technique. Providing a structured environment where key stakeholders can discuss important topics openly results in improved decisions making, ownership and consensus, improved deliverable quality, more effective project teams and reduced time and cost.

WORKSHOP ROOM

- The room in which a workshop is conducted should be large enough to contain the number of participants. The ideal furniture configuration is a "U" shaped table. Adequate walking room should be provided along with separate areas for a refreshment table, an observer's table, and breakout areas. Neither the participants nor the facilitators should feel cramped or closed-in. Lighting should be variable for use with slides, overheads, and/or PC-screen image projection. An example of a Workshop room shows the basic layout.

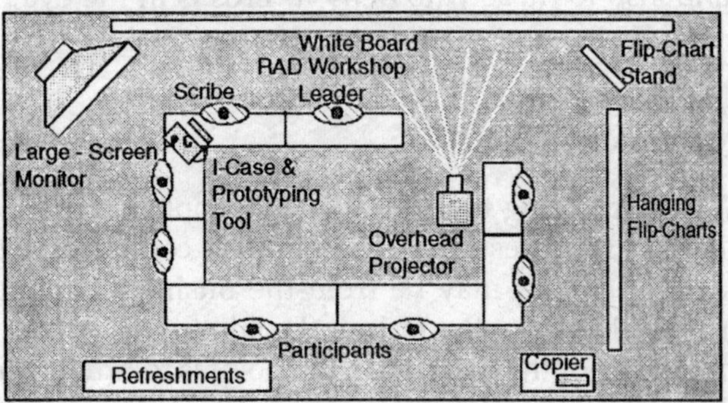

Equipment

Equipment is frequently needed in the rooms in which workshops are conducted. Typical equipment includes:

Traditional items

- One or more large white boards with dry erasable colored markers.
- A kit for building diagrams and specially shaped blank magnets useful for modeling exercises.
- At least two flip charts with extra pads of paper, colored markers, and sufficient wall space to hang and display multiple flip chart sheets. Lined or graph-paper sheets make it easier to write legibly. (More flip charts may be required if the group will work in sub-teams during the workshop.)
- Stickers for structured exercises. Stickers come in multiple colors and large and small sizes. A stapler, scissors, paper clips, and related office equipment are usually included in the kitbag.

Computer Items

- PC with word processing, graphics, and software

development tools. A large screen monitor or projector device helps all participants view the screens clearly and easily.

- Printer to provide participants with models, screen designs and supporting materials.

Electronic Items

- Access to a copier (if not provided in the room) to produce copies of information created.
- Slide projector for use with prepared slides.
- Videotape player and monitor if videotapes are planned to be used.
- Overhead projector and screen, with overhead transparency colored markers, prepared and blank transparencies. An extra projector bulb and sufficient electrical cord length are helpful.
- Tape recorders and telephones should not be used. An instant camera may be useful for photographing white boards and flip charts.

Amenities

- Separate refreshment table (e.g., coffee, juice, and Danish in morning; coffee and/or sodas and cookies in the afternoon).

WORKSHOP LOCATION

Location

Workshops work best when held off-site, that is, away from the normal work location of the participants.

Most hotels and conference centers provide facilities outfitted with the equipment listed above.

Many enterprises have created JAD rooms, group decisions support centers, or facilitated work rooms which can also be used.

If workshops are held on-site, take care to ensure that the participants are focusing on the workshop issues and are not being disrupted by day-to-day operations. Avoid group disintegration.

Duration

Workshops vary in duration. They may range from one day to many days. One, three, and four-day sessions are common and tend to be the most frequently used structure. Complex topics may require multiple workshops.

Specific Hours

Workshops are typically conducted during normal business or working hours. Some sessions go late into the night, but common sense should be used when making scheduling decisions. Workshops are intense events and the participants' motivation and attitude has to be managed properly to maximize their usefulness.

Full and Half-day Sessions

Full day sessions are always preferred, but some cultures and availability constraints may dictate half-day sessions. One advantage to half-day sessions is that the facilitator has time to prepare for the next session. Another advantage is that deliverables can be reviewed, modified, or produced by the scribe(s). With half-day sessions, it is imperative to employ meeting management and behaviour control facilitation techniques. Group effectiveness needs to be maintained.

Marathon Sessions

Great results can be achieved in marathon sessions; however, experience shows that participants (and the facilitator) are not at their best the following morning. Client culture, level of participant, and type of workshop will also impact the length of the workshop day.

WORKSHOP AGENDA

Start-Up

- Welcome remarks from facilitator and/or project manager(s).
- Housekeeping items (rest room locations, message system, smoking areas, etc.)

- Schedule Review.
- Executive Owner kick-off speech (optional, may be performed during Pre-Workshop activities).
- Start-Up items should be limited to 15 to 20 minutes.

Prepare to Work

- Introduction to the workshop technique: Overview of the project purpose and approach. This reinforces comfort levels and sets the work to be done in the next module. Allow no more than 30 minutes.
- Review agenda and make changes as required (helps to establish rapport with group).
- Review and set Rules of Operation.
- Review scope and objectives (i.e., check expectations). At the start of each session, both in the morning, after lunch and at the close of each workshop day, it is typical to review agenda and check expectations.
- Execute ice-breaker or start-up exercise (optional).

Work Module

The Work Module agenda is customized based on the type of workshop; the particular objectives, and special client needs. Moderators should use facilitation techniques to manage the work items performed during this module. Keep to the schedule, but remain flexible for modifications.

Closure Module

- At the end of each workshop day.
- Review Agenda.
- Summarize progress.
- Modify as appropriate.
- Elicit participant feedback and check expectations.
- Always thank participants for their time and contribution.
- Allow a minimum of 15 minutes to accomplish the above.

Closing

- Always review objectives, goals, and agenda items.
- Summarize results to build up ownership.
- As an option, have the Executive Owner give a five minute closing wrap-up.
- Review open issues and check assignments
- Prepare action plan.
- Evaluation and closure. (Current convention is to distribute a workshop evaluation form. Participants' comments are invaluable for improving the workshop technique and for collecting additional perspective information.

Allow at least one hour to bring closure to each workshop.

PARTICIPANT SELECTION

Selection

Participation should be full-time during the workshop, whether full-day or half-day sessions. Participants from the business community (users) should be selected based on their value and ability to contribute to the creation of workshop deliverables. The actual workshop should not be held until all the key participants are available. This may often require the Executive Owner to clear calendars/schedules to get the most knowledgeable users in the workshop.

Visiting participants may be allowed to attend the workshop as silent observers or as subject area experts. Subject experts may be part-time and only scheduled for certain workshop modules or activities.

Preparation

Participants should be briefed prior to attending a workshop. Formal briefing meetings may be held in conjunction with kick-off meetings or separately. Any available materials pertinent to the project such as a list of objectives or coping documents should be provided. Any models which exist may also be distributed.

Participants should also be trained in any and all

diagramming conventions which will be used during the workshops. Example walkthroughs may be required based on the familiarity with information engineering concepts.

Typically a one half day briefing session is all that is required. Individual participants may be given assignments if required for the success of the workshop. Roles and responsibilities, objectives, and workshop concepts should also be introduced. A formal briefing meeting packet is typically distributed to all participants.

Kick Off Meeting Execution

Holding a formal Kick-Off Meeting is one key to successful use of the workshop technique. Whether or not the Kick-Off Meeting is merged with a briefing and participant training meeting, the meeting should be conducted several business days prior to the actual workshop (unless logistics and cost constraints are prohibitive).

The Executive Owner should open the meeting and then turn the meeting over to the facilitator. It is critical to set the expectations of all participants, both users and systems professionals. When combined with a participant briefing session, allow one full-day.

Materials Assembly

A formal briefing book may be prepared and distributed to all participants at the briefing or kick-off sessions. Subsequent documentation or useful model extracts may also be prepared and distributed to participants prior to each subsequent workshop.

Special packages should be assembled for the Executive Owner. Materials required to conduct workshops such as overheads, scripts, exercise walkthroughs, and/or strawman models are the responsibility of the facilitator and scribe. These materials require preparation, reproduction and possibly distribution time.

DOCUMENTATION CONVENTIONS

Deliverables are driven by the methodology, the

workshop objectives and particular client needs. Typical documentation from User Workshops should include:

- List of objectives (project and/or system)
- System/application scope
- Preliminary (and final) list of system functionality
- Tangible and intangible benefits
- Return on investment
- Priority of functions
- Business model diagrams
- User interface designs
- Interface to other systems
- Open issues list
- Action plans and target dates
- Executive summary
- Any additional reports required

Typically, workshops generate one to two days of documentation time for each eight to ten hour workshop day. Allow sufficient resources during the workshop and after the workshop for documentation completion.

SUCCESS OF WORKSHOP

Critical factors affecting the success of the workshop technique include:

- Executive Commitment (resources, time, people).
- Skilled, experienced facilitator or session moderator.
- Reasonable scope.
- Participant commitment and preparation.
- The correct participants, full time.
- Business focus.
- Methodology concepts, principles, and conventions are followed.
- Easily understandable diagramming conventions.
- Proper environment and room layout/facilities.
- Equal participation.

SCIENTIFIC METHOD

OVERVIEW

The Scientific Method is a process for experimentation that

is used to explore observations and answer questions. Scientists use the scientific method to search for cause and effect relationships in nature. In other words, they design an experiment so that changes to one item cause something else to vary in a predictable way.

Just as it does for a professional scientist, the scientific method will help you to focus your science fair project question, construct a hypothesis, design, execute, and evaluate your experiment.

The scientific method is a process for experimentation that is used to explore observations and answer questions. Scientists use the scientific method to search for cause and effect relationships in nature. In other words, they design an experiment so that changes to one item cause something else to vary in a predictable way.

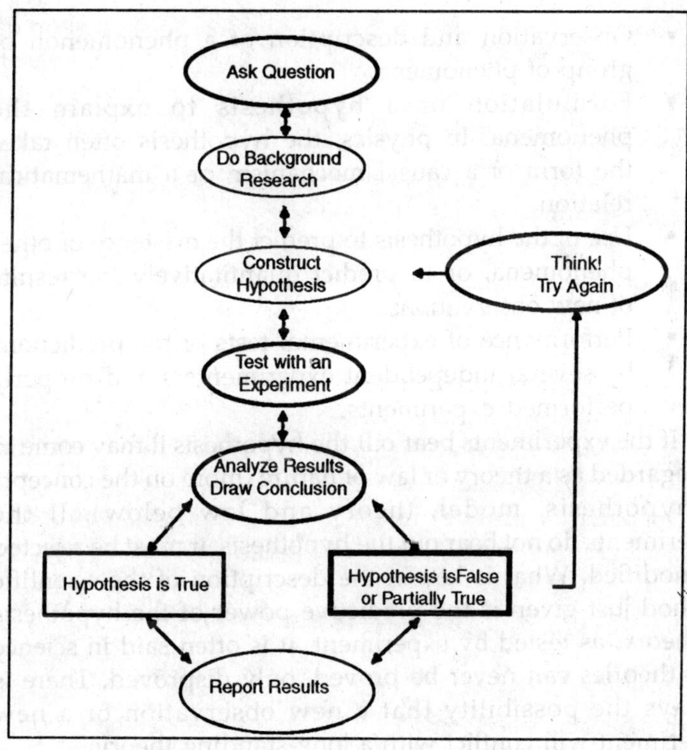

INTRODUCTION TO THE SCIENTIFIC METHOD

The scientific method is the process by which scientists, collectively and over time, endeavor to construct an accurate (that is, reliable, consistent and non-arbitrary) representation of the world. Recognizing that personal and cultural beliefs influence both our perceptions and our interpretations of natural phenomena, we aim through the use of standard procedures and criteria to minimize those influences when developing a theory. As a famous scientist once said, "Smart people (like smart lawyers) can come up with very good explanations for mistaken points of view." In summary, the scientific method attempts to minimize the influence of bias or prejudice in the experimenter when testing an hypothesis or a theory.

STEPS OF SCIENTIFIC METHOD

- Observation and description of a phenomenon or group of phenomena.
- Formulation of a hypothesis to explain the phenomena. In physics, the hypothesis often takes the form of a causal mechanism or a mathematical relation.
- Use of the hypothesis to predict the existence of other phenomena, or to predict quantitatively the results of new observations.
- Performance of experimental tests of the predictions by several independent experimenters and properly performed experiments.

If the experiments bear out the hypothesis it may come to be regarded as a theory or law of nature (more on the concepts of hypothesis, model, theory and law below). If the experiments do not bear out the hypothesis, it must be rejected or modified. What is key in the description of the scientific method just given is the predictive power of the hypothesis or theory, as tested by experiment. It is often said in science that theories can never be proved, only disproved. There is always the possibility that a new observation or a new experiment will conflict with a long-standing theory.

TESTING HYPOTHESES

As just stated, experimental tests may lead either to the confirmation of the hypothesis, or to the ruling out of the hypothesis. The scientific method requires that an hypothesis be ruled out or modified if its predictions are clearly and repeatedly incompatible with experimental tests. Further, no matter how elegant a theory is, its predictions must agree with experimental results if we are to believe that it is a valid description of nature.

In physics, as in every experimental science, "experiment is supreme" and experimental verification of hypothetical predictions is absolutely necessary. Experiments may test the theory directly (for example, the observation of a new particle) or may test for consequences derived from the theory using mathematics and logic (the rate of a radioactive decay process requiring the existence of the new particle).

Note that the necessity of experiment also implies that a theory must be testable. Theories which cannot be tested, because, for instance, they have no observable ramifications (such as, a particle whose characteristics make it unobservable), do not qualify as scientific theories.

If the predictions of a long-standing theory are found to be in disagreement with new experimental results, the theory may be discarded as a description of reality, but it may continue to be applicable within a limited range of measurable parameters. For example, the laws of classical mechanics (Newton's Laws) are valid only when the velocities of interest are much smaller than the speed of light (that is, in algebraic form, when $v/c << 1$).

Since this is the domain of a large portion of human experience, the laws of classical mechanics are widely, usefully and correctly applied in a large range of technological and scientific problems. Yet in nature we observe a domain in which v/c is not small. The motions of objects in this domain, as well as motion in the "classical" domain, are accurately described through the equations of Einstein's theory of relativity. We believe, due to experimental tests, that relativistic theory provides a more general, and therefore more accurate, description of the principles governing our universe, than the earlier "classical" theory. Further, we find that the relativistic equations reduce to the classical equations in the limit $v/c << 1$. Similarly, classical physics is valid only at distances much larger than atomic scales ($x >> 10^{-8}$ m). A description which is valid at all length scales is given by the equations of quantum mechanics.

We are all familiar with theories which had to be discarded in the face of experimental evidence. In the field of astronomy, the earth-centered description of the planetary orbits was overthrown by the Copernican system, in which the sun was placed at the centre of a series of concentric, circular planetary orbits. Later, this theory was modified, as measurements of the planets motions were found to be compatible with elliptical, not circular, orbits, and still later planetary motion was found to be derivable from Newton's laws.

Error in experiments have several sources. First, there is error intrinsic to instruments of measurement. Because this type of error has equal probability of producing a measurement higher or lower numerically than the "true" value, it is called random error. Second, there is non-random or systematic error, due to factors which bias the result in one direction.

No measurement, and therefore no experiment, can be perfectly precise. At the same time, in science we have standard ways of estimating and in some cases reducing errors. Thus it is important to determine the accuracy of a particular measurement and, when stating quantitative results, to quote the measurement error.

A measurement without a quoted error is meaningless. The comparison between experiment and theory is made within the context of experimental errors.

Scientists ask, how many standard deviations are the results from the theoretical prediction? Have all sources of systematic and random errors been properly estimated? This is discussed in more detail in the appendix on *Error Analysis* and in Statistics Lab.

COMMON MISTAKES IN APPLYING THE SCIENTIFIC METHOD

As stated earlier, the scientific method attempts to minimize the influence of the scientist's bias on the outcome of an experiment. That is, when testing an hypothesis or a theory, the scientist may have a preference for one outcome or another, and it is important that this preference not bias the results or their interpretation. The most fundamental error is to mistake the hypothesis for an explanation of a phenomenon, without performing experimental tests. Sometimes "common sense" and "logic" tempt us into believing that no test is needed. There are numerous examples of this, dating from the Greek philosophers to the present day.

Another common mistake is to ignore or rule out data which do not support the hypothesis. Ideally, the experimenter is open to the possibility that the hypothesis is correct or incorrect. Sometimes, however, a scientist may have a strong belief that the hypothesis is true (or false), or feels internal or external pressure to get a specific result. In that case, there may be a psychological tendency to find "something wrong", such as systematic effects, with data which do not support the scientist's expectations, while data which do agree with those expectations may not be checked as carefully. The lesson is that all data must be handled in the same way.

Another common mistake arises from the failure to estimate quantitatively systematic errors (and all errors). There are many examples of discoveries, which were missed by experimenters whose data contained a new phenomenon, but who explained it away as a systematic background. Conversely, there are many examples of alleged "new discoveries" which later proved to be due to systematic errors not accounted for by the "discoverers." In a field where there is active experimentation and open communication among members of the scientific community, the biases of individuals or groups may cancel out, because experimental tests are repeated by different scientists who may have different biases. In addition, different types of experimental setups have different sources of systematic errors. Over a period spanning a variety of experimental tests (usually at least several years), a consensus develops in the community as to which experimental results have stood the test of time.

HYPOTHESES MODELS: THEORIES AND LAWS

In physics and other science disciplines, the words "hypothesis," "model," "theory" and "law" have different connotations in relation to the stage of acceptance or knowledge about a group of phenomena. An hypothesis is a limited statement regarding cause and effect in specific situations; it also refers to our state of knowledge before experimental work has been performed and perhaps even before new phenomena have been predicted. To take an example from daily life, suppose you discover that your car will not start. You may say, "My car does not start because the battery is low." This is your first hypothesis. You may then check whether the lights were left on, or if the engine makes a particular sound when you turn the ignition key. You might actually check the voltage across the terminals of the battery. If you discover that the battery is not low, you might attempt another hypothesis ("The starter is broken"; "This is really not my car.")

The word model is reserved for situations when it is known that the hypothesis has at least limited validity. A often-cited example of this is the Bohr model of the atom, in which, in an analogy to the solar system, the electrons are described has moving in circular orbits around the nucleus. This is not an accurate depiction of what an atom "looks like," but the model succeeds in mathematically representing the energies (but not the correct angular momenta) of the quantum states of the electron in the simplest case, the hydrogen atom. Another example is Hook's Law (which should be called Hook's principle, or Hook's model), which states that the force exerted by a mass attached to a spring is proportional to the amount the spring is stretched. We know that this principle is only valid for small amounts of stretching. The "law" fails when the spring is stretched beyond its elastic limit (it can break). This principle, however, leads to the prediction of simple harmonic motion, and, as a model of the behaviour of a spring, has been versatile in an extremely broad range of applications.

A scientific theory or law represents an hypothesis, or a group of related hypotheses, which has been confirmed through repeated experimental tests. Theories in physics are often formulated in terms of a few concepts and equations, which are identified with "laws of nature," suggesting their universal applicability. Accepted scientific theories and laws become part of our understanding of the universe and the basis for exploring less well-understood areas of knowledge. Theories are not easily discarded; new discoveries are first assumed to fit into the existing theoretical framework. It is only when, after repeated experimental tests, the new phenomenon cannot be accommodated that scientists seriously question the theory and attempt to modify it. The validity that we attach to scientific theories as representing realities of the physical world is to be contrasted with the facile invalidation implied by the expression, "It's only a theory." For example, it is unlikely that a person will step off a tall building on the assumption that they will not fall, because "Gravity is only a theory."

Changes in scientific thought and theories occur, of course, sometimes revolutionizing our view of the world (Kuhn, 1962). Again, the key force for change is the scientific method, and its emphasis on experiment.

CIRCUMSTANCES OF SCIENTIFIC METHOD

While the scientific method is necessary in developing scientific knowledge, it is also useful in everyday problem-solving. What do you do when your telephone doesn't work? Is the problem in the hand set, the cabling inside your house, the hookup outside, or in the workings of the phone company. The process you might go through to solve this problem could involve scientific thinking, and the results might contradict your initial expectations. Like any good scientist, you may question the range of situations (outside of science) in which the scientific method may be applied. From what has been stated above, we determine that the scientific method works best in situations where one can isolate the phenomenon of interest, by eliminating or accounting for extraneous factors, and where one can repeatedly test the system under study after making limited, controlled changes in it.

There are, of course, circumstances when one cannot isolate the phenomena or when one cannot repeat the measurement over and over again. In such cases the results may depend in part on the history of a situation. This often occurs in social interactions between people.

For example, when a lawyer makes arguments in front of a jury in court, she or he cannot try other approaches by repeating the trial over and over again in front of the same jury.

In a new trial, the jury composition will be different. Even the same jury hearing a new set of arguments cannot be expected to forget what they heard before.

CONCLUSION

The scientific method is intricately associated with science, the process of human inquiry that pervades the modern era on many levels. While the method appears simple and logical in description, there is perhaps no more complex question than that of knowing how we come to know things. In this introduction, we have emphasized that the scientific method distinguishes science from other forms of explanation because of its requirement of systematic experimentation.

Just as it does for a professional scientist, the scientific method will help you to focus your science fair project question, construct a hypothesis, design, execute, and evaluate your experiment. The scientific method is the best way yet discovered for winnowing the truth from lies and delusion. The simple version looks something like this:

- Observe some aspect of the universe.
- Invent a tentative description, called a hypothesis that is consistent with what you have observed.
- Use the hypothesis to make predictions.
- Test those predictions by experiments or further

observations and modify the hypothesis in the light of your results.

- Repeat steps 3 and 4 until there are no discrepancies between theory and experiment and/or observation.

When consistency is obtained the hypothesis becomes a theory and provides a coherent set of propositions, which explain a class of phenomena. A theory is then a framework within which observations are explained and predictions are made.

PANEL DISCUSSIONS

OVERVIEW

Panel discussions are especially useful when students are asked to give class presentations or reports as a way of including the entire class in the presentation. Student groups are assigned a topic to research and asked to prepare presentations. Each panelist is then expected to make a very short presentation, before the floor is opened to questions from "the audience". The key to success is to choose topics carefully and to give students sufficient direction to ensure that they are well-prepared for their presentations. You might also want to prepare the "audience", by assigning them various roles. For example, if students are presenting the results of their research into several forms of energy, you might have some of the other students role-play as concerned environmentalists, transportation officials, commuters, and so forth.

INTRODUCTION

A client recently called to say she was going to facilitate a panel for the next business meeting. She had never done so before and asked if somebody could coach her. After the session, she realized that there are some basic skills needed when facilitating a panel of speaker.

TIPS OF PANEL DISCUSSION

To create a seamless and smooth panel discussion here are some tips every facilitator must know:

Meet the Panelists in Advance

The meeting can be a phone call. Get a sense of their styles and message points. Decide how long each person will speak and in what order. Have them send an introductory paragraph.

Consider Logistics

Contact the meeting planner and visit the room. Discuss room set-up, lighting, refreshments, microphones and AV equipment. Decide whether the panelists will sit or stand during their presentations.

Arrive One Hour Early

Check the room, test the microphones. Check seating visibility. Be ready to greet the panelists with a smile. You're the host. Make them feel welcome.

Prepare a Short Bio

Give your bio to the person who will introduce you as the facilitator. Keep it brief-no more than a paragraph.

Make your Opening Remarks

A statement about the topic and the benefits for the audience will prepare the audience to listen. "We expect to have a lively discussion tonight about the state of the economy. Our three speakers have differing view about where to put your money.... Our first speaker...."

Set the Ground Rules

Let the audience know what to expect. "There will be a 30 minute question and answer period after the presentations. Please hold your questions until the end."

Introduce the Speakers

It works best to introduce the first panelist. After the presentation, introduce the next panelist. If you read all the introductions at once, people will forget the information. Practice saying their names and write them out phonetically if the names are difficult.

Act as Time Keeper

Sit in front of the panelists and give them a 5 minute time signal. You can write the number 5 on an index card or you can hold up 5 fingers. If the panelist is running over, give the speaker a wrap up signal. Or interject, "You have 30 seconds to summarize."

Facilitate Questions

It's your job to keep order. Thank the panelists, applaud with the audience and open up the floor for questions. Explain the process. "Please stand, say your first name, and be brief."

If somebody is rambling on, jump in and paraphrase or ask them "What is your question?"

LABORATORY TYPE

Chemistry Laboratories

Chemistry laboratories tend to break down into the following generic spaces: organic chemistry, inorganic chemistry, physical chemistry and analytical chemistry.

Biosciences Laboratories

These laboratories, sometimes also called life sciences laboratories, serve as work spaces for a host of special research interests reflecting the investigators' research direction. They are distinguished by the support space that is required for each laboratory or group of laboratories.

In most ceases, such support space houses: shared equipment, such as centrifuges, freezers, or gas chromatographs; spaces that need to be separated and enclosed for environmental reasons, such as cold rooms, warm rooms or containment laboratories; or spaces that house specialized functions, such as flow cytometry, tissue culture or autoclaving.

Fume hoods, as well as biosafety cabinets and laminar flow hoods, are used in all areas of bioscience research. Storage for chemicals (solvents and acids) must be provided in accordance with applicable codes.

Physical Sciences Laboratories

Physical science laboratories are distinguished from other types of laboratories in a number of ways.

First: There is only a small amount of built-in furniture.

Second: There is an abundance and a variety of electrical power. This, of course, is due to the fact that in most physical sciences research labs the floor space is occupied by an array of mind-boggling apparatus and instrumentation, both home-built and store bought. Almost all of this equipment requires power of varying voltage and amperage... Power and piped services are usually provided from an overhead suspended service carrier.

Computer Science Laboratory

The Computer Science Lab is open to all Computer Science majors and graduate students and students enrolled in any 300+-level Computer Science course. Access may also be granted to other students on a case-by-case basis. The lab consists of ten workstations that are configured as clients of the Computer Science server marlow.cs.wesleyan.edu. The lab is configured for projection from one of the workstations or any other computer. There is also a conference table that seats nine comfortably.

The lab is available 24/7, except when noted on a sign outside the lab door. Access requires the key code, which is provided to Computer Science students and changed on a regular basis. Use of the workstations is restricted to Computer Science students; accounts are managed by the Lab Administrator. Non-CS students are welcome to be in the lab as well, provided there is at least one CS student or faculty member present. You should feel free to use this space even if you are not using the workstations—one of the reasons for the conference table is so that students have a place to work on group projects.

Hardware and Software

Computer Science Lab consist of Hardware and Software. Marlow is a dual-processor server. Each processor is a quad-core Intel Xeon running at 2.33GHz. It has approximately 275GB of disk space. The operating system is RedHat Enterprise GNU/Linux 5. Currently the only available desktop enviornment is Gnome. marlow is also available via ssh, but only from computers on the Wesleyan network. If you wish to log into marlow from outside the Wesleyan network, you must use VPN to first log into the Wesleyan network.

The clients are Intel-based workstations. When a client it turned on, you will be presented with two boot options: 2X ThinClient OS and "local machine." The former loads a client that logs directly into marlow, and is the default. The latter will load a very minimal Windows XP environment that is not connected to the network.

Issues

We are still in the process of configuring both the lab and marlow. Here is a list of known issues; we are working on resolving all of them.

- Marlow does not talk to Wesleyan's Active Directory server yet. The net effect of this is that your marlow password is independent of the password you use for other Wesleyan computing services.
- When you first log on, you are presented with a message to the effect that the authenticity of the host cannot be verified; just click "Yes" to continue connecting.
- Power management on the clients does not work—thus the computers never go to sleep.
- There is no sound once you log on.
- Key repeat does not work.

Rules

We prefer to keep rules to a minimum until they need to be imposed. In general, be respectful of the space and the other students, and we shouldn't have to impose too many. However,

- If there is anyone in the lab, then there must be at least one Computer Science faculty or student in the lab. That is, non-Computer Science students may not be in the lab unless accompanied by someone from Computer Science. This rule may be waived on a case-by-case basis by CS faculty.

- Do not give out the key-code to anyone. Only CS faculty should distribute the key-code.
- If you are the last one to leave the lab, be certain that both doors are closed and locked. Do this even if you are just stepping out for a minute. Equipment that goes missing is unlikely to be replaced, and leaving a door open to an empty lab is a certain way to ensure that some of that equipment goes walking.
- Please turn off any client and monitor that is not in use. They do not take long to boot and, unfortunately, the software that is currently installed prevents power management from putting the computers to sleep. So, if they are left on, they are consuming a non-trivial amount of power and generating heat.

Use of Equipment and Network

- Undergraduate use of all equipment in the university is governed by University or School.
- Regulation permits limited personal use of the equipment and network. However the department pays for most data downloaded from the internet so large downloads of non-academic data is not allowed. Examples which are plainly not permitted: movies and movie trailers, video clips, audio files and software updates for private laptops.
- Also note that traffic to several mirror sites incurs no cost to the department and may be used freely. The cost of downloading from a particular site can be determined using the Information Division Internet Access Cost Tool.
- All students obtaining accounts on Computer Science and Software Engineering machines are required to agree in writing to the conditions, outlined in the Computing and Network Resources Declaration.

- Copyright notices are displayed in all student labs. The University takes a serious stand against copyright infringement; offenses are punishable under various university regulations.

LABORATORY APPLICATIONS

India is one of the huge markets comprising of many manufacturers, exporters and suppliers of laboratory applications. These vendors of laboratory applications are scattered all over indian markets nurturing the requirements of large variety of buyers for laboratory applications who are also scattered throughout india. Different varieties of laboratory applications are available for different industrial purpose. The prime importance for the buyer is to source the quality laboratory applications, which also suits his requirement and pocket/budget thus increasing his production & profits.

PURPOSE OF LABORATORY

Physics is an experimental science. The theoretical concepts and relationships introduced in the lecture part of the course describe the general nature and behaviour of real phenomena. They were, appropriately, discovered by (or inducted from) careful observation and thoughtful analysis of actual experiments. Genuine understanding entails being able to relate the abstract ideas to the particular facts to which they correspond.

The premise of the scientific method is that (observation of) nature is the ultimate judge of the truth of any physical theory. Indeed, experiments designed to prove certain ideas have often ended up showing them to be wrong. Consequently, all physical concepts must be verified experimentally if they are to be accepted as representing laws of nature.

Accordingly, the introductory physics laboratories have the following purposes and goals:

- To provide an experimental foundation for the theoretical concepts introduced in the lectures. It is important that students have an opportunity to verify some of the ideas for themselves.

- To familiarize students with experimental apparatus, the scientific method, and methods of data analysis so that they will have some idea of the inductive process by which the ideas were originated. To teach how to make careful experimental observations and how to think about and draw conclusions from such data.
- To introduce the methods used for estimating and dealing with experimental uncertainties, including simple ideas in probability theory and the distinctions between random (statistical) and systematic "errors." This is essential in understanding what valid conclusions can be deduced from experimental data and that, properly obtained, these conclusions are valid, notwithstanding the uncertainty of the data.
- To learn how to write a technical report which communicates scientific information in a clear and concise manner.
- To introduce new concepts and techniques which have a wide application in experimental science, but have not been introduced in the standard courses. These may require that the student consult additional textbooks.

The laboratory is not a contest whose object is to get the "right answer." The purpose is to learn how to gain knowledge by looking at reality, not an attempt to make reality conform to preconceptions. The important thing is to learn how to be observant, to really see what happens, and to deal with this information with the strictest integrity. And to understand, or learn to understand, the meaning of what happens.

Even if you get results totally at variance with theory (as may happen due to a mistake, or a systematic uncertainty) you will get a high grade if you report it honestly and demonstrate that you understand what you did and how your results occurred. (If you have trouble interpreting your results, contact your TA for help.) On the other hand, if you get perfect agreement with theory by faking your data you will fail. Practical ability to do experiments and analyse data is usually acquired through practice and experience.

Practice is very important in learning any new discipline; such as, for example, a new language. A good lecture may be very helpful but not fully useful without actual practice. In experimental science, practice involves solving many problems (i.e. homework) and performing a variety of experiments (i.e. labs). Practice is essential to being able to make the connection between theory and experience.

LABORATORY NOTEBOOKS

I think it is safe to say that most everyone (including me) can greatly improve their scientific notebook. It is often boring, often repetitive, etc. But it is also always important. The biggest weakness is usually lack of description and interpretation. Make the notebook your diary, in the sense that you communicate with an unknown third person observer. You should aim to provide sufficient information and detail for that third person to understand and repeat your experiments. Sounds simple, but it requires constant motivation and energy.

In setting up your notebooks, it is always necessary to define what one "experiment" consists of. Although the precise definition of an "experiment" is somewhat arbitrary, it is important to think ahead and organize intellectually where your boundaries are likely to lie. The organization of a notebook into an Introduction, Methods, Results, and Conclusions can greatly aid in this planning, as it forces you to define your "experiment".

You should have two levels corresponding to this structure. The first is for each weekly lab, where you need these four components for each lab. The second is a larger overall structure that will encompass two portions of the quarter.

The first corresponds to the first half of the lab experiments covering site-directed mutagenesis through DNA sequencing. The second covers the remainder of the course that is concentrated on hybridization techniques. You should include an overall introduction to the site-directed mutagenesis portion of the course, along with conclusions once you have your DNA sequences.

A detailed description of the format you should use in keeping your notebook is attached. Please read and follow these instructions carefully. One of the most important aspects of a laboratory notebook is taking the time to write down observations and developing interpretations of experiments. DO NOT LIMIT YOUR LAB NOTEBOOK TO SUCCESSFUL EXPERIMENTS! Apparent failures and initially strange observations may be keys to unexpected new directions and will often guide the design of future successes.

GUIDELINES OF LABORATORY NOTEBOOKS

LABORATORY NOTES

General

The main purpose of laboratory notes is, of course, to provide a permanent record of experimental results. To serve this purpose they must be complete and self-explanatory, so that they are readily understandable to others and to oneself years later. They must also be legible, organized and concise. The importance of this cannot be emphasized too often.

There is another purpose of laboratory notes which is almost as important. This is their role in helping the mental processes that are involved in evaluating and setting up proper experiments. A clear statement of the conclusions of an experiment, written down at the end, forces one to think critically about the experiment and its implications. Such a written statement of conclusions is one of the most important parts of the experiment. Furthermore, a clearly written experimental protocol helps to plan an experiment with suitable controls.

A related point is that proper notebook maintenance makes it possible to evaluate an experiment with minimum effort. One should be able to see at a glance the purpose, the results, and the conclusion of the experiment. It is well worth an extraordinary effort to make these concise and clear. At a second glance, one should be able to see how the experiment was set up and how the individual experimental results support the conclusions. The design and utilization of a proper protocol with proper controls are important experiences for the practicing scientist.

One of the most important factors in achieving success in experimental science is nothing more than simple efficiency. Many things cannot be learned or taught, but this can. All of us spend too much time doing experiments that would not be necessary if proper controls had been run in a previous experiment, or if we had been able to think far enough ahead to anticipate results and include the proper work to interpret this result. It is vital to plan carefully and decisively with respect to controls and possible experimental results.

The rule is that new experimental results, once written, cannot be erased. If a reading is taken again or a calculation corrected, the original results should be crossed out and the new results written below. Sometimes the original result turns out to be right on later evaluation or calculation, and it is important to have a record of any change of this kind that is made.

The experimental protocol must be an exact record of the actual experiment. It should not be copied over for the sake of neatness—it should be clear in the first place. Scratch paper should not be used for anything except the most trivial calculations, and usually not even for those. Calculations are more likely to be accurate if entered neatly in the permanent protocol, and very often provides invaluable information later on how a calculation was carried out and a conclusion reached.

CONFORMITY OF FORMAT AND STYLE

There are several compelling reasons to require that members of a research group conform in the format and quality of laboratory notes. The most important point is that if notes are kept in the same manner, anyone can understand anyone else's experiments. For a research group where notebooks accumulate rapidly over the years, this conformity to one style is crucial to anyone trying to understand prior research results.

- The coding system will be as follows:
  - Your initials
  - Roman numeral indicating the number of the notebook
  - Arabic numeral and letter indicating the item on that page

  Example: PSS I.5.c indicates item c on page 5 of my first notebook
- Leave several pages at the beginning of each notebook for a Table of Contents. This should be kept up to date.
- Each experiment should contain:
  - Title
  - Dates (kept in margin)
  - Objective or question asked
  - Protocol: complete and legible description so any person picking up the notebook can understand and repeat the experiment
  - Results
  - Conclusion
- Please try to keep the notebooks concise but accurate so that anyone can repeat or read the experiment.
- Use the right hand page for lab notes, the left hand page for calculations. Tape photos of gels and all other such documentation directly on the page.

Lab Research Notebooks

Table of Contents

Devote the first several pages of the notebook to a Table of Contents:

- Brief, descriptive title (use this in the Table of Contents)
- Dates in margin

Introduction and Purpose

- Brief statement of the purpose of this laboratory exercise/procedure

Procedure

- Descriptive methods; include stock concentrations.
- Describe How experiment is done so any other can understand
- It is important that you include the final concentrations of components.
- Methods: Include a brief description of exactly what was done

Results

- Record observations objectively, stick to the facts, indicate when a point is untrustworthy.
- Reduce data: Graphs, Table, etc., so a rapid overview can be obtained

Conclusions

- Interpret data, be clear in distinguishing what you know from speculation.

Plans

- What are the logical next sets of experiments?

Miscellaneous

- Always refer to samples, spectra, gels, etc. by the sample convention
- Label autoradiograms and sequencing results in same fashion, for sequencing results include sequencing primer

GENERAL GUIDELINES

- Conduct yourself in a responsible manner at all times in the laboratory.
- Follow all written and verbal instructions carefully. If you do not understand a direction or part of a procedure, ask your teacher before proceeding with the activity.
- Never work alone in the laboratory. No student may

work in the science classroom without the presence of the teacher.

- When first entering a science room, do not touch any equipment, chemicals, or other materials in the laboratory area until you are instructed to do so.
- Perform only those experiments authorized by your teacher. Carefully follow all instructions, both written and oral. Unauthorized experiments are not allowed.
- Do not eat food, drink beverages, or chew gum in the laboratory. Do not use laboratory glassware as containers for food or beverages.
- Be prepared for your work in the laboratory. Read all procedures thoroughly before entering the laboratory. Never fool around in the laboratory. Horseplay, practical jokes, and pranks are dangerous and prohibited.
- Always work in a well-ventilated area.
- Observe good housekeeping practices. Work areas should be kept clean and tidy at all times.
- Be alert and proceed with caution at all times in the laboratory. Notify the teacher immediately of any unsafe conditions you observe.
- Dispose of all chemical waste properly. Never mix chemicals in sink drains. Sinks are to be used only for water. Check with your teacher for disposal of chemicals and solutions.
- Labels and equipment instructions must be read carefully before use. Set up and use the equipment as directed by your teacher.
- Keep hands away from face, eyes, mouth, and body while using chemicals or lab equipment. Wash your hands with soap and water after performing all experiments.
- Experiments must be personally monitored at all times. Do not wander around the room, distract other students, startle other students or interfere with the laboratory experiments of others.
- Know the locations and operating procedures of all

safety equipment including: first aid kit(s), and fire extinguisher. Know where the fire alarm and the exits are located.

- Know what to do if there is a fire drill during a laboratory period; containers must be closed, and any electrical equipment turned off.
- Any time chemicals, heat, or glassware are used, students will wear safety goggles. NO EXCEPTIONS TO THIS RULE!
- Contact lenses may be not be worn in the laboratory.
- Dress properly during a laboratory activity. Long hair, dangling jewelry, and loose or baggy clothing are a hazard in the laboratory. Long hair must be tied back, and dangling jewelry and baggy clothing must be secured. Shoes must completely cover the foot. No sandals allowed on lab days.
- A lab coat or smock should be worn during laboratory experiments.
- Report any accident (spill, breakage, etc.) or injury (cut, burn, etc.) to the teacher immediately, no matter how trivial it seems. Do not panic.
- If you or your lab partner is hurt, immediately (and loudly) yell out the teacher's name to get the teacher's attention. Do not panic.
- If a chemical should splash in your eye(s) or on your skin, immediately flush with running water for at least 20 minutes. Immediately (and loudly) yell out the teacher's name to get the teacher's attention.
- All chemicals in the laboratory are to be considered dangerous. Avoid handling chemicals with fingers. Always use a tweezer. When making an observation, keep at least 1 foot away from the specimen. Do not taste, or smell any chemicals.
- Check the label on all chemical bottles twice before removing any of the contents. Take only as much chemical as you need.
- Never return unused chemicals to their original container.

- Never remove chemicals or other materials from the laboratory area.
- Never handle broken glass with your bare hands.Use a brush and dustpan to clean up broken glass. Place broken glass in the designated glass disposal container.
- Examine glassware before each use. Never use chipped, cracked, or dirty glassware.
- If you do not understand how to use a piece of equipment, ASK THE TEACHER FOR HELP!
- Do not immerse hot glassware in cold water. The glassware may shatter.
- Do not operate a hot plate by yourself. Take care that hair, clothing, and hands are a safe distance from the hot plate at all times. Use of hot plate is only allowed in the presence of the teacher.
- Heated glassware remain very hot for a long time. They should be set aside in a designated place to cool, and picked up with caution. Use tongs or heat protective gloves if necessary.
- Never look into a container that is being heated.
- Do not place hot apparatus directly on the laboratory desk. Always use an insulated pad. Allow plenty of time for hot apparatus to cool before touching it.

SYMPOSIUM

Symposium originally referred to a drinking party but has since come to refer to any academic conference, or a style of university class characterized by an openly discursive format, rather than a lecture and question–answer format. The sympotic elegies of Theognis of Megara and two Socratic dialogues, Plato's Symposium and Xenophon's Symposium all describe symposia in the original sense.

TEAM TEACHING

DEFINITION

Team teaching is a strategy that has been around for years,

but creating teams, whether in response to district expectations or as a way of dealing with changes in teaching practice, needs careful thought in order to succeed. While teaming means the partners must reconfigure much of their teaching lives, it can be done successfully.In team teaching a group of teachers, working together, plan, conduct, and evaluate the learning activities for the same group of students.

In practice, team teaching has many different formats but in general it is a means of organising staff into groups to enhance teaching. Teams generally comprise staff members who may represent different areas of subject expertise but who share the same group of students and a common planning period to prepare for the teaching. To facilitate this process a common teaching space is desirable. However, to be effective team teaching requires much more than just a common meeting time and space.

HISTORY OF TEAM TEACHING

In a Team teaching there will be a team of three to five teachers would be assigned to 75 to 150 pupils organized either on a single-grade or multi-grade basis. This recommendation of junior high school reform is where the idea of team teaching developed. Team teaching is now used in all grade levels and across disciplines. When done correctly, this approach has been shown to create bonding opportunities for students and to engage teachers in collaborative, interdisciplinary planning.

Team teaching requires that the faculty is organized so that teachers share a group of students, a common planning time to develop curriculum and instruction in multiple content areas, the same schedule, and that the teachers are in the same physical area of the school.

BENEFITS OF TEAM TEACHING

The need for team teaching is based on the premise that middle school is a transitional period between the traditional elementary structure, where students have one teacher all day, and the high school setting, where students have multiple classes and teachers on a daily basis. Because students coming from a traditional elementary structure are accustomed to having a small group of peers and one teacher, they sometimes become overwhelmed when they have to change classes and have more than one teacher. Research suggests that students who do not feel connected to peers and their teachers often have a higher rate of academic failure. "The formation of interdisciplinary teams has been proposed as one way of reducing student alienation and increasing students' sense of membership... Teams provide students with a greater sense of identity, belonging, and support." Ideally, teams should consist of 120 or fewer students with a student to teacher ratio of 25:1.5 The Carnegie Council on Adolescent Development suggests that the size of teams should be as small as possible depending on the content knowledge and strengths of the teachers.

WHY SHOULD I USE TEAM TEACHING

In view of the additional complexity which team teaching initiatives introduce into departmental organisation and in view of the time needed for staff to adapt to the new structures, it is relevant to ask what benefits accrue from team teaching. How, for instance, does team teaching benefit lecturers, part-time tutors, students, and departments as a whole?

For Lecturers, who so often work alone, team teaching provides a supportive environment that overcomes the isolation of working in self-contained or departmentalized class-rooms. Being exposed to the subject expertise of colleagues, to open critique, to different styles of planning and organisation, as well as methods of class presentation, teachers can develop their approaches to teaching and acquire a greater depth of understanding of the subject matter of the unit or module.

Part-time staff can be drawn moie closely into the department as members of teams than is usually the case, with a resulting increase in integration of course objectives and approaches to teaching.

Team teaching can lead to better student performance in terms of greater independence and assuming responsibility for learning. Exposure to views and skills of more than one teacher can develop a more mature understanding of knowledge often being problematic rather than right or wrong. Learning can become more active and involved. Students could eventually make an input into team planning.

Team teaching aids the professional and interpersonal dynamics of departments leading to closer integration of staff.

In the following extract, the authors describe the instructional advantages of working in teams.

Team teaching is an approach which involves true team work between two qualified instructors who, together, make presentations to an audience. The instructional advantages of team teaching include:

- Lecture-style instruction is eliminated in favour of a dynamic interplay of two minds and personalities. Lectures require students to act as passive receptors of communicated information, but team teaching involves the student in the physical and mental stimulation created by viewing two individuals at work.
- Teaching staff act as a role models for discussion and disagreement. Teaching staff members demonstrate modes of behaving in a disagreement as well as exposing students to the course content.
- Team teaching makes effective use of existing human resources. Acquisition of additional expensive resources or equipment is not required to implement this method: only reorganisation is required to put the team into operation.
- Team teaching has the potential for revitalizing instructional capabilities through a process of dialogue. Team teaching begins with the recognition that the instructor/student link is critical and offers an approach that has been shown to stimulate and provoke, while expanding and enriching student understanding.
- Interest in traditional courses can be stimulated as students share the enthusiasm and intellectual

discourse that the lecturers communicate. Team teaching is not boring. Students are drawn into the situation from the first moment.

- The effective use of facilities is possible. The impersonal nature of large lecture halls can be brought to life by an interactive and dynamic situation.
- Team teaching provides opportunities for interaction with the audience. Implementation.

Implementing a team teaching approach requires administrative encouragement, acceptance of an initial experimental quality, and willingness to take risks. Proof that team teaching works comes not only from the instructors' self-judgment, but from students' evaluations. Above all, team teaching cannot be accomplished by administrative fiat — but administrators need to encourage it.

PLANNING TO IMPLEMENT TEAM TEACHING

Planning, conducting and evaluating team teaching are all important activities. Some of the most important aspects of planning which need to consider in advance of implementing teams are the concerns of staff; the selection of team members; and setting realistic goals for any teaching team in the first instance.

Understanding Staff Concerns

Like any other change or innovation in a department, team teaching will raise concerns among staff members. The full range of concerns will only become clear over time after initial worries are dealt with and team members become comfortable with the innovation. A basic premise of team teaching is that its adoption is not something that happens at one point in time — it extends over time. As users go through the adoption process there will be changes in their concerns.

From a team perspective, the ultimate aim will be to have individual team members reach a stage where they accept joint responsibility for the basic instruction of a group of students. There will be concerns, however, the relevant literature suggests that one way of dealing with these concerns is to recognise that they seem to follow a time cycle. Early concerns usually appear to be procedural e.g., determining roles, setting agendas, keeping records, setting procedures for communicating with outside people, and scheduling teamwork, etc.

Next to appear are student-related concerns such as meeting students' needs, planning to deal with individual students, etc. These are followed by concern among team members for their own professional growth and finally there is concern for the collective well being of the team. This last level is reached when teams are seen as (i) a means of professional self development, (ii) a forum at which ideas about instruction and coordinating curriculum can be shared, and (iii) when students are involved in decision making.

Here are some common concerns about team teaching along with suggestions of what to do to improve the likelihood of overcoming them. The first three of these concerns are usually expressed before the team actually begins functioning while the last is usually expressed after it has functioned for a time.

I do not know enough about team teaching.

Explain the concept of team organisation and the rationale for implementing it. This should include an explanation of how it is envisaged that team teaching will fit with the rest of the departmental programme. Staff need to have a clear idea of the kinds of teaching teams envisaged, what their responsibilities will be and how much of their time will be occupied in teaching in this way.

How will I manage my teaching in the light of the proposed change?

Supplying information usually leads teachers to express personal concerns. Take these concerns seriously. If you do not they become potential barriers to effective implementation. Personal concerns usually expressed about team teaching include:

- Not all team members will contribute equally.

- Teachers do not understand how to make the team work.
- There will be personality conflicts to deal with in addition to the teaching itself.
- A preference for working alone.
- All the work will fall on the team leader/senior subject expert.
- It will be too difficult to cover all the course content.
- Team meetings will be a waste of time.

All in all, concerns usually revolve about inter-personal problems — issues of self doubt, team management and group processes in addition to whether the teaching carried out by this method will be worthwhile.

How is the team going to be managed?

Management questions are concerned with who will be on the team, who will lead it, what will be expected and in what timeframe, how meetings will be conducted, how teaching activities and events will actually be planned, and so on. These should be dealt with as early as possible and not in a casual manner, so that everyone is clear about what their roles and responsibilities will be. As well, once the team begins to function, more routine issues will surface: staff may be bothered by the amount of time involved, the difficulty of keeping track of students, coordinating materials and the work of other team members.

Concern may arise and have to be dealt with while the team is actually functioning or at the time of periodic course reviews. Rather than a single concern, it may be more useful to see it as a category of concerns that focus on the consequences of team actions.

It would be most unusual for the team to find that everything has proceeded as they planned. More usually, they find that there are outcomes as a result of team teaching which they had not anticipated. These outcomes may be to do with student learning or with how the team is functioning. If there are differences between what was planned and what the students are achieving then the team will need to refocus on what is important. To do this the team will have to monitor continually how students are reacting to the team teaching experience. Conscious decisions will have to be taken to emphasise points that may have been missed or correct mistaken impressions. However, concerns may arise apart from those related to student learning. There may be a need for the team to deal with issues of collaboration among its own members. In the same way that the goals associated with student learning need to be monitored and reviewed where necessary, so too do aspects of team behaviour. In both these examples it is apparent that regular meetings of the team need to take place where constructive, professional reflection is encouraged which is itself a team teaching strength.

Selecting Team Members

The composition of any teaching team is a matter which must be considered carefully if that particular team is going to function effectively. While it is possible that teams can be arbitrarily formed it is far more fruitful if they come together in response to needs and interests. Thought needs to be given to selecting team members and defining team roles and these decisions need to be evaluated periodically. The following questions are indicative of the sorts of issues which should be considered:

On what basis should team members be selected?

Team members should not be clones of each other. Why? Because differences in subject expertise, interests, perspectives, back-grounds, and qualification levels, can contribute to the collective strength of a team and the growth of individual team members. Furthermore, the 'mix' of personalities and characteristics add to the experience the students get from interacting with the team.

What is the role of the team leader?

Basically the team leader will be concerned with

- Internal functioning: Setting agendas, keeping records, coordinating schedules ensuring the team 'stays on task' i.e. that it achieves what it sets out to achieve.

- External functioning: Communicating with department heads to ensure that the team is resourced, supported, and meeting departmental goals/expectations, etc.

The Role of Team Members

Team members need to contribute to the team in ways other than simply turning up for classes and meetings. It is essential that all team members contribute to formulating and achieving team goals. To do this, each member must take responsibility for participating in team discussions and planning session and following through on decisions made by the team within the timeframes decided by the team. It is only in this way that a spirit of co-operation and collaboration can be maintained.

Setting Realistic Team Goals

Teams need to have a sense of direction. One finding from the relevant literature of particular interest relates to the time required to develop an effective level of team teaching. When teams are formed from teachers with no previous team experience, it seems to take about three years for them to develop the team teaching process to an efficient and effective level. Hence in setting a time line for teams to achieve realistic goals it is important to ask what will be the aims of team teaching during the first year or semester and what are the longer term goals? The answers to such questions are important in determining priorities for the development of teams. It is unrealistic to expect that all goals and expectations will be met immediately. Rather it is better to consider what it is reasonable to undertake as teachers and to expect from students and at what stage?

TEAM IN ACTION

Planning for Teaching

Assume that it has been decided that team teaching will

go ahead in your department and that you have agreed and been selected to be a member of a team. Assume also that the issues surrounding teams discussed earlier have been attended to and the team is now ready to begin work. Decisions facing yourself and your teaching partners now will focus undoubtedly on planning teaching/learning activities.

You may ask, for instance, in what way will the team use small and large group contexts or independent study? Will it use a large group in an auditorium setting to introduce a topic or convey basic information and background material which all the students need to know? Will the team decide to use a single teacher to make the presentation or will several teachers be used? Will small group discussions relate to large group presentations, or demonstrate skills, or develop a seminar discussion group etc? What of independent study? It is not always taken into consideration but it provides a student or group of students with the opportunity to research or explore a topic of special interest in greater depth outside the formal teaching situation. How will the team use independent study?

This short list of questions underlines the decisions to be made in this area.

What are the programme, unit, and lesson objectives?

What lesson content is to be presented and in what order?

Which content is to be presented by large group presentation?

Which methods and resources are to be used to present the content?

Who will make large group presentations?

What will be discussed during small group meetings?

How will small groups be organized?

Who will be assigned to each small group?

What types of independent study will be appropriate?

What blocks of time will be assigned to large-group, small group and independent study activities?

How will students be assessed?

All of these questions are to do with ongoing interaction with students. A little later the team will have to consider questions such as:

How can the Activities be Improved?

What specific problems have arisen with particular groups of students and how can they be solved?

Irrespective of who asks these questions, they are very realistic and they need to be answered, but the critical issue is who by and how.

Assigning Roles and Responsibilities

Effective teams are systematic in their division of labour, not forgetting that roles may be rotated on a regular basis. In allocating roles, strengths and weaknesses of individual team members need to be taken into account. A brief questionnaire gathering an idea of these strengths and weaknesses might be a good idea before a draft list of responsibilities for the team is discussed.

Catering for Students

While team teachers and their students are usually happy with the community spirit that teams can provide, teamwork also has a considerable effect on classroom management. For example, by planning together, team teachers can clarify teaching policies and behavioural expectations that are applied to students.

Difficult management situations can be analyzed and resolved together resulting in richer discussions and sounder solutions. Teams of teachers can think of ways of improving student motivation, a sense of responsibility, and overall student performance.

Conducting Meetings

Team teaching is group work and as such teams need to develop as functioning groups. In dealing with other team members teamwork is seldom without conflict — professional or personal points of view may clash. Blending differences constructively is a challenge to all team members. To do this it is important to acknowledge team members' strengths, interests, personal and professional goals both in assigning responsibilities and in the conduct of meetings.

RUNNING MEETINGS

For a team to function effectively the team meetings need to run well. They need to clarify expectations for how the team will operate, i.e. clarify management issues and set ground rules for meetings such as:

- How will items get on the Agenda?
- What should be recorded in the minutes?
- Who will do the recording?
- How will decisions be reached?
- How should communication with other teams and members of the department be managed?
- How will a team calendar/schedule be compiled?

MAKING DECISIONS

The main problem encountered in meetings which prevents decisions from being made effectively and efficiently is the difficulty of keeping all team members on task. The team leader needs to ensure that:

- Problems are defined clearly.
- There is time for brainstorming alternatives for action.
- Each alternative is subject to critique.
- A plan of action is selected, implemented and subsequently evaluated.

Evaluating Progress

In a small team, a formal evaluation of progress often seems inappropriate. However, all teams need to set aside some time to evaluate their progress in terms of both teaching the module and with their own development as an effective team. An outside facilitator could be called in to manage this where appropriate. Some questions which might be asked in the context of such an evaluation are:

- Are the goals set for the team's work realistic?
- Have the goals been achieved? to what extent?
- Do all team members participate equally in team decisions?
- Have decisions been carried out?

- Are responsibilities shared among team members?
- Do students benefit from the team's work?
- What areas need more attention?

Maintaining Continuity From Year to Year

In order to ensure the continuity of the module/course when it is presented a second and subsequent times the team needs to maintain clear documentation of the course including:

- The course outline or syllabus;
- Weekly timetables;
- Teachers' notes for each unit;
- Students' notes;
- Teaching materials/written bulletins;
- Copies of tests and examinations;
- Final course evaluations;

Student Evaluations

Carefully maintaining these course documents will ease the task of the course leaders, facilitate the induction of new teachers into the team, and simplify the task of revising the course/module in a rational manner.

Unit V

Biology Laboratory

PRACTICAL WORK IN BIOLOGY

Practical work in Biology comprises of:

- Experimental Design Skills
- Practical Skills
- Presentation
- Interpretation and Evaluation

HYPOTHESIS

- An idea which experiments are designed to test.
- A 'testable' statement.
- A statement that connects the independent and dependent variables.

Example:

- Light intensity will affect the growth rate of plants.
- An increase in temperature will affect the rate of enzyme action.
- Humidity will affect the decay rate of compost.
- Soil moisture will affect slater movement.

INDEPENDENT VARIABLE

Sometimes referred to as the 'experimental variable'.

- The variable which is deliberately changed.
- Should always be plotted on the x-axis of a graph.

Example:

- Light intensity
- Temperature

- Humidity
- Soil moisture

DEPENDENT VARIABLE

- The variable which may change as a result of changes to the independent variable.
- Plotted on the Y-axis of a graph.

Example:

- Rate of plant growth.
- Rate of enzyme action.
- Rate of compost decay.
- Concentration of product formed.
- Number of millipedes in a dark area.

FACTORS HELD CONSTANT

- All factors that are kept the same during an experiment.
- An experiment can only have one independent variable. All other factors must be kept constant if the experiment is to be a "fair test".

Example:

- Temperature, light intensity, amount and source of water, type and amount of fertiliser, soil type of containers (size, shape, nature).
- PH concentration of enzyme, concentration of substrate.

RESOLUTION

- Resolution refers to the smallest increment measurable by the measuring instrument.
- Resolution is a property of the measuring instrument.
- It is determined by the number of digits able to be read from the measuring instrument.
- Resolution refers to individual measurements.

Example:

- High resolution = 0.001g (electronic balance)
- Low resolution = 0.1g (triple beam balance)

PRESENTATION

- All observations and measurements need to be recorded.
- Construct tables with headings and appropriate units.
- Draw graphs which have a title which clearly connects the independent and dependent variables.

Example:

- 'The effect of varying light intensity on the growth rate of plants'.
- Describe the results.

Example:

- As the temperature increased from 00C to 250C the rate of enzyme action increased; from 250C to 300C the rate remained the same.

CHARACTERISTICS OF GRAPHS

- Axes labeled with units
- An appropriate scale (uniform and using most of the axis)
- Accurate plot of points
- Line of best fit

GRAPHS

- The class data was plotted.
- Note choice of axes, scales, and units.
- Describe which is the most appropriate line.

RANDOM ERRORS

- Random error is caused by any factor that randomly affects the measurement of a variable.
- The amount of random error is reflected in the amount of scatter in the data.
- An increase in sample size allows averages to be calculated. This will tend to reduce the effect of random errors.
- Measurements can never be done perfectly and therefore random errors can never be eliminated.

Example:

- Inconsistent reading of scales.
- Inconsistent measuring of volumes in a reaction mix.
- Inconsistent use of a timer.

SYSTEMATIC ERRORS

Systematic errors are present when measured values differ consistently from their true value.

Usually associated with apparatus being faulty or incorrectly calibrated, or experimental design.

Tend to be consistent throughout the experiment therefore taking an average does not correct the problem or give a more accurate value.

SYSTEMATIC ERRORS

- Repeating an experiment may identify systematic errors.
- In repeating, an alternative source of equipment and materials must be used.

Example:

- Incorrectly calibrated electronic balance, or a contaminant in a container or chemical used will give an inconsistent result.
- A consistent result indicates that any conclusion is likely to be valid.

SAMPLE SIZE

- Refers to the number of samples in the experimental group.
- Increasing the number of samples allows averages to be calculated.
- Increasing the number of samples will reduce the effect of random errors and will therefore make the data more consistent and hence reliable.

Example:

- In testing the effect of temperature on enzyme action, you might decide to have 3 trials (or samples) for each temperature.

RELIABILITY

- Reliability refers to the extent which an experiment yields the same results on repeated trials under the same conditions each time.
- Reliability is achieved by minimising the effect of random errors.

Example:

- Ensure that a large number of samples is used.
- Be attentive and careful when taking and recording measurements.

REPEATING THE EXPERIMENT

- Repeating the experiment with the same procedure but different apparatus on different occasions helps to identify systematic errors.
- We repeat an experiment to verify our results, to check the validity of our experimental design, and to be more confident with any conclusions.

Example:

- Repeating a whole experiment on a different occasion, preferably with different experimenters and different subjects, new solutions or equipment etc., to see if results are similar.

VALIDITY

Validity refers to the degree to which an assessment method measures what it is supposed to measure.

Validity is increased by:

- Appropriate experimental design (i.e. it is testing what it claims to test).
- Repeating the experiment (which reveals systematic errors).

Example:

- Consider: hypothesis, variables, controlled factors, size of sample, apparatus, the control, measuring instruments.

RELATIONSHIP BETWEEN PRECISION AND ACCURACY

- High precision
- Low accuracy
- Low precision
- High accuracy (fluke)
- High precision
- High accuracy
- Low precision
- Low accuracy
- Errors still
- Present
- Systematic
- Random
- Random & systematic

RELATIONSHIP BETWEEN PRECISION AND ACCURACY

- P not A
- P and A
- A not P
- Not A not P

PRECISION

- Precision depends on how well random errors are minimised.
- Random errors are present when there is scatter in the measured values.
- Scatter therefore influences precision.
- High scatter reflects low precision.
- Low scatter reflects high precision.

ACCURACY

- Accuracy refers to how close the result of the experiment is to the true value.
- Systematic errors need to be detected if the result is to be accurate.

- The most likely way to detect systematic errors is by repeating the experiment.

Example:

Recalibrate equipment !

PRECISE OR ACCURATE

Student A

pH 4.3 pH 5.0 pH 4.9 pH 4.4 pH 4.7 Mean 4.6

Student B

pH 4.5 pH 4.6 pH 4.6 pH 4.5 pH 4.5 Mean 4.5

RESOLUTION AND PRECISION

The resolution of the stopwatch is 0.01 s but the precision of the data does not match this.

0.13 1.48 1.41 1.44 1.54 1.54 119.5 0.08 1.26 1.21
1.27 1.29 1.25 80 0.08 0.94 0.95 0.93 0.98 0.90
40

Range (s) = ?
Mean time (s) = ?
Time (s) = ?
Distance (cm) = ?

RESOLUTION AND PRECISION

The resolution of the stopwatch is now 0.1 s.

0.1	1.5	1.4	1.4
1.5	1.5	119.5	0.1
1.3	1.2	1.3	1.3
1.3	80	0.1	1.0
1.0	0.9	1.0	0.9
40			

Range (s) = ?
Mean time (s) = ?
Time (s) = ?
Distance (cm) = ?

INTERPRETATION OF DATA

- Written in the third person (stated objectively).
- Inferences can be made when interpreting the data.

- An inference is reasoning based on observation and experience. To infer is to arrive at a decision or opinion by reasoning from known facts.

Example: An increase in temperature influenced the kinetic energy of molecules, therefore increasing the rate of enzyme reaction.

ANALYSIS AND EVALUATION OF THE EXPERIMENT

- Identify sources of, and distinguish between, random and systematic errors.
- List ways to improve procedures of the experiment.
- Comment on suitability and importance of the sample size.
- Comment on the accuracy and precision of the results of the experiment.
- Comment on the value of repeating the experiment.

WRITING A CONCLUSION

- A conclusion is a brief statement related to the initial hypothesis.
- It should be written at the end of each experiment.
- A conclusion supports or refutes the hypothesis.
- Experiments DO NOT PROVE hypotheses.
- Confidence in the validity of a conclusion is dependent upon the quality of the design and the care in execution.

Example:

- This experiment indicates that temperature affects the rate of enzyme reaction.
- No conclusion can be drawn from this experiment due to the large number of uncontrolled factors.

IMPORTANCE OF PRACTICAL WORK

INTRODUCTION

Practical work has a critical part to playin addressing this. It should be thevehicle through which students come toappreciate that science is not exact – notbecause of our failure, but becausemodelling nature is a fascinating, ifextraordinarily difficult, task.

It is the verysimple fact that measurements are noteasy to make. Think of the way globalwarming models depend onmeasurements of sea temperature andthe difficulties in deciding which sea,when, how deep and so on. Theuncertainty associated with thismeasurement can have a critical effect onthe extrapolated slope of globaltemperatures.

This is the sort ofunderstanding that we must place at thecentre of our approach to science.and the effects that uncertainties have onconclusions, and if they can see howevidence is used to structure a scientificclaim, hedged around as it is withqualifications and 'error bars', then theywill be better placed to come to a sound,critical but realistic view. That should beour task. But, how can it be achieved andis there any evidence as to its efficacy?Having collected data, students shouldbe involved in developing a claim basedon that data.

Thisclaim will involve them in weighing theirevidence carefully, and qualifying anddelimiting it. We see this as essential inthat it will develop an understanding ofhow claims link to the underlyingevidence base, and hence develop thesort of critical but open approach to theclaims of others.In summary, we see practical work ascontributing to an understanding of: 1 Basic ideas related to the collection,analysis and interpretation of evidence; 2 How that evidence is weighed in thebalance in the process of making ascientific claim; and 3. How the scientific claim is structuredand delimited and how thatunderstanding can develop a realscientific literacy, which is forensic andempowering rather than explanatoryand patronising.In addressing the questions below weargue that such an understanding isnecessary to combat the rise of anti-scientific 'mumbo-jumbo' that passes forreasoned debate at all levels of societyand which is threatening its rational base.

We believe it to be important, but not inits current format which, driven by thereductionist and debilitating NationalCurriculum, is a waste of time (House ofCommons, 2002). It must be designedfor its particular purpose –

raisingawareness, consolidating an idea,teaching about observation, teachingideas about evidence, giving pupils anopportunity to make their own decisionsin investigations, and so on. Then it canbe motivating and pupils can work attheir own level, i.e. work isdifferentiated by outcome.Good practical work out of theclassroom does all these and introducespupils to 'messy' data, which is vital totheir understanding of how scienceworks and why it is possible forscientists to qualify their predictions anddisagree amongst themselves.

After all,most science they come across in theiradult lives is 'messy' and much is relatedto environmental issues. Fieldworkteaching, in particular, tends toarticulate ideas about evidence well;how to sample, how to handlerepeated/varied data, how manyrepeated readings, comparison ofdifferent measuring methods and usingstatistics to summarise varied data

CONCEPT OF PRACTICAL WORK

Practical work is an industry initiative detailed in conjunction with Lincoln University and is an essential element within an applied course of study. Any practical work needs to be in an area related to student disciplinary and professional interests.

The practical work experience provides opportunities which will enable students to:

Understand the day to day operations involved in the business or on the property.

Apply in practice the values, knowledge and concepts acquired through the academic programme.

Broaden concepts and expand knowledge of practical work opportunities.

Gain an appreciation of some of the social and physical environments in which the business or property operates.

Acquire skills and competencies in collecting and analysing information, written and oral communication, interpersonal and personal skills.

Develop management skills in the areas of report writing,

written presentations and research. Gain experiences and knowledge which will assist in clarifying career interests.

PRACTICAL WORK PROCESS

The Practical Work Unit normally receives offers of work from August each year.

It is the responsibility of individual students to check that any work, intended as practical work, meets the requirements of practical work for their qualification.

Typically, students seeking practical work will:

- Consult the practical work notice board
- Seek full details from folders within the Practical Work Unit
- Note details of any positions in which you are interested
- Contact the employers in accordance with their instructions
- Undertake practical work
- Submit employer verification of work completed to the Practical Work Unit
- Submit practical work associated assignment(s) to the Practical Work Unit.

Note: Employer verification and practical work assignments are required by the annual due date of 31st March each year for returning students.

Final year students must have submitted all employer verification of practical work and assignment(s) by February immediately prior to graduation.

ACTIVITY OF PRACTICAL WORK

Keeping log of Experiments and Mini-Projects

You MUST bring along with you a log book when you attend laboratory sessions. To avoid mix-up of materials of different subjects, you should use one log book for one subject. For instance, keep one log book for Electronic Circuits1, and another for Logic Design. The log book should preferably consist of alternate single-line page and graph paper.

Otherwise, you should bring enough graph papers with you. For some electronics subjects, you should also get your self enough semi-log graph papers with at least three "decades" along the x-axis. So, what is a log book for? The log book is like a "diary" that records everything you see, do and encounter in the lab session. You can have your own style of keeping log of the lab session, but your style must permit readability of the log book by someone else who wishes to study the way you have handled a particular experiment. 'Keeping log' is a compulsory requirement for all practical work. This is true when you become a real engineer one day! Some companies technical and design oriented) require engineers to keep log of all designs, tests, etc., in specific unified formats

Preparation for the Lab Sessions

Normally, you don't walk into the lab without knowing what you are supposed to do in the session. Your subject lecturers usually provide you with all the necessary information regarding nomination of partners, partition of the class, time-tables, venues, experiment titles, etc. well before your first lab session. Usually you should pick up the instruction sheets for all the experiments before you attend the first session (unless otherwise arranged by the lecturers), study the instructions carefully, and if possible, make a preliminary plan for the work. If this is not possible for the very first lab session, you should try to do it for all other remaining lab sessions. All instruction sheets should normally be available to you at last on the first lab session. If not, visit your subject lecturer's website! However, for some special labs, the lecturers may wish to hand out the instructions on spot, especially for those labs that are designed to stimulate quick thinking and analysis.

Recording the use of Apparatus and Instruments

It is extremely important to record all apparatus and instruments used in the experiment. Normally, after writing down the experiment title in the log book, the very next thing you should record is a complete list of apparatus and instruments. Leave some extra space, in case you need to add more items as you go along with the experiment. The way of recording apparatus is worth noting too. Your apparatus list must clearly specify the types and model numbers of the apparatus and instruments. This is an essential part of the logging process as it gives a better chance of diagnosing some possible flaws in an experiment when discrepancies are found at a later stage.

Writing Down What You Actually See and Do

It is worth re-producing some important schematic diagrams in your log book, as well as later in your formal report. Appropriate diagrams help you visualize the physical set-up much more easily than words. You will also find it helpful, after you have left the lab, in recalling your memory about specific set-ups, in the absence of the instruction sheets. Remember that the log book is your "diary"!! A brief and adequate description of the procedure should be included in the log book, especially when you are actually connecting up the set-up in situ. The description given in the instruction sheets may not be as real as it would turn out to be. So, you should take note of the real thing as it appears in front of you. Inevitably, you will encounter problems in the lab session and sometimes you will sort them out yourselves. For future reference and possible diagnosis, you should record all problems encountered during the course of the experiment, e.g., measurement problems, inconsistent observations, etc., however stupid and trivial they are. You may run into them again in future! If you have rectified the problems, with the help of the demonstrator or on your own, spell out the solutions in the log book as well.

Recording and Processing Measured Data

Of course, you will have to record all measured data and results in your logbook. They will be needed for compilation of the formal report. There are several important aspects of data extraction and processing while you are in the lab.

- Clearly tabular data according to the instruction sheet concerned.
- When you are recording a series of data for a range of a given parameter, include enough data to allow a complete characteristic curve to be shown. How? The trick is "use the graph paper and plot as you measure".

Start with some coarsely selected points and gradually include more points in-between to make up the details of a certain characteristic curve which is to be measured. For example, if you are recording the impedance of a simple resonant circuit, you may start with scanning through the whole range of frequencies, and taking values at some extreme points, say 1kHz and 500kHz. Then, take measurements at some coarsely chosen point, say every 50kHz. After you have taken the se measurements, you MUST plot them out immediately on a graph paper. Don't keep the raw data untouched in the lab, and assume you can sort out the details later at home! This won't work! However, if you plot the curve out, you will see immediately where you should insert more points in order to reveal the shape of the curve in more detail. This should be easily done with the help of a partner

- Don't assume you have the right data. Try to determine whether the data you have got are making sense to you. Here, the log book is useful since it can be used as a scratch pad to record all erroneous data as well as to make a quick analysis.
- Always remember to note the range selected in your meter for each datum you take. For example, if you measure a current with a Digital Multimeter, you should write alongside the measured datum the selected in strument range, say 0-100mA.A caution must be exercised when taking measurements with almost all meters. Repeat the measurement with several ranges until you get the best reading. With digital meters, usually, you should select the range to give maximum number of significant digits. With analog meters, make sure the value you measure is

within 10% and 90% of the selected measuring range of the instrument.

- Formal reports: Your subject lecturers will inform you of the requirement of submission of formal reports. In general, you should be prepared to write a formal report for each experiment you have performed in the lab. You should start writing up your report as soon as you have completed the experiment.

Don't wait until you have forgotten every thing! You report must contain the following:

- Title of the experiment
- Date, time and venue
- Name of partner
- Objectives
- list of apparatus with types and model numbers
- Description of procedures
- Schematic diagrams of all setups
- Measured data and graphs9.interpretation of results
- Answers to all questions raised in the instruction sheet
- Discussions of sources of errors
- ALL other things that you have observed in the experiment
- Conclusion: A good report should also present useful discussions and extrapolations of theexperimental work. In the process of writing up, you will find the log bookextremely helpful. In fact, the whole idea of logging is to allow you to recallwhat you have actually seen and done in the lab session. Of course, an early write-up will certainly help since there are still many useful things that you could not be bothered to put in your log book

Locating the Sources of Errors

Errors can be due to obvious or subtle causes. You should attempt to give a critical list of the sources of errors, especially when you observe discrepancies in your measured data. Don't assume the errors are natural and can be ignored. Ask yourself why the results are not consistent with what you expect. Believe it or not, even the simple experiment of verifying a Kirchhoff Current Law equation can appear to make no sense. It could turn out that the sum of currents emerging from a node is non-zero!

When this kind of things happens, don't just ignore it unless you know what causes it. Obviously, in this case, you might have measured the currents with an ammeter, one at a time, and the ammeter has some finite resistance! The key to locating sources of errors is a careful examination of the procedure and actual physical set-up of the experiment. Finally, make possible alterations to minimize errors. In most situations, a change in the physical arrangements and measurement orders can make a lot of differences.

Conclusion

Practical work can be an extremely enlightening part of your training. Makegood use of it! While there are specific objectives for each experiment, you should also aim at acquiring some essential skills in the overall practical work component. At least, one day, you will not be embarrassed for being ignorant of the basic techniques of handling a piece of simple hardware when chances arise for you to deal with it. Finally, I hope you will never again, after enough practical training, fail to see any signals in your circuit just because you have shorted out the essential signal paths with the ground terminal of your CRO leads

FIRST AID

Every employee of a laboratory should have knowledge of emergency first aid and roughly one out of every ten employees of a whole institute should have a valid First Aid certificate including an endorsement for resuscitation. These qualifications should be mentioned on the Staff Record Form model PERS 012 . The management should encourage first aid training and the essential refresher courses by allowing time off and a periodical bonus.

Since no paragraph nor even a chapter can take the place

of a proper first aid training, only some major practical aspects will be mentioned here to provide the basics of emergency first aid. These may be summarized in a SOP or Instruction.

Essential Items and Equipment

- Names and internal phone numbers of employees with First Aid certificate.
- Telephone numbers of physicians and hospitals as well as the general emergency number.
- First Aid kit
- Eye wash fountains or bottles.
- Safety showers (at least one per laboratory).

It is the (delegatable) responsibility of the head of laboratory that these items are in order. A check-list for regular inspection of these points should be made (and kept, for instance, with the First Aid kit).

Items 1 and 2 could be taken care of by issuing a sticker with this information to each employee.

The First Aid kit should be the responsibility of one person who keeps a logbook of regular contents checks and purchased supplements. Tallying used materials from the First Aid kit in practice appears to be illusive. Also eye-wash equipment and safety showers need to be inspected regularly. When an eye-wash bottle has been used, it should be replaced or refilled and the expiration date revised.

Emergency First Aid

- Be alert to unsafe conditions and actions, and call attention to them so that corrections can be made as soon as possible.
- Label all storage areas, refrigerators, etc., appropriately, and keep all chemicals in properly labeled containers.
- Date all bottles when received and when opened.
- Note expiration dates on chemicals.
- Note special storage conditions.

Be familiar with the appropriate protective measures to take when exposed to the following classes of hazardous materials. Information is available from your lab supervisor, DES and the chemistry library:

- Flammables
- Radioactive Compounds
- Corrosives
- Biohazards
- Toxics
- Carcinogens
- Reactives
- Compressed Gases

Segregate chemicals by compatibility groups for storage.

Be aware of the potential interactions of lab furniture and equipment with chemicals used or stored in the lab.

Post warning signs for unusual hazards such as flammable materials, biohazards or other special problems. Pour more concentrated solutions into less concentrated solutions to avoid violent reactions (i.e., Always add acid to water; not water to acid). Avoid distracting any other worker. Practical jokes or horseplay have no place in the laboratory. Use equipment only for its designated purpose. Position and secure apparatus used for hazardous reactions in order to permit manipulation without moving the apparatus until the entire reaction is complete. Sometimes, in case of an accident, there is no time or possibility to await qualified help. In that case, the necessary help needs to be given by others. The most important general points to observe are listed here:

- Stay calm, try to oversee the situation and watch out for danger.
- Try to find out what is wrong with the casualty.
- Take care that the casualty keeps breathing. If breathing stops, try to apply artificial respiration by mouth-to-mouth or mouth-to-nose in sufflation. When unconscious, turn casualty on his/her side with the face tilted to the floor.
- Staunch serious bleeding. If necessary, arterial bleeding may be stopped by pressing a thumb in the wound.
- Do not move the casualty unless he/she is in a

dangerous position (e.g., in case of gas, smoke, fire or electricity), then carefully move casualty to a safe place.

- Put the casualty's mind at rest.
- Call qualified help as soon as possible: medical service, a physician and/or an ambulance, and if necessary, the police. Do not leave casualty unattended.

A few specific accidents that may occur in the laboratory are the following:

Burns

Hold affected parts of the skin for at least 10 minutes in cold water. Try to keep the bum sterile and do not apply ointment.

Corrosive Burns

(e.g. by hydrogen peroxide): wash the affected part of the skin thoroughly with water.

Eye (corrosive) Burns

Wash eye thoroughly with tap water: use an eye fountain or eye-wash bottle or a tubing connected to a tap.

Hydrofluoric Acid Burn

Wash the affected part with dilute ammonia (1-2%) or sodium bicarbonate solution.

Poisoning by Swallowing

- *Corrosive solutions (acids, bases):* Let the casualty drink one or two glasses of water to dilute the poison. Vomiting should not be induced.
- *Petroleum products:* Do not induce vomiting (the products may get into the bronchial tubes).
- *Non-corrosive solutions (e.g. herbicides, fungicides):* Try to induce vomiting. Swallow activated charcoal.

In all these cases must the casualty immediately be taken to a physician or hospital.

PERSONAL SAFETY

Respiratory and Body Protection

- Use fume hoods whenever possible.
- Splash proof safety goggles should be worn at all times in the laboratory.
- Laboratory coat/apron should be worn in the laboratory.
- Appropriate gloves should be worn as needed.
- Appropriate closed-toed shoes should be worn in the laboratory.
- Respirators may only be worn by individuals that have completed respirator training and fit testing through DES and obtained a respirator medical clearance form the University Health Centre.

Personal Hygiene

- Wash hands before leaving laboratory.
- Launder clothing worn in laboratory separately from other clothing.
- Never mouth pipette anything in the lab.
- Never eat, drink or apply cosmetics in a laboratory or areas where chemicals/hazardous agents are stored. (Smoking is prohibited in all areas of University buildings, including laboratories.)
- Never store food in a refrigerator where hazardous materials are stored.
- Never eat or drink from laboratory glassware.
- Avoid wearing contact lenses in the laboratory.
- Avoid situating long hair, loose sleeves/cuffs, rings, bracelets, etc. in close proximity to open flames or operating machinery.
- Keep exposed skin covered. Shorts, sleeveless or short sleeve shirts, skirts or open-toed shoes should not be worn in the laboratory.

Fire Prevention

- Be aware of ignition sources in lab area (open flames, heat, electrical equipment).

- Purchase and store flammable reagents in the smallest quantities available.
- Store flammable liquids that require refrigeration in explosion-proof refrigerators.
- Store flammable liquids in appropriate safety cabinets and/or safety cans.
- Do not store incompatible reagents together.
- Do not store ethers or conjugated dienes for extended periods of time as explosive peroxides could form. Date ethers when received and opened.

Make sure that all electrical cords are in good condition. All electrical outlets should be grounded and should accommodate a 3-pronged plug. Never remove the grounding prong or use an adapter to bypass the grounding on an electrical cord.

Remain out of the area of a fire or personal injury unless it is your responsibility to meet the emergency responders. Meet responders from a safe location.

Be aware of the condition of fire extinguishers. Report any broken seals, damage, low gauge pressure or improper mounting to DES Fire Protection, If the seal has been broken, assume that the fire extinguisher has been used and must be recharged.Report ALL fires by phoning;.

Automatic fire sprinklers must remain clear and unblocked to function properly. Do not store materials within 18" below the sprinkler head.

Housekeeping

Eliminate safety hazards by maintaining laboratory work areas in a good state of order.

Maintain at least two clear passages to laboratory exits.

Always keep tables, fume hoods, floors, aisles and desks clear of unnecessary material.

Wipe down bench tops and other laboratory surfaces after each use with an appropriate cleaning or disinfecting agent.

All equipment should be inspected before use.

Use borosilicate glassware for laboratory work. If

dichromate/sulfuric acid glass cleaner is used in your laboratory, make sure that cleaning is confined to the fume hood as toxic chromyl chlorides are released from the dichromate/sulfuric acid solution.

Better yet, switch to a non-chromate cleaning solution.which will also minimize hazardous waste generation.

If experiments must be left unattended, place a note next to experimental apparatus indicating the chemicals involved, your name and a number where you can be reached in case of an emergency.

Keep the laboratory floor dry at all times. Immediately attend to spills of chemicals or water, and notify other lab workers of potential slipping hazards.

All machinery under repair or adjustment should be properly tagged prior to servicing. All service work should be done by authorized personnel.

Sink traps and floor drains should be flushed and filled with water on a regular basis to prevent the escape of sewer gases or the release of chemical odors in the event of an emergency. Drains which will not be routinely used may be "topped" with 20 - 30 ml of mineral oil to prevent evaporation of water in the trap.

All compressed gas cylinders should be securely chained or clamped to a rack or fixed stationary piece of lab furniture. Mark empty cylinders, but use all safety precautions as if the cylinder were full.

MUSEUM

DEFINITION

- A non-profitmaking, permanent institution in the service of society and of its development, and open to the public, which acquires, conserves, researches, communicates and exhibits, for purposes of study, education and enjoyment, material evidence of people and their environment.
- A public or private nonprofit agency or institution organized on a permanent basis for essentially

educational or aesthetic purposes, which, utilizing a professional staff, owns or utilizes tangible objects, cares for them, and exhibits them to the public on a regular basis.

The Institute of Museum and Library Services (IMLS) uses the Museum and Library Services Act definition as the basis for its eligibility criteria to receive federal funds from IMLS:

- Be organized as a public or private nonprofit institution that exists on a permanent basis for essentially educational or aesthetic reasons
- Care for and own or use tangible objects, whether animate or inanimate, and exhibit these objects on a regular basis through facilities that it owns or operates
- Have at least one professional staff member or the full-time equivalent, whether paid or unpaid, whose primary responsibility is the acquisition, care, or exhibition of the public objects owned or used by the museum
- Be open and provide museum services to the general public for at least 120 days a year

THE MUSEUM

Features in the permanent museum building will include a central hall with large exhibits, a film theater, the main gallery, a picture gallery, temporary and rotating exhibition area, library and study areas and more. The central hall may include a U-2, a section of the Berlin, a "Spy" satellite and other historical War reminders.

The museum has a mobile exhibit on the U-2 Incident of May. The exhibit has been displayed at many museums across the country and internationally. The traveling exhibit has acted as a catalyst for the creation of a permanent Museum. To reserve the mobile exhibit, please contact the Museum. To see more on the museum background, Smithsonian affiliation and more, please refer to the links on the left side of our site.

Online you will find links to virtual exhibits, photo galleries, newsletters and many other collections of cold war related material. In our Gift Store you can purchase artifacts, books, jewelry or simply make a tax deductible donation in support of cold war history preservation.

Exhibits

In addition to our extensive mobile exhibit, the Museum currently hosts a variety of online exhibits, exhibiting artifacts and memorabilia associated with various Cold War related events and activities ranging from Winston Fulton, Missouri speech to the Plan, to the fall of the Wall, the collapse of the Soviet Union and more.

The cold war museum also keeps first hand accounts of the time period and activities, priceless stories from the people who lived the history.

Activities

There are many activities available sponsored by the Museum. Special events include book signings, lectures on cold war history and a Spy Tour of places in Washington associated with famous espionage cases.

There is also a great online trivia game to test your knowledge of the time periods history!

The Cold War

There are many ways to stay in touch with us here at the museum. The best method is to sign up for the Museum's newsletter, The Cold War Times. We have established the Cold Times in order to chronicle the history of the Cold War and notify our subscribers of Cold War anniversaries, events and activities that relate to the Cold War.

Timeline

Located along the bottom of our website pages, our Cold War Timeline section lists major events in Cold War history classified by the decade they occurred - the 40s, 50s, 60s, 70s, 80s, and 90s. Here you will find concise summaries about these significant events, and where possible, links to additional information.

Gift Store

Be sure to visit our gift store, where you will find many unique collectibles from the US, Soviet Union and other sources. Since The Cold War Museum is a non-profit charity, by shopping online through our web site you will be supporting the goals of the Cold War Museum with each purchase.

Summary

The Cold War Museum endeavors to maintain a historically accurate record of the people, places and events of the Cold War. By educating future generations about the fears, divisions, and dangers that the Cold War fostered, the Museum will enable visitors to reflect upon the global geopolitical climate in which many of us grew up.

In addition, The Cold War Museum seeks to develop learning opportunities regarding Cold War implications for public policy, public administration, national security, and international peace and arms control. Through such resources The Cold War Museum will enable future generations to learn from the successes and failures of the past.

The Cold War Museum is cultivating relationships with the Federal Bureau of Investigation (FBI), Central Intelligence Agency (CIA), the Komitet Gosudarstvennoy Besopasnosti (KGB), the National Reconnaissance Office (NRO), and the National Archives, federal, state, and local entities, for-profit and non-profit organizations, worldwide veteran organizations, and individual citizens. The development of these and other relationships will help to establish the features that will be incorporated into the Cold War Museum and enhance the Museum's educational value.

IMPORTANCE OF MUSEUM ENVIRONMENT

One goal of every museum is to make objects accessible to the public, to researchers, and to other institutions. A second goal is to ensure the long-term safety and preservation of the collections. Objects need one set of conditions while people may need another. Achieving both seems impossible.

Managing the museum environment can be difficult since it requires expertise and time. It also requires the efforts of all your staff, as well as the cooperation of the public. But a controlled environment can be achieved, even by small institutions with limited resources.

HEATING, VENTILATION, AND AIR CONDITIONING

Heating, Ventilation, and Air Conditioning (HVAC) is a frequently troublesome area of preservation. Architects often fail to understand the importance of a preservation quality HVAC system, instead specifying units that are better suited to commercial construction. Museum curators often don't know how to describe correctly what it is they need, or what the problems are with the current system.

Museum directors and their boards are sometimes not convinced that controlling the environment is all that important. And preservationists often fail to allow any latitude in the development of an affordable preservation quality environment.

The importance of the environment in which collections are stored should be clearly realized. For example, for every 14° F rise in temperature the deterioration rate of paper (and likely other organic materials) doubles.

Condensation on the inside of windows suggests a potentially serious problem with the institution's relative humidity control.

Humidity is most often associated with an increased probability of mold growth and other forms of biodeterioration. Levels at 60% RH should be considered the threshold for damage - over that level and the museum will eventually have trouble. But because many collections are also hygroscopic, the humidity levels will also affect dimensional stability. For example, some types of wood board can vary up to one inch in length over a foot between 10% and 90% RH. Variation in relative humidity can loosen furniture joints, cause paint to chip from canvas, and cockle paper. In addition, fluctuating relative humidity can lead to chemical reactions.

Metals will corrode, many dyes will fade, and even glass and mineral collections can be damaged.

Staining around the ceiling vents is a sure clue of inadequate filtration.

The quality of the air in the museum will also affect preservation. Particulates are often abrasive and may permanently soil collections. They are also perfect hosts for mold. Particulates increase user discomfort and increase maintenance costs. Gaseous contaminants, such as oxides of nitrogen and sulfur dioxide can attack organic materials by conversion to acids, while ozone is a powerful oxidant, breaking apart every carbon double bond, severely damaging all organic material. Other gaseous pollutants, such as formaldehyde, may be off-gassing from storage cabinets or glues in the museum.

But all of this should not make the creation of a preservation environment sound impossible. Yes, managing the museum environment can be difficult. Environmental control demands expertise, time, and patience. It also requires the coordinated efforts of the entire staff, as well as the informed cooperation of the public, but it can be done.

With some work, and the cooperation of your architect, it is not only possible, but it will also make the library a healthier, and friendlier place for collections, staff and patrons.

The Ideal

When a preservation quality environment is researched the first thing noticed is the lack of agreement between different sources. Some will specify that the correct temperature is 68° F ± 2°, others will suggest a range of 68° to 72°, and so on. Similar problems are encountered when relative humidity, particulate, or gaseous pollution levels are examined.

But there are issues more important than a precise level. Typically, humidity is much more important than temperature and should be controlled first. Further, fluctuations (seasonal and particularly daily) tend to be more damaging than constant levels, whatever they may be.

Ventilation is especially important for libraries, since it not only ensures the health and well-being of staff and patrons (the primary concern of the ASHRAE Standard, Ventilation for Acceptable Indoor Air Quality), but also helps to minimize the potential for mold outbreaks by providing adequate passage of the air through high efficiency filters and maintaining air movement. Pockets of stagnant air are a sure invitation for mold problems and should be carefully avoided by the mechanical engineer.Arrestance vs. Efficiency values for filters using ASHRAE tests.

What all this means to the museum is sometimes hard to understand, but for many institutions it may require:

maintaining a relative humidity between 40% and 55% throughout the year, allowing seasonal fluctuations between the two extremes, but holding daily fluctuations to ± 3%, maintaining temperature between 65° and 75° F throughout the year, allowing seasonal fluctuations between the two extremes, but holding daily fluctuations to ± 5° F, designing filtration to remove at least 50% of particulates using the ASHRAE Dust Spot Efficiency Test, designing gaseous filtration to maintain preservation standards throughout the facility, or using area filtration as necessary, and adequate ventilation to avoid stagnant air pockets, "dead" zones at the ends of ranges and corners of stacks, and similar problems that are conducive to the growth of mold and mildew.

Unfortunately, HVAC or mechanical engineers are most familiar with the American Society of Heating, Refrigerating, and Air Conditioning Engineers (ASHRAE) guide to human comfort, which is very different from that appropriate for collections. Consequently, when architects and mechanical engineers discuss "comfort" and "design" levels, they are almost always expressing concerns that fail to include the needs of collections.

UNDERSTANDING THE EFFECTS OF DIFFERENT TEMPERATURE AND HUMIDITY LEVELS: ISOPERMS

Given the possible range in seemingly acceptable temperature and humidity, how can an institution select an appropriate level? Sometime the choice comes down to a simple cost analysis or to what the present equipment can accomplish.

But recent research by Don Sebera, a consultant to the Commission on Preservation and Access, has developed the concept of "isoperms"—quantitative graphical measures of relative permanence. While currently developed only for paper, efforts are underway to extend the concept to other media such as magnetic tape, textiles, and photographic film. At present, however, the isoperm concept may help us to better understand how different temperature and humidity levels affect the useful life expectancy of organic materials.

In particular, this approach helps us understand otherwise complex questions such as "what is the effect on my collection when the physical plant turns the HVAC system off at night, over weekends, and during holidays?" or "what are the consequences of allowing wider fluctuations in order to contain costs?"

To provide one example, the relative permanence at 95°F and 80% RH is ~ 0.03 (1.00=paper at 68°F and 50% RH for the reference standard). If the paper has an expected useful life of 100 years at the reference standard, under the high temperature and high relative humidity of this example, the expected life is reduced to only 3 years (0.03 x 100). The relative permanence at 50°F and 40% RH is ~ 12. In this example, the expected useful life is increased to about 1200 years!

Without going into great detail, isoperms can also be used to reveal the extent of reduced permanence resulting from cycling collections from high temperatures and relative humidities typical of summer conditions to low temperatures and low humidities typical of winter conditions. Perhaps of even greater importance, isoperms can help minimize the damage from cycling by keeping conditions in relatively high isoperm value levels.

Your institution should become familiar with the use of isoperms and evaluate collection storage conditions not in the context of one "ideal" temperature and relative humidity level, but in the context of long-term permanence.

MAJOR COMPONENTS OF AN HVAC SYSTEM

Without going into detail, a typical large HVAC system will contain a chiller, a cooling tower, a boiler, and one or more air handlers. The chiller provides the cooling, circulating cold water to the various air handler coils. Air passing over these coils is cooled, effectively cooling the museum. The cooling tower is used to dissipate the heat collected by the refrigerants as they are used in the coils. The boiler produces either steam or hot water. Both can be used for heating purposes (used in the coils the same way as the chilled water) or for dehumidification. The air handlers consist of a fan, filtration, and the coil. They are used to distribute the clean cooled or heated air.

Mechanical rooms may look intimidating, but they all contain the same basic equipment.

Smaller institutions may use direct refrigeration units (also called DX or direct expansion units). These units may contain a packaged cooling system (including the coils, filter, and fan) and a condenser mounted outside the building (serving the purpose of a cooling tower in a larger system).

The decision of which to employ is usually determined by the size of the institution and similar factors. But, both can satisfy the preservation needs of a library, if properly designed. Essential elements include:

The use of a constant air volume system which constantly circulates air at full volume. Often the architect or mechanical engineer will use a variable air volume (VAV) system in its place. The VAV system delivers cooled or heated air in proportion to the heating or cooling needed in a specific zone. While this approach saves energy costs, it does so by placing the maintenance of a stable humidity at risk. Such systems also cannot properly filter the air or maintain sufficient air flow to help prevent stagnant air pockets.

The limitation of outside air makeup to that required by the local codes. Museums should not use air economizers, which introduce large amounts of outside air for "free" cooling and heating. These systems make it virtually impossible to maintain stable relative humidities.

Design based on humidity, rather than temperature, control. It is preferable for temperature to fluctuate, rather than RH, and all controls should be designed with this specification in mind.

The use of electronic, rather than very insensitive pneumatic, controls in the occupied spaces, not in the return ductwork.

The use of reheat coils for dehumidification of cooling air and clean steam humidification. Reheat coils allow the air to be super-cooled by the coils, driving off excess moisture, and then to be reheated to the appropriate level. Dehumidification using desiccant drums is not only a costly alternative, but it is more difficult to maintain and may release a fine dust or powder into the air stream. Clean steam dehumidification is preferred over all other humidification techniques.

The use of prefilters and final high efficiency filters, with each bank monitored by a manometer. The use of electrostatic air cleaners should be avoided since they release ozone into the air.

Constant operation of the HVAC system to ensure adequate environmental controls and eliminate sharp spikes and excess fluctuations of temperature and relative humidity.

These essential design features will help ensure that the museum's system is capable of achieving and maintaining a preservation quality environment.

INTERIM AND LOW COST IMPROVEMENTS

A first step in all efforts to improve the museum environment should be sealing the structure—using caulk and weather stripping to make the building weather tight. This step alone will improve the physical condition of the building, reduce air infiltration, reduce pest access, reduce the heating/ cooling load, reduce air pollution, and reduce the particulates in the building. Making the building watertight will reduce the sources of water vapour within the structure and may significantly reduce the relative humidity levels.

Another important step is to recognize that the collections need a more stable environment than staff offices, meeting facilities, and similar areas of the building. By reducing the size of the specially designed HVAC system to cover only the collections and exhibit areas, the costs will be appreciably reduced. Consider establishing safe microclimates in display cases and using materials which will help buffer the environment.

Better cleaning, using damp mops (rather than dust mops) and high efficiency (HEPA) vacuums, will reduce the particulates in the library. Hard floors should be damp mopped every 48 hours and regularly waxed to help prevent them from holding dust. If carpets are used they must be vacuumed at least weekly.

The museum should segregate offending activities, such as smoking, photocopying, and use of laser printers, from the collections.

Only preservation quality materials should be used. Avoid materials which will off-gas and cause additional damage. Emphasize the use of pH neutral, alkaline buffered storage containers. Recently preservation supply companies have introduced storage materials which further buffer collections by incorporating activated charcoal and molecular sieves.

Reduce winter heating. The maintenance of the often encountered winter heating temperature of 76° F will cost 75% more than maintaining a temperature of 68° F. In addition, the cooler temperatures (and somewhat higher relative humidities) are better for the collections.

It may be possible to install a central drain through evaporative pad humidifier on forced air systems. While not as effective or reliable as the in-duct steam system, it may still be an acceptable alternative. Such systems, however, do require additional maintenance.

Supplemental filtration, including gaseous filtration, can be obtained by "add-ons" from companies such as Purafil and the Farr Company. Where only a single room requires the additional protection, the cost for room filtration can be relatively low. It may also be possible to install higher efficiency filters, with only minor modifications to existing fans. Better filtration can also be achieved through the replacement of standard filters with either a combination fiberglass/potassium permanganate filter or perhaps pleated filters which do not significantly increase the pressure drop. However, always be sure to check with a mechanical engineer before changing filters to avoid damaging your system.

MONITORING TEMPERATURE AND HUMIDITY

The levels of temperature and humidity must be quantified. It is not enough to guess that the space is "too dry" or "too humid." It is essential that you measure temperature and humidity at key points throughout the building. To be effective, this monitoring programme must be planned and continuous over at least one change of seasons.

People also have a significant affect on the environment. They raise the temperature and increase the relative humidity in popular exhibition halls. You will want to chart the number of visitors to correlate with the environmental records.

You will also want to keep track of outdoor conditions. It may be that your building and control systems are simply buffering whatever is happening outside, so that during summer thunderstorms the relative humidity inside increases dramatically. Be sure to record any loss of electrical service, so you can determine how long your building can hold constant temperature and humidity levels.

MONITORING EQUIPMENT

The simplest, and least expensive, method of monitoring humidity is offered by the humidity indicator cards. As the humidity increases or decreases, chemically impregnated spots change from blue (dry) through lavender (about 50% RH) to pink (humid). They have a long shelf or use life, but offer only gross measurements.

Example of an Aspirated Psychrometer

Sling psychrometers measure the ambient (dry-bulb) temperature and the temperature of an evaporating water source (wet-bulb; usually a moistened wick surrounding the thermometer bulb). Use of a psychometric chart comparing the two temperatures produces a relative humidity reading. Sling psychrometers require several minutes of vigorous work to maintain the required air flow of 9 to 15 feet per second while the wet bulb temperature is obtained.

The readings may be affected by body moisture, local air movement, and even the fitness of the operator. Aspirated psychrometers use a small battery powered fan to provide a rapid, defined air flow over the wet bulb. They can be very good when calibrated and used correctly.

Major problem areas tend to be contaminants on the wick, an ill-fitting wick, and inadequate air flow resulting from weak batteries. Often it is necessary to get very close to the thermometers to read the wet- and dry-bulb temperatures, which may alter the readings. Unless psychrometers are used by meticulous staff members, they can provide almost useless results. At least one authority suggests that even aspirated psychrometers are both tedious and prone to such severe operator induced errors that they should not be used for calibration purposes.

Many institutions have used dial hygrometers. While there are a large number of models (and associated prices), these are not necessarily the most accurate, or least expensive method of obtaining quantifiable measurements for either temperature or humidity.

The mechanical hygrometer relies on the physical changes of dimension which occur when a material, such as hair, absorbs or desorbs water. They are slow to respond and sensitive to vibration errors. Many of the materials used are subject to aging and often are non-linear, limiting their accurate use to between 25 and 75% RH.

INEXPENSIVE DIGITAL THERMOHYGROMETER

More useful are the recently introduced minimum/ maximum digital hygrometers. A built-in memory function automatically records minimum and maximum readings for both temperature and humidity since the last memory check. This allows conditions to be examined for 24-hour periods, or perhaps overnight or even over weekends. They are small, highly accurate, and very inexpensive.

More expensive hand-held, battery-operated portable thermohygrometers are produced by a number of companies. These instruments usually consist of a display unit and a probe at the end of a lead. The sensors usually consist of a hygroscopic material whose electrical impedance varies with relative humidity. These instruments may also be non-linear at low or high relative humidities and tend to drift over time. When calibration corrections are applied, an accuracy of about ± 3% of the reading is possible (for example, a reading of 50% RH would be within the range of 48.5 to 51.5% RH), although ±4% is more likely (placing the 50% RH reading within the range of 48 to 52% RH). In spite of these problems, most electronic hygrometers are very suitable for museum use. They are fast-responding, easy to ready, easy to transport, and not likely to be affected by normal handling.

Example of a digital thermohygrometer suitable for calibrating equipment.

Hygrothermographs or recording hygrometers incorporate either mechanical or electronic sensors into instruments to record the readings on a moving drum or disk. There are a number of options available and personal preference usually dictates choice. However, electronic sensors are typically better than mechanical sensors, battery operated drives tend to be more functional for most institutions than clock drives, and felt-tip pens tend to be easier and less affected by operator error than inked pens. Some instruments offer remote leads (useful for monitoring closed storage areas or cases without access), high and low alarms, digital readout of current conditions, and AC/DC operation with battery back-up. The resulting charts provide a continuous record of temperature and humidity conditions, offering information on fluctuations which can be correlated with weather and building systems data. One example of a recording hygrothermograph. Data loggers are a new system for measuring and storing temperature and humidity data. Unlike hygrothermographs, data loggers do not provide immediate access to the collected information—they require "down loading" to a computer and use of a software programme. They can, however, collect data for days, weeks, or months (depending on the collection interval) and then allow the resulting data to be graphed or further analyzed. There is no question that it is much easier to obtain statistical analysis from data loggers than hygrothermographs. But it is also important to realise that data loggers, since they use the same technology as other electronic humidity sensors, will drift and have variable sensitivities. Consequently, statistical analysis must not be more demanding than the data is capable of supporting.

A GOOD FIRST STEP

A preventative conservation programme must begin with an intensive museum-wide study which examines the collection, the indoor environment, the building, and the current HVAC system. This type of detailed preservation study provides baseline data and allows you to demonstrate the benefits of improvements. The collection should be examined since different materials require different handling and environmental conditions. Without a knowledge of the condition of the collection and its environmental needs, there is no baseline for any conservation programme.

Monitoring allows the temperature and humidity in every museum space to be quantified. To be effective, the monitoring programme must be well planned and continuous over at least a change of seasons. You will want to reveal both daily and also seasonal fluctuations. The building is the first line of collection defence and a survey can establish whether the museum envelope is buffering the outdoor conditions well enough to reduce the need for the most expensive control equipment. The existing equipment—and its operation—should also be examined.

IMPORTANCE OF MUSEUM LIBRARIES

INTRODUCTION

The purpose of our meeting is to discuss co-operation

between art institutions and their information resources. One could plunge in straight away and try to set formulae and programmes, set targets and target dates. But art institutions did not spring from nowhere and to look back is to begin to understand what our current strategy is, and to build on what is good.

After all, art institutions, whether contemplating the past in museums, or creating the history of today in art schools, in contemporary galleries, and so forth are all involved primarily in the art of preservation. We belong to that dimension of society whose primary task is to guard art efacts, guard the manifest part of the evolution of the human mind. Art institutions who study these art efacts depend on this preservation of the manifest object. So, it will help to look back very briefly at our institutions and at the way co-operation took place in the past.

HISTORY

So where did museums come from? In its most basic form what we call a museum, has come to mean a collection of something. In fact the notion of a museum, according to the Encyclopedia Britannica, springs from the passion for collecting which is deeply rooted in human nature. All civilizations, from the most primitive to the most advanced share the desire to accumulate objects that are beautiful, costly, rare or merely curious. Religious communities, rulers and magnates set up the first collections open to the public, or at least to certain members of it.

An early example is the Athenian Treasury at Delphi. Another early 'collection' was in fact books, Aristotle's Library. The term 'museum' arises with the Musaion, the temple of the Muses, in Alexandria.

This Musaion, however, is also known as the Great Library of Alexandria which was established in the 3rd century AD and which provided the final resting place of Aristotle's famed library. This musaion was in fact a place dedicated to the muses and to study where one engaged oneself in noble disciplines. Thus in its origins a museum was an institution of research, a library and an academy. In time the term museum became strongly identified with a building type, namely, according to the Oxford Dictionary of the English Language, «a buildingused as a repository for the preservation and exhibition of objects illustrative of antiquities, natural history, fine and industrial art». The term also became to be applied to the collection of objects itself.

Collecting blossomed in the middle ages in the great religious institutions which each contained libraries. But collecting here was by commission, in addition to accumulation, both of objects and of manuscripts. The manuscripts of those time ssurvive in the great modern libraries of today. With the Renaissance, collecting as an activity perse reflected the meaning of the word renaissance, rebirth. After all, in classical times Aristotle first collected books, and the dispersal of his library, politically inspired, was experienced as a source of sadness.

This rebirth manifested itself in collecting. Collecting became amania. However, it was a very select mania in that connoisseurs collected for themselves and not for the general public. From the basic satisfaction of the collector's instinct we progressed in time to making use of the collections of objects to suit the needs of study and museums started to open their doors to people who had access to knowledge through education. In modern times the 'public' first gained access to a collection only in1683 when the Ashmolean Museum of Art and Archaeology was founded in Oxford and the first use of the word 'museum' in the English language to refer to a building housing art efacts was in relation to Dr Ashmole's. The great push came in1793 when the new Museum National du Louvre was founded with the specific intention of making it possible for the people to view the objects collected together, and so to educate them.

However, broadly speaking, connoisseurship remained the driving force in the act of collecting and the aim of education remained only implicit. In the US, however, a sense of cultural isolation can be discerned in the creation of museums, and education as a purpose became a strong and overt driving force. Education has remained a very strong component of museums since then.

LIBRARIES

As more and more museums were created in thc 19th century libraries were regarded as an essential part of the museum. For example, the Boston Museum created a reference library in 1875, and a library was envisaged as an integral part by the founders of the Metropolitan Museum. The German National Museum created in 1852 in Nuremberg established a library and archive to collect documentation on the history of German art.

One purpose of a museum library was seen to be to provide documentation on the objects within the specific museum. The museum library was seen as a tool to provide support to the museum staff alone and museum-libraries were not regarded as for the public at all and in many instances they retain to this day the character of a private library. Where the library collections have become known to be very strong in a specific subject, scholars and connoisseurs have been allowed in as a favour, and they predominantly gain access through their relationships with museum curators.

However, some museums realised that they could physically collect only a very small amount of objects but to study these objects one would need to view many more examples than the museum could house. In these museums, libraries were developed as extensions to the museum objects. Whilst the museums tried to obtain one or two examples of an object, the museum library collected books in which examples of hundreds more objects of the same type were illustrated.

Thc Library in the Victoria and Albert Museum in London is one such example. In1837 the British Government created a School of Design because it felt that design in Britain was inferior to other countries. The School of Design aimed to educate artisans of all the crafts and to do so it collected both plaster-casts of objects and illustrated books. In fact, books were regarded as of such importance that the first staff-member of the School of Design to be appointed was the Librarian. It was the Librarian's job to acquire books in which examples of well-designed objects were illustrated. After the Great Exhibition in London, the Government decided to set up a Museum of Manufactures and to this end purchased a large number of the best art efacts from the Exhibition so that craftspeople could study actual objects from many nations.

But because it was desirable that artists and craftspeople should view as many objects in their trade as possible, a library of illustrated books was an essential extension of the Museum's collection. It was therefore decided to incorporate the Library of the School of Design into this new museum.

By the time this museum established its own home in South Kensington in the mid-1850s the library began to be called the National Art Library.

But implicit in the nature of the material that libraries collect, one can discern a third purpose of a museum-library, namely to view the book not only as an information-carrying device, but as an object in its own right and the librarian also as a curator.

TAKING FIELD TRIP

- *Plan*: Look for a destination or an experience that builds on children's interests. Then ask yourself: Is it compatible with children's attention spans? Will there be long lines? Places to sit? Are there many "do-not— touch" temptations? What will children gain from the experience?
- *Experience*: If possible, take the trip yourself beforehand. Check to make sure it meets your criteria for a successful experience. Also note locations of bathrooms, parking, places for children to have lunch or snacks, and any safety concerns. Don't forget to confirm directions for drivers.
- *Focus*: Trips mean so much more when children are prepared for the experience. Many trips also lend themselves to culminating activities, such as drawings, exhibits, class books, and photo albums.

And, of course, you can never go wrong with a combination of both.

- *Prepare*: Talk about rules: who will walk together, how to behave on the bus, and so on. Make sure name tags are sturdy and won't fall off. (Pinning them to the back of children's shirts or coats works well. They're easy for adults to read, and children aren't tempted to remove them.) Include the school's phone number and the number of the bus taking you back.
- *Include*: Along with permission slips, send home information about where you're going and why, what children should wear and bring, the cost, departure and arrival times, lunch provisions, and transportation.
- *Support*: Give each volunteer informational sheets stating when to arrive, where to go, what to wear and bring, how to reach you beforehand with any questions, and goals for the trip - and include your thanks.
- *Don't forget*: Bring along emergency information: A list of parents' phone numbers, allergy concerns, and children's special physical needs. Make sure you have a first-aid kit and, if necessary, sunscreen.
- *Record*: When you get back, jot down your thoughts - high points, tips to remember, great contacts - for your field-trip file. This way, you'll have information to use another year and to share with other teachers.

SAFETY OF FIELD TRIP

Field trips are a highlight for children in school or at day care, and as parents it's important to make sure your children are safe on their outing.

Here are some safety guidelines to be aware of before you sign that next permission slip:

- Find out if the caregiver visits places before outings to check for safety features.
- Make sure the trip is right for your child. Keep in

mind that children under age 4 do better on shorter trips and in the morning.

- Be sure there are enough adults to supervise the children. Volunteer to go along when possible.
- Get information about every trip and be sure to sign a permission slip.
- Talk with your children ahead of time about where they are going and what will happen on the field trip. Go over basic safety rules.
- Be sure you know what is involved for each trip. If you do not feel it is right for your child, make alternate plans for that day.

Responsibility

Before your child leaves on the trip, make sure of the following:

- The children are assigned to groups with the adults.
- The caregiver goes over safety rules with the children and adult helpers before each trip.
- Each child wears a tag with the school name and phone number on it. The children's names should not be on the tags.
- Supervising adults count children frequently during the outing and pay close attention to each child in their group. They avoid getting caught up chatting with each other.

It is especially important to count the children when leaving a vehicle at the field trip site and when returning to the centre or child care home.

- No child should ever be left alone in any vehicle for any reason.
- Be sure there are federally approved car seats for children to use when riding in a vehicle. Car seats need to be properly secured in the back seat of the vehicle, and the children must be belted.

PROCEDURE IN FIELD TRIP

Each field trip needs some specific planning for everything

to run smoothly. Teachers should always make sure to include the following:

Letter Home

This explains where the class will be going, the purpose of the trip, costs, requests for chaperones, and a tear-off permission slip to go on the trip. Also inquire as to whether a child will need medication during the trip.

Chaperone letter

Thanking volunteers ahead of time works great! The teacher also can outline her/his expectations of chaperones for the trip, their responsibilities, and any extra materials the class or chaperone might need (such as a picnic blanket, cameras, etc.).

Scavenger Hunt

Develop a simple, fun, and guaranteed successful activity for the children to do during the bus trip. Ask adults to help out. This will reduce problems on the bus.

"I need . . . " paper

The day before the trip, work with the students to write an "I need . . . " paper. This would included: a bag lunch with a small drink, weather appropriate clothing, a good night's sleep, a nutritious breakfast, and, of course, manners and a smile. Have students take home and share with parent(s).

Name Tags

This is a great way to squeeze in some economics! The day before the trip, establish a production line to create name tags for the students. Within an hour the class will have the best name tags available!

Thank you Letter

In their groups, children can write a simple thank you for the adult chaperone(s) who went with them. They can all work on one note or each child can write his/her own. If a classmate's parent was a chaperone, that child can take the letter home.

Other letters can be mailed. Thank you letter to staff at field trip site.

The class can write a thank you note to the staff at the field trip site. This can be written on chart paper, recording individual or whole class messages. Illustrations may accompany this note.

Plan Ahead

When arranging for your field trip visits, anticipate the needs of your group. Provide time and opportunity to use bathroom facilities, and a location for snacks and meals whether at restaurant facilities or at a rest area where a bag lunch can be enjoyed, and allow students ample time to enjoy the primary sites of your trip.

Get Directions Maps

The direction map will help you visiting and consult with the host facility (ies) to determine the amount of time required for their programs and for travel between facilities and events. For maps to the Jordan Planetarium, click here.

Make the Field Trip Relevant

Spend time with your group discussing and learning about the subjects addressed at the sites that you are going to visit. Most sites have materials that can be used in advance that help to focus your group's attention on the lessons that can be gained from this visit. The Planetarium offers Cosmic Classroom guides for each star show, so that your class will be fully prepared for their visit to the planetarium.

Organize

In the weeks leading up to a field trip, get permission slips from every student's family allowing the student to participate in the field trip. Be sure that it includes a telephone number where guardians and parents can be reached on the day of the field trip.

This is also the time to solicit the help of parents and teachers to be chaperones during the field trip. State law requires at least one chaperone for every ten students in a school class. Additional adults are usually very helpful, but adults who have to bring other siblings may be bringing unwanted distractions.

With children's groups, it is often wise to assign a chaperone to a specific group of children, so that the task of counting heads and carrying out directions does not fall entirely on the shoulders of one or two leaders.

Collect all of the monies that are required from each student before leaving home, and organize the payments into separate envelopes for each of the facilities that you will be visiting.

AQUARIUM MAINTENANCE

DEFINITION

Aquarium is

- A tank, often fitted with life-support equipment, specifically constructed for housing living aquatic organisms for exhibition, aquaculture, or scientific study, of dimensions appropriate to enclosure within a building
- An exhibit of living organisms in one or several separate containers, intended to give the impression of a window into an aquatic habitat

The aquarium is set up and running, the fish are schooling happily, and everything is going to plan. Try not to get too comfortable watching the fish swim by yet. To keep it all functioning will require regular care and maintenance.

The exact upkeep procedures and their frequency will differ depending on the individual aquariums in question. The following is a guide that can help you establish the correct aquarium care procedures for your circumstances.

As a general estimation you should be willing set aside 10 minutes per day and about an hour once a week. If this routine is going to clash with your schedule then perhaps keeping an aquarium is not for you.

GENERAL MAINTENANCE TIPS

- Never change more than 40% of aquarium water at a time.
- Never empty the entire aquarium to clean it. This causes undue stress on fish and will disturb the biological balance of your aquarium.
- Only change half of your filter media at a time, to retain the established biological balance.
- NEVER use soap or any detergent on your aquarium or any products used in or around your aquarium.
- When cleaning the inside glass of your aquarium, avoid picking up pieces of gravel, as this will scratch the glass.
- Limit the amount of times you put your hands in the water. Oils and films may cause stress in fish.

Things to do Daily

- Observe all aquarium inhabitants. Perform a quick visual check to ensure that there is no disease, injury, and/or abnormal behaviour.
- Verify temperature and confirm that all support equipment is functioning correctly (filters, heaters, lighting, etc.).
- Remove any dead fish, plants, or obvious debris (such as plant leaves attached to intake strainer of filter).

Weekly

- Perform a partial water change, 5 to 10 per cent is recommended. Use a gravel washer to extract trapped waste from the gravel. Partial water changes on a regular basis will provide stable water quality and maintain ideal conditions.
- Clean fluorescent tube(s) and fixture. This will maintain consistent light levels.
- Clean inner and outer glass surfaces. This will eliminate any algae accumulation and ensure full viewing pleasure.

Monthly

- Check supplies, food, water conditioners and all other regularly used items.
- This will help the fish to thrive and you to have a great display in your house.

Daily Care

Each day aquarium fish require feeding. You should feed only what will be eaten in a few minutes. If there is any food left after 5 minutes remove it from the water before it decays. Alternately you can keep a freshwater snail to clean up any excess fish food.

While feeding do a head check to account for all of your fish. If any have been died it is best to find them sooner rather than later. This will allow the decaying body to be removed and any possible fatality causes to be corrected.

Also check that the filter and heater are functioning correctly. Sometimes plugs can be accidentally pulled from the wall or appliances can develop a fault. Be sure to switch off all aquarium appliances before placing your hands in the water. If your filter has lost a significant amount of it's flow follow the filter maintenance procedure below.

If you have no lid on your aquarium it may be worth considering the water level. If your days are hot and the evaporation high replace the lost water with new de-chlorinated water. Aquarium heaters can easily burn out if the water level drops below the correct operation level.

Weekly Care

Each week at least 25% of the aquarium water should be changed. This is necessary for the removal of toxic nitrate which is the end product of biological filtration.

Remove a quarter of the water before topping up to the full level. The new water should be de-chlorinated and adjusted to match the temperature, pH and hardness of the original water. When making the replacement more water will be added than what is removed so as to replace evaporated water.

If your aquarium has illumination some algae removal may be required. This and other glass scum can be removed using an algae magnet, a non abrasive scourer or even some clean cotton cloth and patience.

You may consider only cleaning the front viewing pane. Doing so will allow more surfaces for beneficial microorganisms to live upon. Such cleaning may be unrequited in aquariums with cleaning species such as bristlenose catfish.

A weekly feeding of live or frozen food is excellent for the health of all fish species. On a regular basis be sure to include some extra tidbit in your fish's diet.

Filter Maintenance

Aquarium filters are best cleaned as required. When the water flow has slowed down substantially it is time for a clean.

Depending upon your type of filter it will contain one of more filter media. Charcoal should be discarded and replaced. Sponges of fibre should be replaced or cleaned. When cleaned be sure to use only aquarium water so that useful bacteria can be preserved. New sponges of fibre can be seeded with a little gunk from the unclean filter to kick start the maturation process

Under gravel filters should be left for up to six months between maintenance. The gravel filter will continue to function as long as it's structure does not become clogged. If the aquarium floor is looking blocked with refuse siphon of these debris with care. Try not to disturb the aquarium substrate substantially as it's biological filtering capacity will be diminished.

Unit VI

Text Books

INTRODUCTION

Biology literally means "the study of life". Biology is such a broad field, covering the minute workings of chemical machines inside our cells, to broad scale concepts of ecosystems and global climate change.

Biologists study intimate details of the human brain, the composition of our genes, and even the functioning of our reproductive system. Biologists recently all but completed the deciphering of the human genome, the sequence of deoxyribonucleic acid (DNA) bases that may determine much of our innate capabilities and predispositions to certain forms of behaviour and illnesses.

DNA sequences have played major roles in criminal cases as well as the impeachment of President Clinton (the stain at least did not lie). We are bombarded with headlines about possible health risks from favourite foods as well as the potential benefits of eating other foods such as cooked tomatoes. Infomercials tout the benefits of metabolism-adjusting drugs for weight loss. Many Americans are turning to herbal remedies to ease arthritis pain, improve memory, as well as improve our moods.

Can a biology book give you the answers to these questions? No, but it will enable you learn how to sift through the biases of investigators, the press, and others in a quest to critically evaluate the question. To be honest, five years after you are through with this class it is doubtful you would remember all the details of metabolism. However, you will know where to look and maybe a little about the process of science that will allow you to make an informed decision.

BIOLOGY TEXTBOOK

Biology is an authoritative majors textbook with evolution as a unifying theme. It is distinguished from other texts by its strong emphasis on natural selection and the evolutionary process that explains biodiversity.

Not only has the book been thoroughly updated to reflect rapid advances, there is more emphasis today on the teaching of concepts and this has led to significant changes in how the material is presented. Technology also plays a greater role in teaching and this Online Learning Centre and BioCourse.Com provide professors and students alike with an abundance of resources. Five considerations influenced this revision. They are:

- Focus on concepts.
- Reinforcing ideas.
- Emphasizing relevance to students.
- Keeping up with new developments.
- Careful editing.

Because of the lack of solid creationist-based biological textbooks at the secondary level, much work in the area of curriculum development needs to be done. From this author's perspective, the ICR tenets of Scientific and Biblical Creationism should serve as the starting point and unifying theme of biology textbooks and the development of biological science materials. Use of the ICR tenets:

- Assists the curriculum developer in combating the tenets of false science and worldview of the National Association of Biology Teachers and other evolutionary groups.
- Allows for the development of a broad-scoped curriculum allowing the curriculum developer to show how science affects all areas of the life endeavor.
- Assists the creationist curriculum developer in showing clearly and decisively that the creationist

worldview is a total and logically satisfying worldview.

- Allows the developer to integrate a creationist worldview throughout the text materials in response to textbooks such as Modern Biology
- Would focus the content within a microevolution framework.
- Would focus the content on a correct view of the nature of man. Man would be viewed as a created being in fully human form right from the start.

Our world has been shaped by an extraordinary diversity of living organisms. The Sun's light is harvested by bacteria, algae, and plants, while every feasible source of chemical energy, from hydrogen gas to carbon monoxide to phenol is exploited by some microbe. Life thrives in the most extreme environments, from Antarctic rocks to scalding undersea vents to crevices miles beneath the Earth's crust.

Organisms are sensitive to the slightest variations in their environment: Bacteria find their way by sensing the Earth's magnetic fields, moths find their mates from a few molecules' scent, and owls see their prey from afar on a moonless night. Birds can use specialized tools to help them extract food, bees coordinate the activity of their hive, and human societies use language and technology to overcome the limitations of their biology.

All of these diverse functions are achieved by the same fundamental biochemical system. Genetic information stored in the sequence of bases in DNA is transcribed into RNA and then translated into sequences of amino acids that construct and maintain the organism. The engineering of organisms is as remarkable as its consequences. DNA sequences can be replicated with less than one error in a billion bases. Proteins at ambient temperatures can catalyze reactions that human chemists can achieve only under extreme conditions and with much coarser specificity.

Interactions between DNA and proteins regulate precise patterns of gene expression that allow the reliable construction of complex organs—most impressively, the intricate connections in the brain that generate elaborate behavioral programs. All of this is determined by a remarkably compact genome; the human DNA sequence, for example, encodes less information than is stored in a personal computer.

We know, at least in outline, how the DNA sequence is translated into proteins, how these proteins effect metabolism and regulate gene expression, and how multicellular organisms develop reliably from a single cell.

We also know, at least in outline, how the diverse organisms now living came to be. All of them (and us) descend from one "universal ancestor" that lived about 3.5 billion years ago.

That ancestor itself descended from a much simpler organism in which RNA carried out the present roles of both DNA and protein. Thus, all the biochemical, morphological, and behavioral diversity around us descends from a few original genes.

The exquisite biological devices we now see appear as though carefully designed for their present purposes, and this appearance of design was long taken as evidence of an intelligent Creator. We now know that biological function is constructed and maintained by natural selection: the gradual accumulation of variations that arose by chance and that were preserved because they aided the reproduction of their carriers.

The theory of evolution is a synthesis of Darwinian natural selection with Mendelian genetics. It allows us to ask not just how present-day life evolved, but also why it is as it is: Why do organisms develop from a single cell?; Why is the genetic code as it is?; and Why is there sexual reproduction?

EVOLUTION ABOUT BIOLOGY BOOK

Evolution is designed to serve as the primary text for undergraduate courses in evolution. It differs from currently available alternatives in containing more molecular biology than is traditionally the case.

But this is not at the expense of traditional evolutionary theory. Indeed, a glance at the Table of Contents and the authors' interests reveals the range of material covered in this book. The authors are world-renowned in population genetics, bacterial genomics, paleontology, human genetics, and developmental biology.

The integration of molecular biology and evolutionary biology reflects the current direction of much research among evolutionary scientists.

EVOLUTION IS DIVIDED INTO FOUR PARTS

Part I

Is a history of evolutionary biology and of molecular biology. Most evolution textbooks include a discussion of how the ideas underpinning evolutionary theory arose. The first striking difference in *Evolution* is that the history of experiments and ideas in the development of molecular biology is also discussed.

This approach reflects the more prominent role that findings from molecular biology have in the current text.

Part II

Describes the history of life on Earth. This is a narrative account from the origin of life up to the evolution of humans (although evolution of humans is dealt with in greater detail in Part IV. The emphasis is on the major transitions in genetic organization and the novel adaptations that have evolved.

The diversity of life is also highlighted. The impact of molecular biology is clear in this part of the book: Chapters herein make extensive use of information gained in recent years from the complete sequences of the genomes of several organisms and also from the rather detailed knowledge we now have on the molecular mechanisms of developmental biology.

Part III

Covers the evolutionary processes that account for the series of events discussed in Part II. Thus, how variation arises and how selection acts on it are considered in detail. The bulk of the material in this part of the book is typically covered in most evolution textbooks, though in the current text, examples used to illustrate the theory are more often chosen from molecular sources than is traditionally the case.

Part IV

Is dedicated to human evolution and diversity. Once again, the huge influence of molecular biology on this field is reflected in the extent to which DNA markers, rather than bones and skulls, are emphasized (though the bones are not ignored).

Additional chapters, found on the Web only, deal with the methods and models used in studying evolutionary biology. Again, the role of molecular biology and genomics is paramount in the phylogenetic reconstruction methods that are described.

UNIT VII

Curriculum in Biology

PRINCIPLE OF BIOLOGY SCIENCE CURRICULUM

Biology Science and its applications play a significant role in our everyday lives, from the challenge of developing vaccines to exploring Mars. During the next decade, the demand for scientists and engineers is expected to increase at more than double the rate for all other occupations. The ultimate goal is for all students to understand their surroundings and the relationships within these surroundings.

CURRICULUM BASIC

A very broad, encompassing topic that goes beyond mere academic studies and instruction, curriculum consists of three categories: formal curriculum, hidden curriculum, and extra-curriculum. The most common part of curriculum is what the teacher directly conveys to each student in the form of lessons in the basic subjects. Often, this is the type people assume to be the only form curriculum takes. Hidden curriculum includes everything that goes on in and outside of the classroom that is not being readily taught by the teacher. When playing an academic related game, for example, the students learn winning and losing as well as how it feels to do either. Extra-curriculum involves the experiences and knowledge derived from activities outside the school day, like sports teams, academic clubs, music and drama. Students learn things like leadership and how to work cooperatively with their peers.

All of these components are necessary when providing

the best curriculum for the students. For testing, perhaps, the most important becomes the direct instruction of the cold hard facts needed to pass certain written tests. The other two areas, however, are important in the way of preparing the students for life after their school career is over. The leadership skills obtained from extra-curriculum activities as well as the underlying information conveyed from hidden curriculum add to the students' ability to relate to people and things in the real world.

Curriculum has numerous definitions, which can be slightly confusing. In its broadest sense a curriculum may refer to all courses offered at a school. This is particularly true of schools at the university level, where the diversity of a curriculum might be an attractive point to a potential student.

A curriculum may also refer to a defined and prescribed course of studies, which students must fulfill in order to pass a certain level of education. For example, an elementary school might discuss how its curriculum, or its entire sum of lessons and teachings, is designed to improve national testing scores or help students learn the basics. An individual teacher might also refer to his or her curriculum, meaning all the subjects that will be taught during a school year.

On the other hand, a high school might refer to a curriculum as the courses required in order to receive one's diploma. They might also refer to curriculum in exactly the same way as the elementary school, and use curriculum to mean both individual courses needed to pass, and the overall offering of courses, which help prepare a student for life after high school.

Usually, students in high school and colleges have some degree of choice in pursuing their education. They often have an individual curriculum which helps them attain a degree or to specialize in a certain field. Even at the high school level, curriculum may be separated into courses that make one eligible to attend certain colleges, and courses that will merely earn students a diploma.

Some high schools have curriculum specially designed for students who plan to work in a trade after finishing high school. In those cases, a high school may offer certification in secretarial or construction skills when a student follows a specific curriculum.

ROLE OF TEACHERS

This primer for teachers (prospective and practicing) asks students to question the historical present and their relation to it, and in so doing, to construct their own understandings of what it means to teach, to study, to become "educated." Curriculum theory is presented as the interdisciplinary study of educational experience. The mental concept of curriculum studies as a "complicated conversation" is explored.

Within this framework, Pinar offers a compelling interpretation of contemporary "school reform" policies and practices, and an explication of curriculum theory's power to bring forth understanding, resistance, and change. His argument is this: Public education today is dominated by a conservative agenda based on a business model of education focused on the "bottom line" (test scores).

The origins of this agenda go back to the 1950s, when gendered anxieties over the Cold War and racialized anxieties over school desegregation coded public education (not for the first time) as "feminized" and "black." The nature of many politicians' and some parents' criticisms of public education is intelligible only as a recoding of these gendered and racialized anxieties, deferred and displaced from their originating events onto "school reform."

This has rendered the classroom a privatized and racialized domestic sphere which politicians—mostly (white) men—endeavor to control, disguised by apparently commonsense claims of "accountability." What is dangerously at stake is academic freedom and control of the curriculum—what teachers are permitted to teach, what children are permitted to study.

This text offers both an understanding of the problem and a way to address it. Pinar uses the concept of *currere*—the Latin infinitive of curriculum—to describe an autobiographical method that provides a strategy for self-study, a way for both individuals and groups to understand their situations, leading to action. Through *currere*, it is possible for educators to begin to reconstruct the public sphere—now a "shopping mall" in which citizens and students have been reduced to consumers—by connecting academic knowledge to their students (and their own) subjectivities, to society, and to the historical moment. In doing so, they can take back (relative) intellectual freedom and rebuild schooling to speak to persisting problems of race, class, and gender. It is this link, this promise of education for our private-and-public lives as Indians that curriculum theory enables.

CURRICULUM DESIGN

INTRODUCTION

- Defining and delivering an effective curriculum is THE most important professional responsibility for Science.
- Science in higher education has shown an almost exemplary concern for teaching.
- Concern and care for education in Biological Science has been a major factor in allowing the technology to diffuse so rapidly.
- Several published *examples of possible syllabus* was one of the most ambitious educational projects ever undertaken in Biological Science higher education. Unusually, it was subject to careful evaluation and assessment through individual case studies and overall user feedback. Nobody, least of all its originators, would claim it to be perfect, but it gave a 'kick start' to many educational developments. More recently, the methods used in the development of a Biology Science curriculum, have been described and initiated.
- The *Proceedings of a number of international workshops* concerned with Biology Science education. Almost all of the major conferences include a 'stream' relating to Biology Science education and training.

- The Science community has produced many *general teaching resources*. Examples include a number of, low-cost, systems that run happily on basic hardware, some very useful vendor training products, 'teaching' computer-based tutorial systems, and some carefully designed packaged 'distance learning' materials making use of standard instructions.
- Increasingly, these materials are being made available to anyone who has access via WWW. A good place to start a search for these materials is:
  - The Department of Computers has taken an initiative in Teaching for Science and other Computer Courses.
  - That at Madras University there are various Biology Science related courses.
- Many curriculum design issues remain unresolved.
- There is no single correct answer. Biology Science curricula will vary, for example, by:
  - Level and student background
  - Delivery mechanism
  - Intended outcomes
  - Instructor preferences
- There is thus a responsibility to *design* the Science curriculum correctly to suit local circumstances, resources and student needs. Sample curricula can help, but a more general approach is to develop methodologies for curriculum design. An analogy we might use is between specific computer programmes (curricula) and the more general idea of programming languages (the methods and toolkits used).

CURRICULUM AS A SYSTEM

- There is no clear, accepted definition of the word curriculum. The dictionary definition is *a course of study*, but this gives little away and educational theorists invariably give a much wider definition that includes:

- Explicit statements of ideology underlying the instruction (why are you teaching it, and why is the teaching the way it is?
- General long-term aims.
- Specific, testable, short-term objectives (what will they be able to do as a result of following the course?)
- Resources to be used.
- The delivery methods to be employed (how is it to be taught?)
- Timing of the units and their sequencing.
- Assessment procedures and the balance of assessments to be made.
- A methodology for evaluating how well the course has been received.

- A curriculum is more than a course title and list of topics or even set of lecture notes. These constitute a *syllabus* and this is only one component of a curriculum.
- A simple model of the curriculum sees it as an interacting system made up of aims and objectives, assessment and evaluation (not the same thing), teaching methods and content.
- The implications of this system view are:
  - Because changes in any one of these elements will force changes in all the others, curriculum design is a complex and difficult process, similar in many ways to the development of a software system. A commercial Science is very similar to a curriculum. Both have a high intellectual, conceptual and technical content, but note how differently they are usually produced. More often than not in higher education the curriculum is the work of a single individual or small team following no clear design methodology, often under extreme pressure of time, and with no process documentation on the way. A large team following a formal design methodology will

produce a commercial Science and documentation will form a very important part of the process.

- For completeness, all the elements defined above should be considered and present.
- In theory you could start at any point in the system and begin to design the curriculum, what matters is that all the elements and their linkages are known.

- *As an exercise, think through how these approaches might be used in a practical curriculum design.*

CURRICULUM DESIGN METHODOLOGIES

- GIS curricula should be designed and there are a number of formal models of the design process that are surprisingly similar to those proposed in software engineering Some questions to ask are:
  - Why is the course being taught?
  - What new knowledge, skills and attitudes do I expect my students to develop?
  - If so, what experiences do I need to provide for them?
  - Will all students benefit from the same experiences?
  - What range of experiences is possible?
  - What resources are available? What am I comfortable with, and what would I like to experiment with?
  - How will I know if the course is progressing as intended?
  - How will I know if it succeeds?

Designing Approaches: Design through aims and objectives or intended learning outcomes.

- This is the equivalent of a *top down* approach_to software development. It starts from a clear statement of broad educational aims, refines these into a series of explicit and testable objectives, and then devises teaching strategies, content and assessment methods to meet these aims and objectives. As with software engineering, so most of the relevant educational literature tends to favour this approach.

- An educational AIM is a broad statement of the overall motivations for the course such as *to develop an understanding of the theory behind Biology* Science *and to develop skills in the application of* Science *to problems in environmental management*. In contrast an educational objective is a precise statement written in such a way that it easily translates into something that can be assessed in some way such as *to understand by a practical example the basic principles of semiautomatic digitizing*.
- Educationalists recognize taxonomy of *educational objectives*. Bloom's taxonomy has six major categories from knowledge, through comprehension, application, analysis and synthesis to evaluation. The ordering of these categories is intended to be broadly hierarchical, each measuring a more complex behaviour than its predecessor and also subsuming it.
- The difficulty of specifying aims and objectives has led many educationalists to argue that it is better to specify a series of intended learning outcomes. Examples are provided at the head of this, and all the other, units in the Core Curriculum. The key is to specify something that the student should be able to do after following the course. For example, the aim we used above might translate into an ILO such as *'after completing this module, you should be able to use a semiautomatic digitiser to input and structure basic vector data in the ARC/INFO system'*. Notice that this is very easily converted into a task that students would have to complete in the laboratory. Without such a laboratory exercise, the same ILO might be *'after completing this module, you will be able to state how line data on a map can be captured for input into the ARC/INFO using a semiautomatic digitizer*. At a higher

level in the taxonomy of objectives, students might have an ILO, which asks them to take an evaluative view *'after completing this module you will be able to list the advantages and disadvantages of semiautomatic digitizing related to raster scanning as input for line data into the ARC/INFO'.*

- The advantages of both aims and objectives and ILOs are that they:
  - Communicates teacher's intentions clearly and unequivocally
  - Provide an immediate framework for course structure and content
  - Guide the selection of appropriate teaching and learning resources
  - Help both evaluation and assessment.
- The major problem with this very formal approach in which everything is written down in advance is that once started, it is hard to change tack, possibly as a response to student feedback on the course or changing circumstances.

DESIGN BY SUBJECT MATTER

- An obvious way to design a curriculum is to write down a set of topics that will be taught. Many instructors have started at syllabus and content, specifying WHAT should be taught and then gone on to consider all the other elements. This is a *content driven* approach to curriculum design and this approach is the one that has necessarily been taken by almost all the published examples in Science. This is an approach that software engineers would recognize as bottom up. There are at least six reasons why this approach should be modified:

Research evidence shows that *syllabus content is not what most influences student learning*. It is the precisely extra components that turn a syllabus of topics into a curriculum, such as attitudes to study, assessment tasks and so on, that most define what they ultimately remember and use in later life.

- A published syllabus may actually hide the real content. Educationalists also talk of the importance of andhidden' curriculum and various departmental cultures. These form a hidden agenda of implicit demands, which may run totally counter to the explicit syllabus. In practice, assessment in the form of the examination questions set often reveals this hidden curriculum, which is why the study of past examination papers is such a useful student revision method.
- *Content dates rapidly.* What is currently fashionable in research is often ephemera, to be replaced very rapidly by other materials. This is particularly likely to be the case in a rapidly expanding field like Biological Science.
- Course content always undergoes a series of *pedagogic transformations* on the way from teacher to taught which filter and transform it. Thus the real 'content' of a course can be defined in several ways. Is it what was originally intended should be taught, what was actually delivered, what was added to this by teacher/student interaction, what the students actually wrote down, what they remembered, or what they took from the course into the world of work?

$$C \Rightarrow C1 \Rightarrow C2 \Rightarrow C3 \Rightarrow C4 \Rightarrow etc$$

C = what it was intended to teach.

C1 = what actually was taught.

C2 = what the students actually wrote down.

C3 = this content after modification by the students additional work and interaction with others.

C4 = this content as it was remembered and reproduced

Note:

- Each transformation will be noisy.
- The absence of any clear feedback loops.

- Designs, which build up in this way, can be

perfectly rational but there is a tendency for designers to lose sight of the overall course structure when using this approach.

— These two approaches are the most common, but Gold et al recognize four other possible approaches:

DESIGN FOR POWER

- It may well be that Science course designers are not totally free to design as they see fit. In many countries the Science teaching might be part of some specified national, even international scheme in which others have specified many aspects of the curriculum 'in power'. An example is where the instruction is part of a professional development or continuing professional development scheme such as those operated by some of the professions.

Design Building on Teacher Motivations

- A seemingly radical approach to curriculum design that may be far more common than instructors like to recognize is a design, which simply builds on the motivations, experience and interest of those delivering the course. Purists will argue that this will give an unbalanced view of GIS, but there are several arguments in its favour. First, the instructor will be knowledgeable and enthusiastic and hence teach 'better'. Secondly, this enthusiasm may well be transmitted to students who respond by working harder and with greater commitment. The final result could well be a better experience than that of a course given by instructors less at ease with the material and less enthusiastic. This type of curriculum at BA/ BS level often leads good students directly into Graduate School, but this is likely to be a some cost in general awareness of the field for those who do not.

Design for Resource Availability

- Given that there is a large number of Science education resources such as machine tutorials, CD-ROM, WWW sites, published pencil and paper exercises, text books and vendor instruction manuals it is possible to design a curriculum that builds on these resources. In USA, it is relatively common for introductory classes to be based very closely around a standard, specified course text. There is a different tradition in UK, but the logic of this approach is beginning to be more widely accepted. It has the advantage of providing a clear 'map' of what is to be covered and in what sequence, allows students time to work on the materials out of class and thus reduces the number of steps in what above was called the pedagogic transformations.

Student Centered Design for Individual Needs and Knowledge

- Finally, and possibly the most challenging approach of all, *student-centered design* that begins by an examination of individual student needs and attempts to provide course materials to meet them. The problem with this model is that only seldom do educators 'listen to the learner' and, even if they did, it is by no means clear that students would have a correct perception of the field. The student's learning environment is a complex one that includes far more than just the formal programme of instruction. It includes interaction with other students, browsing the library, talks with parents, and so on. It should be apparent that this approach must recognize that students adopt very different learning styles, so that what is good for one may be totally inappropriate for another.
  - The importance of feedback and critical evaluation. These six approaches to curriculum

design are theoretical models. Any one of them is unlikely to be followed in its entirety, either as a 'top down' or as a 'bottom up' system. In practice, almost everyone will choose middle *out* strategy those designs by refinement of a central core of materials that most probably already exist. The important point is that there is a design and that all the elements of the curriculum system have been thought about.

DILEMMAS FOR BIOLOGICAL SCIENCE CURRICULUM DESIGN

- In common with many new technologies, Science has a number of characteristics that make formal curriculum design difficult:
- *Speed of development.*
  - Biological Science has evolved very rapidly relative to the speed at which developments can possibly be incorporated into curriculum structure. This has had a number of consequences. Until recently, it has meant that there has been a shortage of faculty/instructors able to teach about it. Normally, in education there is a reasonable supply of qualified educators willing to enter into it. These instructors are able to draw on models of curriculum practice based on their own experiences or have a background in research and applications that leads to a pretty clear idea of what should make up a curriculum. None of these conditions is met in Science education.
- *Education or training*
  - GIS is usually introduced as a technology or an industry that is technology driven, yet it rests on top of many years of work in *spatial information science* (SIS). This 'education or training' debate permeates almost all the curriculum. It clearly

must influence the overall aims and objectives, but it also affects the modes of delivery and the content that is offered. The dilemma is to choose between education in the concepts of SIS and training in the use of a specific system. In part this is to do with the levels of skill needed for a variety of possible future involvements with Science, from operative to system designer. No single curriculum could hope to meet all these requirements.

- Science *or xIS*
  - Where x can be S (spatial), L (land), M (Management) or even a redefined G (geoscience). There are a number of different conceptions of the field of Biological Science, depending on the background and prejudices we bring to it. For better or worse, the use of the word 'geographic' has meant that responsibility for education in Science has mostly rested in academic Departments of Science. This is both a strength and a weakness. It is a strength because many of the antecedents of Biological Science, such as computer-cartography, remote sensing and spatial analysis, were firmly located in the same place and have remained so. It is a weakness because many of the technical underpinnings of Science are difficult to teach in the same context. Again, no one single approach can hope to meets all these needs. From a curriculum design point of view, it is doubtful if anyone from a purely geographical background is able adequately to balance the material that goes into the curriculum or to specify educational aims and objectives that fully address what a complete education in Science should provide.
- *Breadth or depth*
  - For a full education in Biological Science,

students need the breadth of vision to understand not only the scientific and societal problems to which it might be applied, but also the complex managerial, legal and ethical questions that might arise from this use. At the same time, they must also have the depth of understanding to be able to play. In the hardball version it is necessary to know about and apply concepts from data base management, computer programming, and so on, to real world problems with the inevitably 'messy' data. In his view, teaching students about the use of Science using a 'filled' raster system is essentially playing the 'softball' variation, 'played on a smaller field, with a larger, more easily handled ball designed for summer camps and picnics where everyone can take part'. There is nothing wrong with softball, provided we do not pretend that it is hardball and this is not simply a question of curriculum content. Most of the basic concepts of Science are capable of being dealt with either as a shallow concept or in depth. Balancing breadth against depth may well be the most important curriculum design problem of all.

- *Hands on or hands off*
  - In producing a curriculum for Biological Science, it is almost certain that students will need to access as powerful a system as is possible within the usual budgetary constraints. Although desirable as an end in itself, 'hands on' has some unfortunate consequences.
- *Option or integrator*
  - A fifth dilemma concerns how we relate Science to the rest of whatever curriculum we happen to teach. At least two models are possible.
  - Biological Science is a sub-set of some other discipline, to be taught as an elective within the context of a course in some other 'real' discipline.

The difficulties that this view is creating for academic Science. The obvious weakness of this model is that it tends to generate teaching in breadth rather than in depth and risks marginalizing the entire enterprise.

— Biological Science is a cover set integrating materials from parts of several other disciplines into one distinct science of spatial information that is worthy of study in its own right.

- *About* Science *or with* Science
  — Finally, although a lot of people are teaching and learning about something called Science, far fewer seem to be teaching *with* it, that is, using Science better to teach some other discipline.

CONCLUSION

- Designing a curriculum for Biological Science is not a simple matter and there is no single 'best' answer either in the form of the curriculum or even the methodology adopted for its design. A final question we might ask is whether or not it is possible to determine if the result is any good. One way is by always including a careful student of the course once it has been given. Evaluation of this sort is essential and should always be treated seriously, allowing sufficient time in class for any survey questionnaire to be filled out and with the results carefully summarized. It is good practice to post a notice giving the results of the evaluation and providing instructors commentary.
- Is it possible to anticipate whether or not the curriculum meets its aims? One simple test to apply makes use of the set of *guiding principles of good education* proposed by Association of Higher Education. According to these a good curriculum should:
  — Encourage staff/student contact.
  — Encourage co-operation between students.

— Encourage active learning.
— Provide prompt feedback on performance of both teacher and taught.
— Emphasis 'time on the task'.
— Respect the diverse talents and ways of learning brought to the course by the students.
— Evaluate itself.
— Display a clarity of aims and objectives.
— Make use of the educational literature.

Unit VIII

Educational Technology

PROJECTED AIDS

Projected aids are those that require audiovisual equipment in order to be presented properly. Some of the aids included in this category are slides, filmstrips, overhead transparencies and motion pictures.

It is important to remember that most nonpro- jected aids may be adapted for use as projected aids. A chart, for example, can be photographed and made into a slide.

OPTICALLY PROJECTED AIDS

Optically projected aids include the opaque projector, overhead transparency projector, videotapes (and associated equipment) and the Carousel slide projector.

Opaque Projector

The opaque projector has two basic applications. First, it can be used to project graphs, photographs and other aids that are too small to be seen but should be shown in their actual form to your audience.

It may also be used for enlarging clippings, maps, photographs and other items so they can be traced proportionally correct and in complete detail. The projector permits you to project an illustration or other material out of a book without damaging the publication, The "opaque" uses a 1,000-watt projection lamp and is equipped with a 4 1/2-inch diameter, 22-inch focal length lens. The projector comes with an opaque object-holding device and a conveyor belt loading mechanism that permits uninterrupted projection. It also has an optical pointer that permits details anywhere on the screen to be pointed out by a projected light spot.

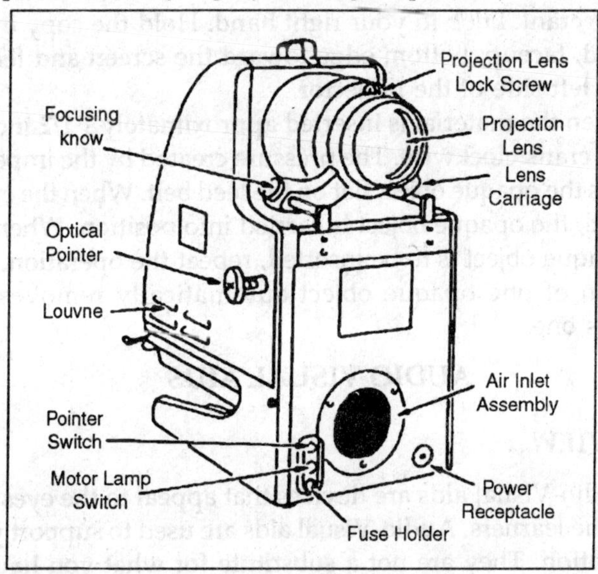

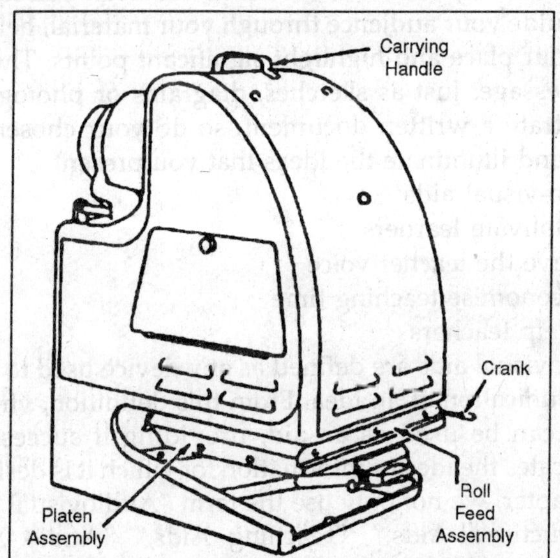

The roll feed assembly provides a means for handling

opaque objects of any length up to 10 inches wide. The thickness of the object should not exceed 1/32 of an inch. To operate the roll feed assembly, stand behind the projector and hold the crank knob in your right hand. Hold the copy in the left hand, faceup, bottom edge toward the screen and feed it into the left side of the projector.

When the material is inserted approximately 1 1/2 inches, turn the crank clockwise. The pressure created by the impelled air holds the opaque object flat on the feed belt. When the crank is turned, the opaque object is carried into position. When the next opaque object is to be inserted, repeat the operation. The insertion of one opaque object automatically removes the previous one.

AUDIO-VISUAL AIDS

OVERVIEW

Audio-Visual aids are devices that appeal to the eyes and ears of the learners. Audio-Visual aids are used to support your presentation. They are not a substitute for what you have to say, but guide your audience through your material, help you to keep your place and highlight significant points. They are *not* the message. Just as sketches, diagrams or photographs may illustrate a written document, so do your chosen aids illustrate and illuminate the ideas that you present.

Audio-visual aids:

- Motivate learners
- Save the teacher voice
- Economise teaching time
- Help teachers

Audiovisual aids are defined as any device used to aid in the communication of an idea. From this definition, virtually anything can be used as an aid, providing it successfully communicates the idea or information for which it is designed. In this chapter, we not only use the term "Audiovisual Aids" but "Instructional Aids," "Teaching Aids," "Audio Aids," and "Visual Aids" as well. An audiovisual product is any audiovisual (AV) item such as still photography, motion picture, audio or video tape, slide or filmstrip, that is prepared singly or in combination to communicate information or to elicit a desired audience response. Even though early aids, such as maps and drawings, are still in use, advances in the audiovisual field have opened up new methods of presenting these aids, such as videotapes and multimedia equip- ment which allow more professional and entertaining presentations to be presented. Most of the visual aids covered in this chapter can be grouped into the following categories—non-projected aids and projected aids.

TYPES OF AUDIO VISUAL AIDS

Realia

Realia are people and real objects that give us information. "People" means anybody in the environment: students, teachers, visiting native speakers, etc. The teacher can make use of his/her movements, gestures, signals, mimics, and hands. Real objects should be small enough to bring into the classroom but large enough to be clearly seen. Real objects can be used for various purposes, such as teaching pronunciation, vocabulary, grammar, etc.

For example, you may bring a map into the classroom and use it to practice comparative and superlative adjectives (Which country in Europe is bigger than X?); to practice passives (Where is "orange" grown in Türkiye?); etc. Other examples of reali are clock faces, toys, brochures, catalogues, magazine and newspapers, board games, posters, wrappers, labels and logos from various products, records, stamps, coins, old tickets, ticket stubs, postcards, programmes, timetables, calendars, containers, cans, bottles, flags, menus, puppets, etc.

Pictures

Most learners are visual minded, so pictures are a great help in teaching. They remind the learner of the meaning and help him/her communicate. They help the teacher save his/ her voice. Also the same pictures may be used for several purposes, and for review purposes.

When selecting a picture, some points should be kept in mind:

- The picture should be large enough for the entire class to see clearly. Small pictures can be used for pair work, group work, and games.
- The picture should illustrate, at first glance, the point under the study.
- The coloured pictures are more effective than black and white ones and can be used for many purposes.
- The picture should fit into cultural pattern of the learner.
- The picture should tell the learner something familiar to connect it with real life.
- The pictures should be labelled to ease classroom practice.
- Pictures should not be confusing.

Blackboard

It is the most common visual aid available to the teachers. When using blackboard, some points should be kept in mind:

- Start each lesson with a clean blackboard.
- Organise the material effectively so that students can easily understand what you are trying to do.
- Number items that belong together.
- Leave only the correct forms on the blackboard. If you are analysing an incorrect form, correct it and then erase it.
- Write legibly and large enough so that the students can read without difficulty.
- Erase the board frequently. Do not leave a mess of material on it.
- Do not write unnecessary material on the board.
- Use coloured chalk/ marker for special effect.
- Watch your own spelling and punctuation for correctness.
- Underline the main points written on the board.
- Erase all unnecessary material at the end of the class hour.

Flashcards

These are pieces of cards large enough for the whole class to see. These may either drawings, magazine cut-outs, pictures, written words or numbers. They are called flash cards because they are shown to the class for a short time. The words, phrases or sentences written on them should be written in thick, high and block letters. These cards are held up for the class to see, and they can be used for a great variety of activities.

Wall Charts

These are large pictures with a lot of in them. They are used for question-and-answer work, for oral composition, for practising adjectives, and for discussing the relations of objects and people. They may display different scenes, landscapes, or may develop a situation, or tell a story in one or sequential pictures. They are especially useful to display things which cannot be brought into the classroom.

Pocket Charts

Pocket charts are investigative tools which use pictures as stimulus to encourage people to assess and analyse a given situation. "Pockets" are made of cloth, paper or cardboard and are attached to a poster-sized piece of paper or cloth. Rows and columns of pockets are arranged into a matrix. Drawings serve as captions for the columns of pockets. In general, the combination of activities in a pocket chart exercise - participating in the creation of a display, looking closely at it, and discussing it - has proven to be a successful means of generating participation and consensus in both community and classroom settings.

A major advantage of this tool is that it can be put together with whatever materials are available. The materials needed are: a set of pictures (photos or drawings) which represent areas in which data are needed; a clear space to set the pictures up at the head of as many columns as their are pictures; a bunch of ballots (slips of paper, straw, cloth, leaves); and receptacles (cloth pockets, pots, jars) for ballots under each column. A large rectangular cloth with pre-sewn rows and columns of pockets can serve as a re-usable, standard pocket chart.

Tape Recorder and Tapes

They present exercises related to class work and homework. These aim at improving the listening and speaking skills. In teaching environment, the audio material may be accompanied by visual material. For instance, while doing exercises they may look at visuals which are cues for substituting, completing, answering, etc.

A tape recorder should have a rich volume, a meter counter. The teacher may record radio broadcast, interviews with visiting native speakers, the students in class (who then correct themselves), or any other material suitable to give his/her students practice in listening comprehension or speaking.

Slides

The most commonly used visual aids are 35mm slides, overhead transparencies, and computer-generated slides. Slides are probably one of the most common and easily accessible mediums for projecting large images in classrooms, lecture halls. Nowadays, many schools have necessary equipment with slide projectors and long extension cords for the remotes. You will also need a slide carousel so that you can put all of your slides in the order that you'll view them. [Remember: slides need to be put in upside down and backwards.] Slides are nice and easy to use, but creating them can be expensive.

Slides can be created from any object, event, or image. You simply have to point a camera at it, with the proper film, and take a picture. You can also make 'copy slides' from illustrations/photos, books, magazines, other colour or Black & White prints, radiographs, posters, gels, three dimensional objects of varying size, people, and more. Slides can also be made from computer files. Burn-ins are a special type of slide. With a burn-in you can take a B&W image, line drawing, or text and burn it as another colour onto another slide.

OHP

You can read the related pages from there. In addition to them, overhead transparencies are also very helpful materials for the teachers.

You can either write down your notes as you talk using a Visa-Via pen or have them pre-made.

Most schools are equipped with overhead projectors, but since they are not very portable teachers may not prefer them. You may also find the overhead inconvenient because they are loud and the bright light makes it difficult for some people to read. However, it offers a cheap and immediate solution to visual aid needs.

How to Make Overheads

There are three ways of making an overhead.

- You can hand write your text and pictures using an overhead pen. This may look unprofessional, but gives immediate, cheap results.
- You can photocopy text and images onto a special type of heat resilient transparency. First cut-and-paste your desired images and text onto a white sheet of paper.
- The third way to make transparencies is to print onto the transparency directly from a computer. This process can be used for presentations you've put together on the computer using programs like Word and Power Point.

Note: There are several different types of transparencies out there. They're not all made to withstand the high temperatures of copiers or laser printers. Be careful, with the wrong material you can not only melt your overhead, but you can also ruin the machine you used to make them.

Video/tv Filmstrips

As a teacher always watch them and listen to their soundtracks before using them in class. You may teach vocabulary, grammar, culture, pronunciation, etc. through video films.

PLANNING AUDIOVISUAL AIDS

Audiovisual aids-including overhead transparencies, flip charts, slides, chalkboards (and occasionally film and video)-can supply added impact and clarity to your, presentation. You can use A/-V to visually reinforce the points made verbally in your presentation, to summarize the points you will make, as well as those you have already made, and to visually clarify important concepts and analogies. Audiovisual aids not only help your target group follow your presentation, but they provide support to the presenter by helping to keep, you on track.

The key to preparing effective audiovisual aids is to remember that they are only aids. Their role is to add a visual dimension to the points that you made orally. They cannot make those points for you; they can only reinforce them. When you plan for audiovisual aids, follow these simple guidelines:

- DO use them to summarize or show the sequence of content.
- DO use them to visually interpret statistics by preparing charts and graphs that illustrate what you will say.
- DO use them to illustrate and reinforce your support statements.
- DO use them to add visual clarity to your concepts and ideas.
- DO use them to focus the attention of the target group on key points.
- DON'T project copies of printed or written text. Instead, summarize the information and show only the key points on the visual aids. If the group must read every word, use handouts for reading, either before or after your presentation.
- DON'T put yourself in the role of aiding your visuals: A presentation is primarily an oral form of communication. If your only function is to read the information on your overheads or slides, the target group will become easily bored.
- DON'T use copies of your transparencies as

handouts. They reinforce what you are saying— they don't say it for you. If you want your target group to remember what you meant, you'll need to provide written text in addition to any key point summaries or charts that you need for your transparencies.

- DON'T use charts, graphs, or tables that contain more information than you want to provide. The group will have difficulty focusing on the point that you're tying to make.

Choosing Appropriate Media

You may wish to combine different types of media in a single presentation. The media used most often are overhead projection transparencies, flip charts, slides, blackboards, and handouts. You may occasionally use videotapes and/or films.

Plan to practice using several different media in this course. You will find that practicing will increase your comfort level, and therefore afford you the flexibility of choosing the most appropriate medium. In the future, use the following guidelines to help you choose the media best suited to your presentation:

TYPES OF MEDIA AND THEIR USES

Overhead Transparencies: Used for displaying charts and graphs. High visibility for large groups. Showing summaries, sequences, relationships, and process steps.

Flip Charts: Used for small groups (under 20). Ad lib charting and graphing. Showing summaries and sequences. Listing, recording, outlining. Developing charts. Instructions. Reinforcing group contributions.

Blackboards/Whiteboards: Spontaneous presentations. Listing/recording. When no other media is available.

Slides: Displaying high quality artwork. Displaying a series of photos. Demonstrating- a "hands-on" process. Creating a mood, or inspiring.

Videotapes and Films: Demonstrating a process. Creating a mood, or inspiring. Presenting* testimonials. Supplementing presentation ideas.

Written Handouts: Providing background information. "Sending home" your ideas. Reminder of follow-up activities. Providing a record of presentation. Weighting a variety of alternatives. Clarifying abstract or complex topics.

OVERHEAD TRANSPARENCIES

Overhead transparencies are inexpensive, easily prepared, and highly effective visual aids for target groups of five or more people. With smaller target groups, choose overhead transparencies as your primary A/V medium if the target group prefers a somewhat formal mode of communication. With small groups, overhead projection may tend to distance you from the target group and limit personal interaction. If you are presenting to a relatively informal group of less than five people, you may wish to use transparencies only to display charts and graphs.

If costs very little to add colour to your charts and graphs, using special transparency markers and adhesive colour film. If fact, some ordinary markers will work perfectly we on transparency film.

You can use overhead projections in full light in any size room. There are three simple guidelines for preparing effective transparencies: Visibility, clarity, and simplicity

Visibility

Lettering should be neat and at least a quarter inch high. You should be able to read the original at a distance of seven feet. Computers make very effective, highly visible transparencies. If a computer is not available, use a typewriter equipped with a special "Orator" typeface, or a special lettering system designed for overhead transparencies, or "rub-off' lettering (available at any art supply store) to provide readable lettering. If you must hand-print, be sure that your printing is neat and even. Use all capital letters, and write with a black, felt-tipped pen.

Clarity

Everything displayed on an overhead transparency

should be instantly recognized by the target group. Label all elements of your charts and graphs. Use colour or shading Ito emphasize and clarify key elements. Be sure to title every transparency.

Simplicity

Try to limit each original to one point or comparison. Use a maximum of six or seven words per line. No more than six lines should be included in a single transparency. Use a horizontal format whenever possible so that the projected image will fit the shape of most standard screens.

Flip Charts and Boards

Flip charts are often the ideal visual aid for small target groups. You can prepare your chart pages in advance for maximum clarity and impact.

The flip chart can also be used to "ad lib," or give the appearance of spontaneity. Prepared flip charts can be used to show pre-drawn charts, graphs, and diagrams, or you can draw them "on the spot."

Chalkboards may be used in the same ways as flip charts. But the space they provide is more limited and the medium is less permanent.

If possible, draw important charts on chalkboards before the presentation and mask them with paper. Be sure to consider what information you will be able to erase during the presentation and what you will save for reference at a later point.

The guidelines for preparing effective flip charts and boards include the following:

- Always title each page.
- Print clearly. For maximum visibility, letters should be at least one inch high for each ten feet of distance from viewers.
- Use pictures, diagrams, and symbols whenever possible.
- Skip a sheet between prepared flip pages to avoid "bleed through."

- Leave room for "ad lib" flip pages (plan when you'll ad lib).
- If you plan to ad lib, make sure you have at least two markers with you—one will always run out of ink.

SLIDES, VIDEO, AND FILMS

Slides, videotapes, and films are included in the same category because! they all require professional preparation. These media can have a very dramatic effect if properly selected. However, unless you are using media that is available through the company library or training centre or your library, all three of these media types are expensive.

Slides may occasionally be in your budget, but very few people have the budget to produce quality videotapes or, even more expensive, films to supplement a presentation. If you can afford to use slides, video, or film in your presentation, be sure the media you select reinforce and enhance what you have to say, and that the media do not contradict your presentation points. The guidelines for using slides, tapes, and films include the following:

- Check the room layout and locate light switches and dimmers. Films and slides must be shown in a darkened room.
- Make sure the media are up to date, unless you intend to contrast old and new.
- Make sure that the images (and sound) are clear—free of static and other interference.
- Know how to use the equipment—or enlist the aid of a projection assistant for your rehearsal and delivery.
- Make sure that the media are compelling and interesting to the target group.
- If you are using slides, check to make sure that they are all in order and facing in the right direction (not upside down).
- Check your equipment. Make sure it can project the media you want to use, in the manner that you want

to use it. Verify that it is in good working condition and that all cables, wires, plugs, etc., are in place and ready to go.

- Load and advance the tape or film to the starting point before the meeting begins. Check sound levels and image clarity.
- Plan what you will do if the equipment breaks down.

Written Handouts

When providing written text, remember that you won't be there to explain or remind the target group of what you mean. Written communications should be as brief as possible, but they must also be meaningful to the reader, whether they are read a week before your presentation or a year after. They should always be:

Clear

Written in language that the target group can easily understand and follow.

Relevant

Do not simply provide data. Explain why the information should be read and what it means. Explanations should not repeat your entire presentation, but should capsulate it.

Specific

Do not give your target group a mass of reading material that they do not need. Make sure that all documentation is absolutely necessary.

AUDIO VIDEO PLAYER

Video Audio Player can play video audio multimedia files such as mp3 wmv mpeg mpg m1v dat wma wav aiff au aif mid midi rmi snd avi asf VCD etc. If you have installed more audio or video decoders codecs, the player can play more video and audio files. The player is easy to use, has small size and mini interface.

The AS3532 is an innovative music player subsystem

whose core is based on a newly developed audio engine and audio post-processor which act as co-processors to an ARM central programmable unit.

The audio engine, in a fully hardwired context, executes the decompression and playback of most popular compressed audio formats, like MP3, WMA and AAC for the least amount of power consumption with zero CPU load.

The audio post-processor implements an Asynchronous Sample Rate Converter (ASRC) with near transparent quality, a multi-channel mixer with limiting function and a 10 bands graphics equalizer and supports 192 KHz sample rates at 24 bits dynamic range for high definition audio processing.

Three sets of I2S outputs can independently control stereo speakers, subwoofer and headphone or line outputs; these can also be utilized as multi-channel audio outputs. The AS3532 audio subsystem additionally includes a stereo PDM digital microphone input thereby completing all audio requirements for new generation mobile phones.

Interfaces included in the AS3532 can support either peer mode to a baseband phone IC or a "Black Box" companion music sub-system. In the latter case, the IC provides direct support for latest generation removable and embedded flash memory types with 4/8/16-bit hardware ECC, for MLC NAND Flash, iNAND, LBA NAND, moviNAND, oneNAND and removable card formats like SD2.0, MMC+, CE-ATA, MS PRO and CF.

An on-chip 512Kbytes buffer memory in the AS3532 music player IC allows single chip support of all key audio formats, compressed, lossless and high definition, polyphonic sequenced content, wavetable synthesizer, 3D positional sound, virtualizer engines and other digital audio effects.

The AS3532 is complemented by a comprehensive software suite that has matured over three generations of products delivered in the multimedia player market.

The SDK has passed the stringent test criteria of the Certified for Windows Vista programme for downloadable content.

VIDEO AUDIO PLAYER

HOW TO USE:

Please launch the programme. Click Open Media Files buttons to select audio video files. the control panel support flexible playback operation: play, pause, stop, skip forward, skip backward, play previous file, play next file.

Drag the edge of right or left side of the player, you can move the player position.

WORKING WITH AUDIO

You can have one video track and up to eight audio tracks on a single timeline. But a DVD player can play only one audio track at any given moment. Generally the main sound track of your project goes on the Audio 1 track. That sound track can be one of several types of audio—from monaural to digital surround sound.

Other tracks might be dubbed versions of the sound track, director comments, or teacher instructions.

All audio tracks need to be complete within themselves. For example, if you want the same background music and sound effects to be heard in each dubbed language track, you must mix them with the dubbed voice track in another editing application like Adobe Audition before you import them into an Encore DVD project.

Timeline Audio File Type Conflicts

You face a couple of limitations when working with audio and video clips in the Timeline Viewer. While you can string together a variety of video and still image file types on the Video track, you can't mix some file types.

Don't combine audio clips from an MPG file with any other audio clip on the same audio track.

Don't combine audio clips with different channel counts on the same track.

Don't combine DTS (Digital Theater Sound) and other audio clips on a single track.

You can overcome these limitations by putting the conflicting audio clips on different audio tracks, but that means the only way viewers can hear the various audio clips is to quickly switch to the other audio tracks as they watch the DVD. This is an impractical solution.

The simple solution is to not mix these incompatible audio file types in the same timeline.

- Import the following files from the Encore DVD 2.0 CIB Assets/Video and Audio folder: Behind the Scenes.avi, Party Life-video.m2v, and Party Life-audio.wav.
- Create a new timeline by right-clicking on Behind the Scenes.avi in the Project panel and choosing New > Timeline.

Since Behind the Scenes.avi is an audio/video file, this timeline will have clips in both the Video and Audio 1 tracks.

Creating a Timeline Using an Audio File

In addition to selecting a video (or audio/video) clip as the starting point when creating a new timeline, you can make a timeline by starting with only an audio clip. It works in basically the same way as creating a timeline with a video. In this case select an audio-only file and then either choose File > New > Timeline or right-click on the audio file and choose New > Timeline.

- Drag any photo file from the Project panel to the video track.

  It falls directly after the Behind the Scenes.avi clip. The purpose is to create a gap in the audio track to facilitate the next few steps in this exercise.
- Drag Party Life-video.m2v from the Project panel to the video track.

  This is an elementary MPEG-2 video file (it doesn't have an audio track). It ends up where you'd expect it, following the two clips in the Video track.
- Drag Party Life-audio.wav to the to the Audio 1

track. Encore DVD automatically places it directly to the right of (after) the Behind the Scenes.avi audio clip, not under Party Life-video.m2v. This is the default behaviour for any clip you add to any track in the Timeline. Newly added clips always snap to the beginning of the timeline or directly after the last clip in the selected track.

- Drag the Party Life-audio.wav clip so its first frame lines up directly under the Party Life-video.m2v clip's first frame.

  Depending on how much you've zoomed in the view of the Timeline, the audio clip might not line up exactly.
- Move the Current Time Indicator (CTI) to the first frame of the Party Life-video. m2v clip on the Video track by pressing the Page Down or Page Up keys.

NOTE

Page Down and Page Up keyboard shortcuts move the CTI right or left respectively to the first (or last) frame of the next clip on any track in the timeline.

- Zoom in the Timeline view by pressing the equal key several times (or use the Zoom slider or its buttons).

Note

Encore DVD will centre the zoom on the CTI, which in this case expands the view directly over or near the first frame of the Party Life-video.m2v clip.

- Drag the audio clip so its first frame lines up directly at the CTI. You'll note that the Snap feature helps you place the audio exactly where you want to put it.

Adding Audio Tracks

Adding audio tracks is easy. Simply right-click in the Timeline and choose Add Audio Track, or drag an audio clip below the lowest audio track to have Encore DVD automatically add an audio track.

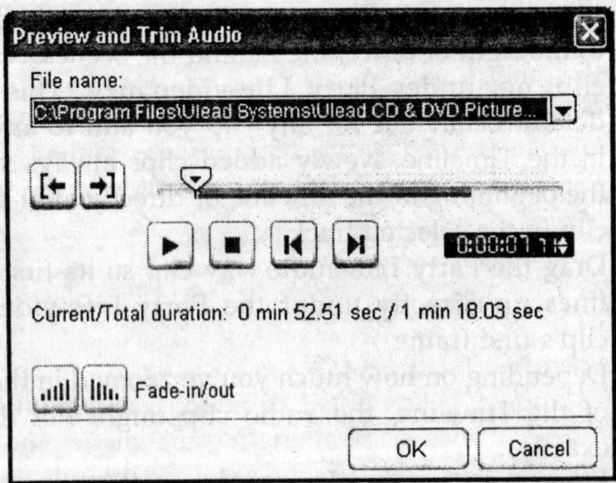

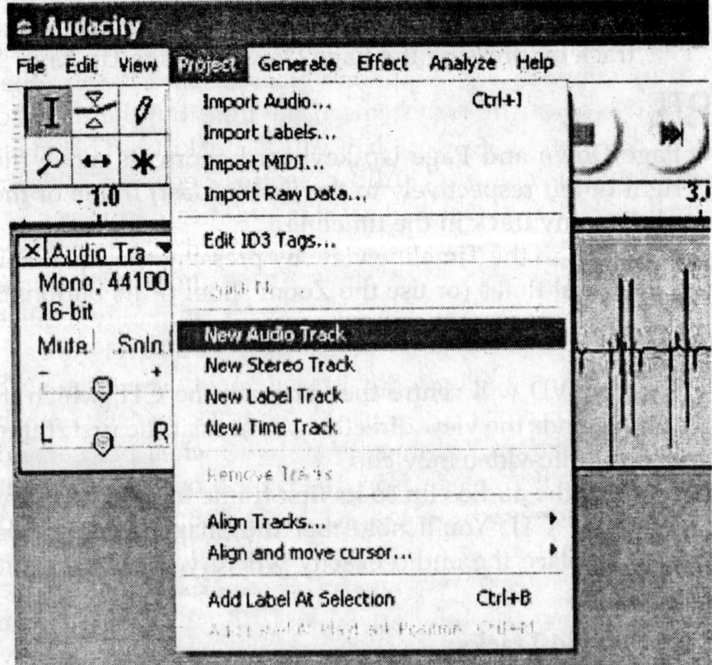

Once added, there are a couple of options in each audio track:

- As is the case for those viewing your finished DVD, you can listen to only one audio track in the Timeline

Viewer at a time. To listen to a particular track, click the empty square on the left end of the track and that will turn on the audio speaker icon and mute the other tracks.

- If you are adding audio in different languages, choose the appropriate language code from the Language menu on the left side of the audio track.

TAPES AND CDS

DEFINITION OF TAPES

The compact audio cassette audio storage medium, sometimes known as the music cassette, was introduced by Philips in 1963. It consists of a length of magnetic tape inside a protective plastic shell. 4 tracks are available on the tape, giving 2 stereo tracks - one for playing with the cassette inserted with its 'A' side up, and the other with the 'B' side up, thus mimicking gramophone records. There were other magnetic tape cartridge systems at the time, but the compact cassette succeeded through Philips' backing. The mass production of compact audio cassettes began in 1965 in Germany, as did commercial sales of pre-recorded music.

The cassette was a massive step forward in convenience from reel-to-reel recording, though the limitations of the cassette's size and speed compared poorly in quality. Unlike the open reel format, the two stereo tracks lie adjacent to each other rather than a 1/3 and 2/4 arrangement. The tape is $^{1}/8$ inch wide (3.175mm), with each stereo track being $^{1}/32$ inch wide (0.079375mm) and moves at $1^{7}/8$ inches per second (47.625 mm/s). For comparison, the typical open reel format was ¼ inch wide (each stereo track being $^{1}/16$ inch wide) and running at either 3¾ or 7½ inches per second.

The original magnetic material was based on ferrite (Fe_2O_3), but then chromium dioxide (CrO_2) and more exotic materials were used in order to improve sound quality to try to match those of vinyl records. These had different bias requirements, requiring more complicated equipment.

A variety of noise reduction schemes were used to increase

fidelity, Dolby B being almost universal for both prerecorded tapes and home recording. By the late 1980s, sound fidelity on equipment by manufacturers such as Nakamichi and Tandberg far surpassed the levels expected of the medium by early detractors and on suitable audio equipment could challenge the sound quality of the compact disc.

Tape length was usually measured in minutes total playing time, and the most popular varieties were C60 (30 minutes per side), C90, and C120 (usually thinner tape, more likely to be destroyed in use - especially the C120). Some vendors were more generous than others, providing 132 m or 135 m rather than 129 m for a C90 cassette. C180 and even C240 tapes were available at one time, but these were extremely thin and fragile and suffered badly from effects such as print-through which made them unsuitable for general use.

The cassette had originally been intended for use in dictation machines, but quickly became a medium for distributing prerecorded music - particularly through Philips' record company, PolyGram - with an option for home recording use. Cassettes were also used for purposes such as journalism, field history, meeting transcripts and so on. In the 1980s, Tascam introduced the Port studio, a four-track recorder for home studio use, which increased the audio quality possible on cassette by doubling the tape speed and using DBX noise reduction.

Most cassettes were sold blank and used for recording the owner's records (as backup or to make compilations), their friends' records or music from the radio. However, many claimed that the medium was ideal for spreading new music and would increase sales, and strongly defended at least their right to copy their own records onto tape. In the late 1970s, Sony brought out the Walkman, a small portable cassette player, which greatly increased the consumption of music in this manner. Cassettes were also a boon to people wishing to make bootlegs.

Many home computers of the 1980s, notably the TRS-80, Commodore 64, ZX Spectrum, Amstrad CPC and BBC Micro used cassettes as a cheap alternative to floppy disks as a storage medium for programs and data. Data rates were typically 500 to 2000 bps, although some games used special faster loading routines, up to around 4000 bps. A rate of 2000 bps equates to a capacity of around 660 kb per side of a 90 minute tape.

DEFINITION OF CD

CD stands for Compact Disc. Compact Disc refers to both the disc and the digital audio playback format developed by Philips and Sony in which audio is digitally encoded, similar to the way computer data is encoded, into pits on a disc. Essentially, the encoding system used in the CD format is a mathematical representation of the music that is recorded. The CD was introduced in 1982 and is still in use.

INTRODUCTION

The history of the compact disk (CD) started with the videodisk in the form of Video Long Play (VLP) read-only systems. The videodisk did not become a commercial success, even once a few write-once optical disks of different formats and sizes were introduced. These were analog systems.

In about 1982, the CD-DA (compact disk-digital audio) was introduced to the market jointly by Phillips and Sony. It stored a high-quality stereo audio signal in a digital form. These systems became a huge success.

In 1985, the compact disk-digital audio technology was extended for computer storage, thanks again to cooperation between Phillips and Sony. This was called a CD-ROM (compact disk-read only memory) and later became a standard

ECMA-119, which specifies the CD-ROM physical format. The logical format of the CD-ROM is specified in the ISO standard 9660 and allows data access through file name and directories.

The next step, CD-I (compact disk-interactive) was again created by Philips and Sony and announced in 1986. The CD-ROM/XA (/extended architecture) was introduced in 1988. Philips, Sony, and Microsoft specified digital optical formats for several media and published the specifications. CD-WORM (write once read many times) technology was initiated in 1990, as well as CD-MO (magneto-optical). The main reason for the great success of CD-DA and CD-ROM technology is a set of standards jointly developed by Sony and Phillips which, essentially specify the following:

Macroscopic and microscopic physical structure and design of the compact disk.

Compact disk data format that specifies space for data, address information, and error correction codes.

Error correction code (ECC) scheme, with room for additional data and ECC. The CD-ROM standards, also created by Sony and Phillips, use the same disk and scanning technology, and the same mastering and replication technique as used for CD-DA. The only difference between CD-DA and CD-ROM is in the data format, more powerful ECC, and more precise data addressing for CD-ROM. Most of the following explanation applies equally applied to CD-DA and CD-ROM.

OHP

DEFINITION

The Overhead Projector, or "OHP" is one of the most frequently used tools in education and training today. It may be facing a challenge from the data projector, but it is still more flexible and useful for all except uninterrupted, rehearsed presentations.

INTRODUCTION

An overhead projector is a very basic but reliable form of projector. The overhead projector displays images onto a screen or wall. It consists of a large box containing a cooling fan and an extremely bright light, with a long arm extended above it. At the end of the arm is a mirror that catches and redirects the light towards the screen.

An overhead projector can be used to enlarge images onto the screen or wall for audiences to view. Transparencies can be placed onto the projector to be viewed by both the audience and the speaker. The overhead projector was once a common feature in both classrooms and business meetings. Recently, it has seen a decline in use, as more sophisticated computer based projectors are favored.

The overhead projector was first seen during World War II. It was used as a tool to train large numbers of servicemen. In the 1950s and 60s, it crossed over into the classroom as an educational tool, and then into the business world as a training tool. The overhead projector reached its sales peak in the 1990s, when almost every classroom and business place in America had one installed.

The overhead projector is best used when the screen is approximately 6 to 12 feet (about 2-4 meters) from the projector. There are overheads that can increase the distance between projector and screen, but these are usually custom built and the cost is greatly increased. The biggest difference that can be seen between overhead projectors is the type of optics used.

There are three main types of optics that can be used in the overhead projector. Folded optics or chamber optics have a mirror placed in between the lamp and the lens. There are a number of benefits in using a folded optic projector as opposed to the more common direct optic projector. The resolution is a lot clearer, and there is more light used to project the image. There is approximately 50% more light available with a folded optic than with a direct optic projector.

Another type of optic is the reflected light optic. This has a specially designed lens that is backed by a mirror. The light source directs light to the lens, and the light is reflected by the mirror. The reflected light is directed back through the lens and onto the main projective lens. The light is then focused to a second mirror and onto the screen.The reflected light optic is used more in portable overhead projectors, and the cooling system, light source and main projection optics are all placed in one unit.

The entire projector can be folded down into a case for portability. Although still used in many classrooms around the world, the overhead projector may sadly be on the decline. However, some critics still favour the overhead projector for reliability and claim it is far easier to use than the more sophisticated projectors.

TIPS FOR USING OHP

- It's sucking eggs time again! Get the OHP set up for optimum image size, focused, etc. before the class starts. Make sure everyone can see.
- Once you are sure of the above, you have no need to look at the screen. You can concentrate on the class.
- So do not point to material on the screen itself. Use a pen or other pointer on the stage of the OHP. If your hand is at all shaky, lay the pointer down on the OHP stage. Standing in front of the screen to point out salient topics: means that you are tempted to talk to the screen and not the class means that some of the image is projected onto you, and there is a large obscuring shadow on the screen.
- The only exception is when you are projecting onto a whiteboard, and writing/drawing on the board to elaborate on the image. Even this can usually be dealt with more effectively by writing on an overlaid transparency on the OHP stage.

Do not leave an old OHT showing when you have moved on to talk about something else. Switch off between OHTs, or at least between sequences.

TRANSPARENCIES

INTRODUCTION

With improvement of software has come an increase in

the use of transparencies, especially among those who create ads. Industry-wide, printing companies are striving to find balance with the designers' creativity and the mechanics of what will work in the pressroom. Publishers' goal is to have what is seen on-screen in the designer's office match what prints.

TRANSPARENCY DEFINITION

An effect applied to an object which allows items beneath it to show through. Some examples of trans-

parencies are: drop shadows, feathering, opacity of less than 100%, blending modes, inner/outer glow effect, and opacity masks.

CREATING TRANSPARENCIES

The transparency adapter enables you to manipulate images in such a way that particular shades and colors become transparent. When you run the image as part of an HTML document, the transparent area will be invisible. This is particular useful for isolating objects and eliminating the backgrounds and shadows. You can focus attention on the African art objects, without drawing attention to anything else that may have been included in the photograph.

Creating transparencies is a rather simple ten-step process, but it is also rather specific:

Use Fetch to download the image you wish to convert into a transparency. Transparencies must be gif images. But you can start with a jpg. You will just have to convert it to a gif before continuing.

Open Photoshop. Remember that Photoshop is like a word- processor, and each image is like a word-processing document. You will not see your image when you start Photoshop. All you will see are the pallets that you can use to manipulate images. To look at your image, click on File in the top left, and then select Open. Find your image and click on Open.

If you selected a jpg, you will now need to change it to a gif. Click on Mode and select "indexed colour." You may notice that the screen will go haywire for a second as it adjusts its colors from one format to another. If you selected a gif, you can ignore this step.

A new window will appear in the middle of the screen with a number of options. You will also see a portion of your image. The critical thing in this window is the collection of three little buttons near the middle: a hand, a magnifying glass, and an eye dropper.

If you click on the hand, you can move around in your image. To do this, click the image and—while still holding the mouse button down—move the mouse.

If you click on the magnifying glass, you can zoom in within your image. Just click anywhere on the image. If you double- click on the magnifying glass, you will see your entire image.

Finally, the eye-dropper is what you actually use to create a transparency.

To make a transparency, use the eye-dropper to click on any part of the image which you wish to become transparent. Photoshop will isolate that particular colour, and will look for everywhere else in the image where that colour appears. It will replace that colour with a dull gray. When you are finished, everything in that gray will be transparent.

You will probably need to click the eye dropper a number of times, since most images have a broad range of colour in their backgrounds. By holding the mouse button down, you can move the eye-dropper around, sweeping up every colour you touch.

When you are finished, click the "OK" button. Photoshop will immediately require you to save the image. The default name it gives will be the original name for the image plus ".gif". For example, if your original name was "mask.gif", the new name will be "mask.gif.gif.". You can change the name, however, and in this case you might want to name it something like "transparency.gif".

Your transparency is now finished. You can exit Photoshop.

Remember that you must upload the image with Fetch.

In addition, if you gave it a new name you will need to alter your HTML document so that it shows the new image.

TRANSPARENCY PAPER

It is a type of paper which is designed for use with overhead projectors. This paper is clear, so that things printed or written on the paper can be clearly seen when light is passed through the paper to make a projection. In addition to being used with projectors, transparency paper can also be useful for overlays and lightboxes. Art supply and office supply stores are good resources for transparency paper.

The earliest transparency papers were made from specially-treated wood pulp papers. Modern versions could more accurately be termed "transparency film," since they are classically made from clear plastic films. The advantage to using transparency paper as opposed to to traditional paper is that the opacity of regular paper can interfere with the projection or clarity of an image. The use of overhead projectors is on the decline, but this specialized paper can be useful for other applications, and it continues to be produced by several paper companies.

Some companies make transparency paper which can safely be run through a printer, so that people can make prints and copies of prepared presentations. However, caution should be used before running this type of paper through a printer, because some transparency sheets will melt or warp when they are run through a printer. Paper which has been specifically marked as safe for use with a printer is the best choice, as a partially-melted piece of transparency film can gum up the works of a laser printer or copier considerably.

SLIDE PROJECTOR

DEFINITION

A slide projector is an opto-mechanical device to view photographic slides. It has four main elements: a fan-cooled electric light bulb or other light source, a reflector and "condensing" lens to direct the light to the slide, a holder for the slide and a focusing lens. Light passes through the transparent slide and lens, and the resulting image is enlarged and projected onto a perpendicular flat screen so the audience can view its reflection. Alternatively the image may be projected onto a translucent "rear projection" screen, often used for continuous automatic display for close viewing.

The resolution and colour brilliance of good quality 35mm slides projected onto a high quality screen far exceed that of modern in-home video.

Common in the 1950s and 1960s households as an alternate to television or movie entertainment, family members and friends would gather, darken the living room and show slides of recent holidays or vacations, an often boring affair that incited heckling, catcalls and sleep.

In-home photographic slides and slide projectors have largely been replaced by low cost paper prints, digital cameras, DVD media, video display monitors and digital projectors.

USEFUL FEATURES

Remote focus can be extremely useful, as most people find it easier to focus their projector accurately while standing close to the screen than from the back of the presentation room.

Auto focus can also simplify the setup process, but is most useful as a means to ensure that each slide in a given tray stays in as sharp a focus as the first.

An extra lamp module will allow you to get up and running quickly should a projection lamp fail during a presentation. (Simply pull out the whole module and slide in the new.) The newer Ektapro projectors can include a dual-lamp module, which automatically switches to a new lamp when the old one fails.

A preview screen allows you to look at a tray of slides in your presentation room without having to show them to your audience.

A reading light is not actually for reading, but is included to allow you to identify a tray or look at an individual slide in a darkened room.

Ru to project any slide in your tray at any time.

HOW CHOOSE A SLIDE PROJECTOR

Comparing slide projectors from spec sheets is a little more difficult than you might expect, because the items you most

want to compare–image quality, brightness, and reliability–aren't given in the specs.

On the other hand, the technology has come far enough that these three items really aren't a big issue. If you stick with a projector built for professional use, the main question becomes one of the features you need versus the budget you have available.

THE MOST IMPORTANT SPECIFICATIONS

- The focal length of the lens you choose for your new projector determines the screen size you can fill at a given distance. The following table shows the approximate throw distance needed (from film plane to screen) for various screens and focal lengths.

Because most people use their projectors in different rooms at different times, zoom lenses are the most popular sells.

- Compatibility can be an issue if you plan to use your projector with a dissolve unit or multi-image programmer, particularly if you're considering a projector mainly intended for home use. By and large, the projectors in this catalog will work with the majority of programmers available, but it makes sense to check before you buy.

	Screen width			
Lens	60"	70"	84"	96"
35 mm.	5.2	6.0	7.3	8.3
50 mm.	7.4	8.6	10.4	11.9
90 mm.	13.3	15.6	18.7	21.3
100 mm.	14.8	17.3	20.7	23.7
150 mm.	22.2	25.9	31.1	35.6
200 mm.	29.6	34.6	41.5	47.4
250 mm.	37.0	43.2	51.9	59.3

- Slide changing time refers to the minimum time it takes to cycle each slide in and out of the projection gate. This, again, is a consideration if you're planning to use your projector with a multi-image programme.

TYPES OF SLIDE PROJECTORS AND THEIR OPERATING TIPS

There are many kinds of slide projectors and each one uses a different technology.

- The Carousel slide projectors have circular trays, which consist of 20 to 140 slide holders. A stepper motor rotates these trays, and another corresponding system drops each slide in front of the light bulb to be projected. The trays can be horizontal or upright, though horizontal trays are more frequently seen.
- In case of Dual slide projectors, these have a number of holder trays that are made up of an inner and outer ring. Every ring can be advanced and can be put in independently and they can also be locked together. Two or more slides can be put in and they can be projected simultaneously.
- Unlike Dual slide projectors, Single slide projectors have only one holder slot that is built into a compact case, which also contains the bulb and lenses. These projectors can project only one slide at a time. Every

time the slide has to be removed and loaded manually. The slides are generally compact and can be carried conveniently to any place. They are often more in tune with larger slide formats.

- Viewer slide projectors display slide images on built-in viewing screens and the holders along with the projection mechanism are contained in a case behind the screen. The screen can be used for previewing images before they are projected onto a bigger screen.
- Slide cube projectors are called so as they have cube-shaped holders where slides are stacked in uniformly one on top of the other. Each slide is put into a circular plate and projected onto a preview screen before it is enlarged and one might include up to 40 cubes, each holding 36 to 44 slides.
- The other type of projector is the Stereo Slide projector which can project two images at a time and that can be from single holders or separate holders. There is a polarizing lens in front of the slides, which projects every image with a different polarization. As a result of which the image that comes up is three-dimensional and we get a more detailed picture than a single slide image.

RADIO AND TELEVISION

HISTORY ABOUT RADIO

By the early 1930s, radio had acquired an industry status in many countries. Amplitude Modulated (AM) frequency was used for radio broadcasting prior to FM frequency. In 1937, Edwin Armstrong invented the Frequency Modulated (FM) radio that used FM frequency. The first commercial FM radio broadcast was made in December 1941 at Nashville. The advent of FM radio further increased the listener base on account of the level of clarity in the broadcast.

However, the advent of TV during the 1940s severely eroded the listener base of the radio industry. The ban exerted on media during World War II added to the industry's woes.

Post war, the TV industry grew at an incredible pace. During its initial years, TV shows were primarily adaptations of existing radio shows. However, in the mid-1950s, TV shows created a distinctive identity for themselves in the field of entertainment and communication. In the next two decades TV media extended its roots to all corners of the world and became an inseparable part of almost every household. As a result radio programming experienced a decline in popularity.

Many of the leading radio broadcasting companies shifted their focus to TV programming on account of the shift in the audience preferences. Consequently the radio industry suffered from inadequate funding. In spite of all these, in the 1950s, radio still remained one of the major mass communication media.

In 1954, the number of radios in the world (257 million) exceeded, for the first time, the number of newspapers printed daily (256) million. The advent of the transistor and FM stereo, in the 1950s and 1960s respectively, also contributed to the increase in the listener base because of its size, style, and portability and improved quality of broadcasting. By the early 1970s, the FM band overtook the AM band across the world and gained popularity among the young listeners.

The industry faced another setback with the advent of satellite broadcasting technology during the mid- 1970s. This technology enabled TV networks to show their programs all over the world. In the 1980s, the satellite TV industry established itself firmly, reaching out to millions of subscribers all over the world, generating huge revenues through advertisements. And in the 1990s, the Internet evolved as a major communication channel, linking people across the world via computers. The Internet soon became a craze across the world and was very popular with the younger generation during the late 1990s.

In light of these developments, many analysts forecasted the end of radio broadcasting. However, many of them commented that radio broadcasting had successfully withstood competition from TV and satellite broadcasting, and would remain one of the major sources of mass communication across the world, despite the Internet. Portability and free accessibility of radio indoors and outdoors mainly contributed to the success of radio broadcasting worldwide. In small and developing countries radio broadcasting remains a major means of communication. Some analysts also were also of the opinion that radio broadcasting would retain its popularity in future on account of recent technological developments in field like digital radio and satellite radio, which would allow it to survive and progress alongside with other advanced media.

RADIO WORKING

A radio wave is an electromagnetic wave propagated by an antenna. Radio waves have different frequencies. The listener can tune the radio receiver to a specific frequency to catch a specific radio signal. For example, all FM radio stations transmit in a band of frequencies between 88 megahertz (millions of cycles per second) and 108 megahertz, and any listener who tunes his radio receiver to a frequency falling in this range would have access to that specific FM radio station's programs. Common radio frequency bands include

- FM – 88 MHz to 108 MHz
- AM – 535 KHz to 1.7 MHz
- Citizen Band (CB) Radio – 26.96 MHz to 27.41 MHz
- Short Wave Radio – 5.9 MHz to 26.1 MHz.

Every radio setup consists of two parts, the Transmitter and the Receiver. The transmitter receives the message, encodes it onto a sine wave (a continuously varying electromagnetic wave) and transmits it with radio waves. The receiver receives the radio waves and decodes the message from the sine wave it received. The transmitter and the receiver use antennas to radiate and capture radio signals. The function of the antenna in a radio transmitter is to send radio waves into space, and in a radio receiver, it is to capture the transmitter's power to the maximum extent and route it to the tuner. The size of the antenna depends on the frequency of the signal to be transmitted or received.

A radio station transmits the sine waves, with information

(programs) encoded on them, into space with help of an antenna. These sine waves are captured by antenna at the receiving station (radio set). The sine waves themselves do not contain any information and are modulated so as to hold information. Normally, sine waves are modulated in three ways:

- Pulse Modulation (PM): In PM, the sine wave is turned on and off at specific intervals. This is an easy way of sending coded messages. Usage of PM is comparatively less.
- Amplitude Modulation (AM): In AM, the amplitude of the sine waves (its peak to peak voltage) differs. AM is the most commonly used mode across the world.
- Frequency Modulation: In FM, the transmitter's sine wave frequency changes very slightly, based on the information signal. FM is largely immune to static (not useful or empty transmissions), which enhances the effectiveness of transmissions.

The sine waves with encoded messages are captured by antenna and sent to the tuner in the receiving station. The tuner's function is to separate one from the other, the thousands of sine waves received by the antenna. Tuners use the resonance principle, i.e. they resonate and amplify at one sine wave frequency, ignoring all other sine wave frequencies. They thus enable radio to receive only one sine wave frequency. The decoding of the information on sine waves in that particular frequency is done with the help of a demodulator or detector in the radio (detector defers from one radio type to the another). The radio amplifies this decoded information and sends it to the speakers, from where the listener listens to the information.

TELEVISION

Since Marconi's invention of wireless telegraphy in 1897, the imagination of many inventors have been sparked with the notion of sending images as well as sound, wirelessly. The first documented notion of sending components of pictures over a series of multiple circuits is credited to George Carey. An inventor suggested the possibility of sending an image over a single wire by rapidly scanning parts of the picture in succession.

Edwin Belin, who held the patent for the transmission of photographs by wire as well as fibre optics and radar, demonstrated a mechanical scanning device that was an early precursor to modern television. Belin's machine took flashes of light and directed them at a selenium element connected to an electronic device that produced sound waves. These sound waves could be received in another location and remodulated into flashes of light on a mirror. Up until this point, the concept behind television was established, but it wasn't until electronic scanning of imagery (the breaking up of images into tiny points of light for transmission over radio waves), was invented, that modern television received its start. But here is where the controversy really heats up. The credit as to who was the inventor of modern television really comes down to two different people in two different places both working on the same problem at about the same time: A Russian-born American inventor working for Westinghouse, and Philo Taylor Farnsworth, a privately backed farm boy from the state of Utah. "Zworykin had a patent, but Farnsworth had a picture..."

Vladimir Zworykin demonstrates electronic television, 1929

Zworykin is usually credited as being the father of modern television. This was because the patent for the heart of the TV, the electron scanning tube, was first applied for by Zworykin in 1923, under the name of an iconoscope. The iconoscope was an electronic image scanner - essentially a primitive television camera. Farnsworth was the first of the two inventors to successfully demonstrate the transmission of television signals, which he did on September 7, 1927, using a scanning tube of his own design. Farnsworth received a patent for his electron scanning tube in 1930. Zworykin was not able to duplicate Farnsworth's achievements until 1934 and his patent for a scanning tube was not issued until 1938. The truth of the matter is this, that while Zworykin applied for the patent for his iconoscope in 1923, the invention was not functional until some years later and all earlier efforts were of such poor quality that Westinghouse officials ordered him to work on something "more useful."

A Scottish engineer and entrepreneur who 'achieved his first transmissions of simple face shapes in 1924 using mechanical television. Baird held his first public demonstration of 'television' at the London department store Selfridges on Oxford Street in London. In this demonstration, he had not yet obtained adequate half-tones in the moving pictures, and only silhouettes were visible.' - *MZTV*

John Logie Bard with his mechanicall TV

In the late thirties, when RCA and Zworykin, who was now working for RCA, tried to claim rights to the essence of television, it became evident that Farnsworth held the priority patent in the technology. The president of RCA sought to control television the same way that they controlled radio and vowed that, "RCA earns royalties, it does not pay them," and a 50 million dollar legal battle subsequently ensued.

In the height of the legal battle for patent priority, Farnsworth's high school science teacher was subpoenaed and traveled to Washington to testify that as a 14 year old, Farnsworth had shared his ideas of his television scanning tube with his teacher.

Philo Famsworth with his Television

With patent priority status ruled in favour of Farnsworth, RCA for the first time in its history, began paying royalties for television in 1939.

CCTV

DEFINITION

CCTV, Closed Circuit Television, is a TV system that does not broadcast TV signals to public but transmits them over to limited monitor(s). CCTV system usually utilizes CCD video cameras (to produce the video), cable or wireless transmitters/ receivers or Internet (to transmit the video), and monitors (to see the video). CCTV system is not only applied to the security and surveillance purpose but also to the other fields like laboratory in schools or in private companies, even to production lines in factories. As the application of CCTV system increased, the CCTV industry has developed variety of CCTV equipment like Time Lapse VCRs, combiners, infrared illuminators, Pan/Tilt, etc. The most recent development is web camera server which uses the Internet for remote surveillance.

Also we can say that, CCTV (closed circuit television) is a television system in which signals are not publicly distributed; cameras are connected to television monitor s in a limited area such as a store, an office building, or on a college campus. CCTV is commonly used in surveillance systems.

USE OF CCTV

The most obvious and common use for CCTV is for security. This type of installation is used in a variety of locations such as stores, banks, and government buildings. However, there are so many other uses. It can be used for monitoring traffic. It is used in sports stadiums to focus on the audience. It can be hidden in trains and buses to detect vandalism. It can be used to monitor animals in a zoo. It can even be used to reproduce infrared vision. The applications are almost limitless.

CONSTRUCTION OF CCTV

It all starts with the camera. This creates the picture that is transmitted to the control area. Most CCTV cameras are not fitted with lenses. They must be obtained separately and screwed on. There is a standard screw thread although there are different mounts. Not all lenses have focus adjustment. Most have iris adjustment. Some wide angle lenses do not have a focus ring. There is a BNC jack for connecting the video cable. In the case of line powered cameras, this coaxial cable also provides power. The monitor is what receives the signal that the camera creates. A CCTV monitor is similar to a television set but it does not have tuning circuits.

Simple CCTV systems consist of a camera connected to a monitor with coaxial cable. This cable also carries the power needed for the camera. This is called a line powered camera.

The Pye Observation System was such a system and was popular during the early days of CCTV. It was affordable and could be set up with a minimum of difficulty. The next big step in the technology was allowing for four cameras to be connected to the monitor simultaneously. The view could be programmed to cycle through the available cameras or go to a particular camera chosen by the user.

MULTIMEDIA COMPUTER

DEFINITION

Multimedia computer is such type of Computer, which is used to present text, graphics, video, animation, and sound in an integrated way. Long touted as the future revolution in computing, multimedia applications were, until the mid-90s, uncommon due to the expensive hardware required. With increases in performance and decreases in price, however, multimedia is now commonplace. Nearly all PCs are capable of displaying video, though the resolution available depends on the power of the computer's video adapter and CPU.

USES OF MULTIMEDIA COMPUTER

Multimedia computers will serve you best in the following tasks:

- Editing Video: Editing, adding effects, animating or converting file types with programs like PowerDirector, ShowBiz or Ulead VideoStudio.
- Audio Editing: Creating music mixes, recording Internet radio, converting file types or restoring music with programs like Dexter Audio Editor, GoldWave Digital Audio or Blaze Media Pro.
- Photo Editing: Editing images, creating slide shows or photo galleries with programs like Adobe Photoshop Elements, PhotoImpact or Digital Image Suite.
- Burning DVDs: Creating/copying slides shows, burning backup DVDs, restoring or converting/

compressing files with programs like DVD Cloner, 1Click DVD Copy or Clone DVD.

- Organizing Photos: Organize, archive, or share your family's digital photo album with programs like Adobe Photoshop Album, Digital Image or Corel Photo Album.
- Recording Television/Music: Recording programs utilizing software like Genuine Windows XP Media Centre 2005.
- If you are primarily interested in watching or storing DVDs, recording TV, listening to Internet radio or managing your music files, you may want to consider a Media Centre PC, which is more like an entertainment centre component than a desktop.

In this site, you'll find articles related to multimedia computers, as well as comprehensive reviews and a side–by–side comparison to help you make an informed decision on which computer is right for you.

QUALITIES OF MULTIMEDIA COMPUTER

Multimedia computers require higher quality components than general use computers. We looked at several different systems from a variety of providers, and then compared their ability to handle media applications. We selected products with a retail price of under 32,500 and were marketed as "multimedia" computers.

Below are the criteria used to evaluate multimedia computers:

- Processor: The processor should run at a minimum of 3.0GHz, with a front bus speed of 800MHz. Those that offer dual or quad-core processors are better at running multiple applications and thus, rated better.
- Memory: Multimedia requires a large amount of memory. The best computers offer at least a 500GB hard drive and 2GB of RAM.
- Graphics Card: An exceptional graphics card is required for playing and recording DVDs, TV, digital video and games successfully. The best multimedia

PCs come with at least a 256MB card.

- Multimedia Features: Systems configured for multimedia should include a DVD burner/reader, surround sound, and inputs for connecting video, peripherals and other media devices.
- Accessories: Accessories include keyboard, mouse, software, monitor or other devices. Software can be costly, so it is nice if the system comes ready to run with an operating system and the ability to burn DVDs and edit videos, photos or audio.
- Value/Price: Cost effective computers offer above average features at a below average price.
- Customer Service: Setting up a system can get complicated, so it is useful if the manufacturer offers helpful customer service by telephone, email and chat. Some companies may publish a comprehensive online FAQ or tutorial, as well as offer driver and software downloads.

NON PROJECTED AIDS

DEFINITION

Non-projected aids are those that do not require the use of audiovisual equipment such as a projector and screen. Included in this category are charts, graphs, maps, illustrations, photographs, brochures, and handouts.

CHARTS

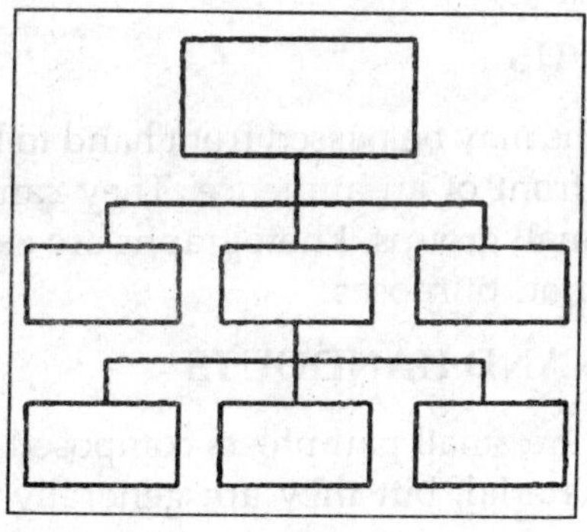

Charts are in common use almost every- where. A chart is a diagram which shows relationships. An example of a chart is shown in figure below. The organizational chart is one of the most widely used. This chart shows the various branches of a particular organization. Air and sea maps that are used for navigation purposes are also charts.

GRAPH

These aids show comparisons between figures. Four types of graphs are illustrated in figure above. The bar graph is one of the most commonly used. Graphs are useful when the information being presented compares figures from time to time or from several sources. For example, a budget meeting may utilize graphs to show the increases and decreases of the budget over several years.

MAPS

Maps are graphic representations of the surface of the earth. Maps are usually drawn to scale. The type that you are most likely to encounter is the world map, used in conference rooms, classrooms, and in briefing rooms.

ILLUSTRATIONS

Illustrations are the most versatile of any aid covered here. All aids make use of illustrations to some degree in their planning stages, and perhaps even in their final form. Charts, cartoons, maps, and signs are illustrations that are often used to present or clarify an idea.

PHOTOGRAPHS

Photographs may be passed from hand to hand or posted on a board in front of an audience. They can be used most effectively in small groups. Photographs are extensively used for documentation purposes.

BROCHURES AND HANDOUTS

Brochures are small pamphlets composed of illustrations and printed material, but they are generally much briefer than handouts. When given to students or an audience, these materials should help the people understand the presentation. Handouts are normally retained by the audience for purposes of reference and later review used to tion. Long after the presentation, they can be review important points of the presentations.

COMPUTER-ASSISTED INSTRUCTION

DEFINITION

Computer-assisted instruction (CAI) is a narrower term and most often refers to drill-and-practice, tutorial, or simulation activities offered either by themselves or as supplements to traditional, teacher directed instruction. Computer Assisted Instruction (CAI) is a legitimate method of instruction, equal to other traditional types of teaching in terms of learning and time involvement reported two studies that showed small but significant achievement gains in the average examination scores of CAI classes as compared to traditional classes. In six studies, retention of the information showed no significant difference between CAI and conventional methods of instruction. The time required to learn from CAI compared to conventional methods also was not significantly different.

The past decade has seen a growth in the number and quality of available instructional software packages for nursing education, which have many advantages: flexible, self-paced, easily monitored and updated, and provide feedback on progress. CAI is useful in teaching decision making; developed on a case simulation approach, it can assist the student in the steps of the nursing process. The findings of a study conducted at the University of Texas Health Science Centre in San Antonio showed that CAI was at least equivalent to the traditional nursing process strategy in terms of critical thinking outcomes and was demonstrated to have some advantages over traditional nursing process in terms of student satisfaction and time efficiency, which could make it a superior strategy. Another study found that students using computer based instruction had higher examination averages and they had more positive attitudes toward their instructional method than conventionally taught students.

Some faculty members may find it hard to locate good case materials and others are not sure how to go about teaching a case study. A potential fear is that the discussion will degenerate into a "pointless exchange of personal opinions."

- Review the problem-solving objectives for the class session.
- Prepare the materials the students will read.
- Consider critical issues and topics yet to be covered.
- Make notes after each class session, and use them to review.
- Hypothesize how the case will develop.
- Consider each student's background and experiences.
- Considering your personal attitude toward the case study issue to prevent biases from emerging.
- Developing opening comments and closing summaries for each case.

Dowd and Davidhizar warn that instructors must be willing to relinquish control over the learning process when they implement student-centered strategies like the case study approach. Both successes and failures will occur; both should be used as feedback in developing subsequent learning experiences. The danger when student-centered approaches fail is that instructors quickly return to more familiar teacher-centered approaches such as lecturing.

INVENTION OF CAI

The findings offered in this summary emerge from an analysis of the 59 research reports cited in the References section of the annotated bibliography. Each of these reports documents some relationship(s) between computer-based learning and student outcomes. Twenty eight are research studies, 22 are reviews, and 9 are meta-analyses of research studies. Twelve of the documents focus on elementary students, 19 are concerned with secondary students, 7 cover the elementary-secondary range, 5 involve subjects spanning the elementary-postsecondary range, and the age/grade levels of subjects are not specified in 16 of the reports.

Most of the studies involved American students, but Israeli and Canadian subjects are also represented. Other specific populations serving as subjects in the documents include economically disadvantaged students (4), special education students (5), remedial students (2), and Hispanic students (2). The rest of the documents either concerned general student populations or did not specify characteristics of their subjects.

The 59 reports were concerned with the effects one or more of the following types of educational computer use on student outcomes: CAI (35), CBE in general (15), the use of word processors for written composition (5), computer-managed instruction (3), programming (2), and simulations (4).

The effects of computer use on a large number of outcome areas were examined, including academic achievement in general (30), in mathematics (13), in language arts (8), in reading (3), in science (2), in problem-solving skills (2), and in health and social studies (1 each). Studies also focused on students' attitudes toward the content of courses in which computers were used (21), toward computers themselves (19), toward school in general (6), toward the quality of instruction in courses with computer activities (4), and toward themselves as learners (4). Other outcome areas include learning rate (10), learning retention (9), locus of control and motivation, computer literacy, and cooperation/helping (4 each).

Beyond these outcome-focused reports, the General References section of the bibliography cites 18 additional reports on related topics, such as teacher training to conduct CAI effectively, cost-effectiveness of CAI, discussions of current and potential applications of computers in education, and examinations of students' favorable attitudes toward computer activities.

ADVANTAGES OF CAI TO STUDENTS

Students say they like working with computers because computers:

- Are infinitely patient
- Never get tired
- Never get frustrated or angry
- Allow students to work privately
- Never forget to correct or praise
- Are fun and entertaining
- Individualize learning
- Are self-paced
- Do not embarrass students who make mistakes
- Make it possible to experiment with different options
- Give immediate feedback
- Are more objective than teachers
- Free teachers for more meaningful contact with students
- Are impartial to race or ethnicity
- Are great motivators
- Give a sense of control over learning
- Are excellent for drill and practice
- Call for using sight, hearing, and touch
- Teach in small increments
- Help students improve their spelling
- Build proficiency in computer use, which will be valuable later in life
- Eliminate the drudgery of doing certain learning activities by hand (e.g., drawing graphs)
- Work rapidly—closer to the rate of human thought.

QUALITIES OF CAI

The use of CAI as a supplement to conventional instruction produces higher achievement than the use of conventional instruction alone.

Research is inconclusive regarding the comparative effectiveness of conventional instruction alone and CAI alone.

Computer-based education (CAI and other computer applications) produce higher achievement than conventional instruction alone.

Student use of word processors to develop writing skills leads to higher-quality written work than other writing methods (paper and pencil, conventional typewriters).

Students learn material faster with CAI than with conventional instruction alone.

Students retain what they have learned better with CAI than with conventional instruction alone.

The use of CAI leads to more positive attitudes toward computers, course content, quality of instruction, school in general, and self-as-learner than the use of conventional instruction alone.

The use of CAI is associated with other beneficial outcomes, including greater internal locus of control, school attendance, motivation/time-on-task, and student-student cooperation and collaboration than the use of conventional instruction alone.

CAI is more beneficial for younger students than older ones.

CAI is more beneficial with lower-achieving students than with higher-achieving ones.

Economically disadvantaged students benefit more from CAI than students from higher socioeconomic backgrounds.

CAI is more effective for teaching lower-cognitive material than higher-cognitive material.

Most handicapped students, including learning disabled, mentally retarded, hearing impaired, emotionally disturbed, and language disordered, achieve at higher levels with CAI than with conventional instruction alone.

There are no significant differences in the effectiveness of CAI with male and female students.

Students' fondness for CAI activities centers around the immediate, objective, and positive feedback provided by these activities.

CAI activities appear to be at least as cost effective as— and sometimes more cost-effective than— other instructional methods, such as teacher-directed instruction and tutoring.

DEVELOPMENT OF CAI

CAI can be proceed by using the following directions as shown below:

Click here to save the self-extracting zip file to your desktop. Create a new folder on your desktop named "CAI Template." Double click on the saved file (cai.exe) to begin the self-extractor. Extract the files to the "CAI Template" folder. Copy the "CAI Template" folder.

Rename the copied folder to represent the topic of your CAI; for example, "Acute Renal Failure CAI." Make a similar copy of the "CAI Template" folder for each new CAI (always preserving the CAI Template folder for future development). Open the index.htm file in the newly renamed folder using your preferred html editor.

Replace the text in the index file as directed; save the file (using the same file name) after changes are made.

Modify each file in the newly renamed folder using the html editor; save each file (using the same file name) after changes are made.

Transfer the the newly renamed folder containing the modified files from the hard drive of your computer to your web page using a file transfer protocol (FTP) utility such as WS-FTP LE (free to educational users) or ask your IT department for assistance. Place a link to the newly renamed folder on a web page that introduces the CAI and gives the student instructions for completion - your first CAI is ready to go!

EFFECT OF CAI

The purpose of this study was to determine how computer-assisted-instruction improves student performance among various types of students. 161 middle school students of various programme types: special education, non-English proficient, limited English proficient, and regular education, completed instructional units using a computer programme, Corner Stone. Regular education students were found to have made greater pretest-posttest gains than special education students using an ANCOVA test, $F1, 156, 0.95, = 15.59$, $p < 0.0001$.

Collectively, the students showed significant pretest-posttest gains, $t160, 0.95 = 6.02$, $p < 0.0001$ using a dependent t-test. The direction of future research was suggested based on the results.

There is no doubt that technology has become incorporated into our school systems. Computers are used not only as a means of helping schools analyse data, computers have become a pervasive tool toward optimizing student learning. For example, students are regularly using the Internet to gather and assimilate information for use in research assignments.

They are preparing "electronic" presentations using computer presentation programs and LCD projectors. They are using word processing programs to create various other reports. Students are even using spreadsheets to increase their experiences with mathematical concepts. In addition, many schools have incorporated interactive computer-assisted-instruction into their programme to provide students opportunities to master specific educational objectives or standards.

INTERNET

HISTORY OF INTERNET

The Internet was the result of some visionary thinking by people in the early 1960s. J.C.R. Licklider of MIT, first proposed a global network of computers in 1962, and moved over to the Defence Advanced Research Projects Agency (DARPA) in late 1962.Lawrence Roberts of MIT moved over to DARPA in 1966 and developed his plan for ARPANET. The initial infrastructure for Internet was established in 1969 to provide a secure and survivable communications network for organizations engaged in defence-related research.

Over the following two decades, it evolved into a fast, convenient, low cost means for universities and research institutions to electronically exchange information and messages. The spread of personal computers in businesses, government, schools and homes coupled with the growth of local area networks during the 1980s and early 1990s provided a means for million of individual users to link into the system.

These developments propelled the growth of the Internet from a thousand or so networks in the mid-1980s to about 60,000 connected networks in mid-1995.By the middle of 1997, the Internet was available to an estimated 100 million register users worldwide.

OVERVIEW

The Internet was the result of some visionary thinking by people in the early 1960s who saw great potential value in allowing computers to share information on research and development in scientific and military fields. J.C.R. Licklider of MIT, first proposed a global network of computers in 1962, and moved over to the Defence Advanced Research Projects Agency (DARPA) in late 1962 to head the work to develop it. Leonard Kleinrock of MIT and later UCLA developed the theory of packet switching, which was to form the basis of Internet connections.

Lawrence Roberts of MIT connected a Massachusetts computer with a California computer in 1965 over dial-up telephone lines. It showed the feasibility of wide area networking, but also showed that the telephone line's circuit switching was inadequate. Kleinrock's packet switching theory was confirmed. Roberts moved over to DARPA in 1966 and developed his plan for ARPANET. These visionaries and many more left unnamed here are the real founders of the Internet.

When Senator Ted Kennedy heard in 1968 that the pioneering Massachusetts company BBN had won the ARPA contract for an "interface message processor (IMP)," he sent a congratulatory telegram to BBN for their ecumenical spirit in winning the "interfaith message processor" contract.

The Internet, then known as ARPANET, was brought online in 1969 under a contract let by the renamed Advanced Research Projects Agency (ARPA) which initially connected four major computers at universities in the southwestern US (UCLA, Stanford Research Institute, UCSB, and the University of Utah). The contract was carried out by BBN of Cambridge, MA under Bob Kahn and went online in December 1969. By June 1970, MIT, Harvard, BBN, and Systems Development

Corp (SDC) in Santa Monica, Cal. were added. By January 1971, Stanford, MIT's Lincoln Labs, Carnegie-Mellon, and Case-Western Reserve U were added. In months to come, NASA/Ames, Mitre, Burroughs, RAND, and the U of Illinois plugged in. After that, there were far too many to keep listing here.

The First to Use the Internet

Charley Kline at UCLA sent the first packets on ARPANet as he tried to connect to Stanford Research Institute on Oct 29, 1969. The system crashed as he reached the G in LOGIN!

The Internet was designed in part to provide a communications network that would work even if some of the sites were destroyed by nuclear attack. If the most direct route was not available, routers would direct traffic around the network via alternate routes.

The early Internet was used by computer experts, engineers, scientists, and librarians. There was nothing friendly about it. There were no home or office personal computers in those days, and anyone who used it, whether a computer professional or an engineer or scientist or librarian, had to learn to use a very complex system.

Did Al Gore invent the Internet?

According to a CNN transcript of an interview with Wolf Blitzer, Al Gore said, "During my service in the United States Congress, I took the initiative in creating the Internet." Al Gore was not yet in Congress in 1969 when ARPANET started or in 1974 when the term Internet first came into use. Gore was elected to Congress in 1976. In fairness, Bob Kahn and Vint Cerf acknowledge in a paper titled Al Gore and the Internet that Gore has probably done more than any other elected official to support the growth and development of the Internet from the 1970's to the present .

E-mail was adapted for ARPANET by Ray Tomlinson of BBN in 1972. He picked the @ symbol from the available symbols on his teletype to link the username and address. The telnet protocol, enabling logging on to a remote computer, was published as a Request for Comments (RFC) in 1972. RFC's are a means of sharing developmental work throughout community. The ftp protocol, enabling file transfers between Internet sites, was published as an RFC in 1973, and from then on RFC's were available electronically to anyone who had use of the ftp protocol.

Libraries began automating and networking their catalogs in the late 1960s independent from ARPA. The visionary Frederick G. Kilgour of the Ohio College Library Centre led networking of Ohio libraries during the '60s and '70s. In the mid 1970s more regional consortia from New England, the Southwest states, and the Middle Atlantic states, etc., joined with Ohio to form a national, later international, network. Automated catalogs, not very user-friendly at first, became available to the world, first through telnet or the awkward IBM variant TN3270 and only many years later, through the web. See The History of OCLC

Ethernet, a protocol for many local networks, appeared in 1974, an outgrowth of Harvard student Bob Metcalfe's dissertation on "Packet Networks." The dissertation was initially rejected by the University for not being analytical enough. It later won acceptance when he added some more equations to it.

The Internet matured in the 70's as a result of the TCP/IP architecture first proposed by Bob Kahn at BBN and further developed by Kahn and Vint Cerf at Stanford and others throughout the 70's. It was adopted by the Defence Department in 1980 replacing the earlier Network Control Protocol (NCP) and universally adopted by 1983.

The Unix to Unix Copy Protocol (UUCP) was invented in 1978 at Bell Labs. Usenet was started in 1979 based on UUCP. Newsgroups, which are discussion groups focusing on a topic, followed, providing a means of exchanging information throughout the world . While Usenet is not considered as part of the Internet, since it does not share the use of TCP/IP, it linked unix systems around the world, and many Internet sites took advantage of the availability of newsgroups. It was a significant part of the community building that took place on the networks.

Similarly, BITNET connected IBM mainframes around the educational community and the world to provide mail services beginning in 1981. Listserv software was developed for this network and later others. Gateways were developed to connect BITNET with the Internet and allowed exchange of e-mail, particularly for e-mail discussion lists. These listservs and other forms of e-mail discussion lists formed another major element in the community building that was taking place.

In 1986, the National Science Foundation funded NSFNet as a cross country 56 Kbps backbone for the Internet. They maintained their sponsorship for nearly a decade, setting rules for its non-commercial government and research uses.

As the commands for e-mail, FTP, and telnet were standardized, it became a lot easier for non-technical people to learn to use the nets. It was not easy by today's standards by any means, but it did open up use of the Internet to many more people in universities in particular. Other departments besides the libraries, computer, physics, and engineering departments found ways to make good use of the nets—to communicate with colleagues around the world and to share files and resources.

While the number of sites on the Internet was small, it was fairly easy to keep track of the resources of interest that were available. But as more and more universities and organizations—and their libraries— connected, the Internet became harder and harder to track. There was more and more need for tools to index the resources that were available.

The first effort, other than library catalogs, to index the Internet was created in 1989, as Peter Deutsch and his crew at McGill University in Montreal, created an archiver for ftp sites, which they named Archie. This software would periodically reach out to all known openly available ftp sites, list their files, and build a searchable index of the software. The commands to search Archie were unix commands, and it took some knowledge of unix to use it to its full capability.

McGill University, which hosted the first Archie, found out one day that half the Internet traffic going into Canada from the United States was accessing Archie. Administrators were concerned that the University was subsidizing such a volume of traffic, and closed down Archie to outside access. Fortunately, by that time, there were many more Archies available.

At about the same time, Brewster Kahle, then at Thinking Machines, Corp. developed his Wide Area Information Server (WAIS), which would index the full text of files in a database and allow searches of the files. There were several versions with varying degrees of complexity and capability developed, but the simplest of these were made available to everyone on the nets. At its peak, Thinking Machines maintained pointers to over 600 databases around the world which had been indexed by WAIS. They included such things as the full set of Usenet Frequently Asked Questions files, the full documentation of working papers such as RFC's by those developing the Internet's standards, and much more. Like Archie, its interface was far from intuitive, and it took some effort to learn to use it well.

Peter Scott of the University of Saskatchewan, recognizing the need to bring together information about all the telnet-accessible library catalogs on the web, as well as other telnet resources, brought out his Hytelnet catalog in 1990. It gave a single place to get information about library catalogs and other telnet resources and how to use them. He maintained it for years, and added HyWebCat in 1997 to provide information on web-based catalogs.

In 1991, the first really friendly interface to the Internet was developed at the University of Minnesota. The University wanted to develop a simple menu system to access files and information on campus through their local network. A debate followed between mainframe adherents and those who believed in smaller systems with client-server architecture. The mainframe adherents "won" the debate initially, but since the client-server advocates said they could put up a prototype very quickly, they were given the go-ahead to do a demonstration system. The demonstration system was called a gopher after the U of Minnesota mascot—the golden gopher. The gopher proved to be very prolific, and within a few years there were over 10,000 gophers around the world. It takes no knowledge of unix or computer architecture to use. In a gopher system, you type or click on a number to select the menu selection you want. Gopher's usability was enhanced much more when the University of Nevada at Reno developed the VERONICA searchable index of gopher menus. It was purported to be an acronym for Very Easy Rodent-Oriented Netwide Index to Computerized Archives.

A spider crawled gopher menus around the world, collecting links and retrieving them for the index. It was so popular that it was very hard to connect to, even though a number of other VERONICA sites were developed to ease the load. Similar indexing software was developed for single sites, called JUGHEAD. Peter Deutsch, who developed Archie, always insisted that Archie was short for Archiver, and had nothing to do with the comic strip. He was disgusted when VERONICA and JUGHEAD appeared.

In 1989 another significant event took place in making the nets easier to use. Tim Berners-Lee and others at the European Laboratory for Particle Physics, more popularly known as CERN, proposed a new protocol for information distribution. This protocol, which became the World Wide Web in 1991, was based on hypertext—a system of embedding links in text to link to other text, which you have been using every time you selected a text link while reading these pages. Although started before gopher, it was slower to develop

USE OF INTERNET

Finding General Information About a Subject

The Web is like a huge encyclopedia of information - in some ways it's even better. The volume of information you'll find on the Web is amazing. For every topic that you've ever wondered about, there's bound to be someone who's written a Web page about it.

Finding Online Encyclopedias

Many of these are now offering a subscription service

which lets you search through the complete text of the encyclopedia. There are also many free ecyclopedias that may give you a cut-down version of what you would find in a complete encyclopedia.

Accessing of Information

One of the great things about the Web is that it puts information into your hands that you might otherwise have to pay for or find out by less convenient means.

Finding World Clock Timings

Current local times for cities all over the world - even knows about daylight savings.

Knowing Foreign Exchange Rates

Get a table with exchange rates to and from any other currency.

Village Cinemas

Find out movie times without having to search for a paper.

Correspond with faraway friends

Email offers a cheap and easy alternative to traditional methods of correspondence. It's faster and easier than writing snail mail and cheaper than using the telephone. Of course, there are disadvantages too. It's not as personal as a handwritten letter - and not as reliable either. If you spell the name of the street wrong in a conventional address, it's not too difficult for the post office to work out what you mean. However if you spell anything wrong in an email address, your mail won't be delivered. Find out more about Email

To Meet People

The Web is generally a very friendly place. People love getting email from strangers, and friendships are quick to form from casual correspondence. The "impersonal" aspect of email tends to encourage people to reveal surprisingly personal things about themselves. When you know you will never have to meet someone face-to-face, you may find it easier to tell them your darkest secrets. Cyber-friendships have often developed into real life ones too. Many people have even found love on the Nel, and have gone on to marry their cyber-partner.

To Discuss Their Interests with like-minded People

Did you think you were alone in your obsession with a singer, TV programme, author, hobby? Chances are there's and Internet group for people like you, discussing every little detail of your obsession right now. The Republic of Pemberley is a discussion board for "Pride and Prejudice" (by Jane Austen) obsessives. The Society of Barefoot Living is for people who go barefoot - everywhere!

To Have Fun

There's no doubt that the Internet is a fun place to be. There's plenty to keep you occupied on a rainy day. Here's just a few of the many frivolous things to do on the Web: The Waitakere Rovers Kiwiness Quiz. Send virtual flowers, Misheard Song Lyrics.

To Learn

Online distance education courses can give you an opportunity to gain a qualification over the Internet.

To Read the News

The Indian Express Press On-Line is the first Indian newspaper to make it on to the Web. The Ecnomic Times is always up to date with the latest (Indian) news.

To Find Software

The Internet contains a wealth of useful downloadable shareware. Some pieces of shareware are limited versions of the full piece of software, other are time limited trials. Other shareware is free for educational institutes, or for non-commercial purposes. Shareware.com is a shareware archive that lets you search by keyword.

To Buy Things

The security of on-line shopping is still questionable, but as long as you are dealing with a reputable company or Web Site the risks are minimal. Amazon Books is a huge American book store (they exist only on the Web and are very reputable). Their prices are very good - it's can be much cheaper to buy books from here than from NZ book stores, especially if you buy several at once to keep the shipping cost down.

Why do People Put Things on the Web?

To advertise a product. Most company Web sites start up as a big advertisement for their products and services. It may be hard to see why anyone would willingly visit a 10 page ad - but these advertisements are very useful to anyone genuinely interested in finding out about their products. Companies may also give away some information for free as an incentive for people to visit their pages. Adobe Systems Incorporated - a good way to find out the facts about the excellent software that Adobe offers.

To Sell a Product

Internet shopping (e-commerce) is still in its infancy - it takes a very good marketing strategy to actually make money out of selling items over the Web, but that doesn't stop lots of people from trying. Amazon Books - one of the most successful (perhaps the most successful) e-businesses.

To Make Money

A popular way to make money out of the Web is from advertising revenue. Popular sites have banners at the top of the page enticing people to click them and be taken to the advertiser's Web site. These banners are generally animated and very appealing, with mysterious messages to make users wonder where they will be taken.

For each person that clicks the ad, the host site gets commission. Making money this way is only successful if the site gets lots of visitors (thousands a day); so the sites must be very useful and offer something of real value to their visitors.

The Alta Vista Search Engine is an example of a site that makes money from banner advertisements. The Internet Movie Database offers a very useful and fun service - it's financed by advertising and sponsorship.

To Share Their Knowledge with the World

Many individuals write Web pages to share information about their interests or hobbies. They don't expect to make any money out of it - they just feel that the Web has given them so much information that the least they can do is put something into it that may be useful for others.

Other rewards come from the prestige of having their site recognised as something good and the contact inspired by their pages with others sharing the same interest.

IMPACT OF THE INTERNET

There has been a huge, worldwide explosion in the use of the Internet. It is already changing the way we work, shop, bank and also the way we live.

Why the Internet has Grown

The PC is becoming commonplace in many homes and there is a general acceptance that this is a way forward. Analogue phone lines are being replaced by faster digital lines (ISDN). Even faster high-speed digital connections will soon be delivered to households, offering a whole day connection to the Net. Many countries around the world are developing in communication technology via satellite, wireless and cable to enhance worldwide Internet access. Access to the Internet and its services have already become available through the use of digital TVs and mobile phones. The use of the Internet by many business, organisations and the general public has led to a rapid increase in the number of sites.

Clearly all these developments are going to change the way we work, live and experience life.

The Internet and the Way We Work

Information technology has had an impact on the way we

work for quite some time, but the Internet has now added electronic mail (email), tele working and video conferencing to the workplace.

Tele Working

The ability to work from home by means of a PC or laptop and since some communications link are increasing, and there are a number of benefits to the employer:

Office running costs and overheads (rates, electricity, heating etc.) can be reduced, which in turn may reduce the need for office space. Travel-related problems may be reduced.

It may tempt better staff to come and work for the company.

However, employers need to be able to trust their staff and be prepared to have less direct control over them.

Benefits for The Employee Include

- You can work from the comfort of your own home.
- There is no time wasted travelling and no travel costs.
- It enables you to work around the needs of your family and/or children, giving you greater flexibility.
- It is more convenient - you can plan the working day to suit you, which could help reduce stress levels.

Drawbacks Include

- There is less opportunity to meet up with people and share ideas therefore teamwork is more difficult.
- There may be more temptation to spend time on non-work-related activities.

Video Conferencing

Video conferencing means using computers to provide a video-link between two or more people. Instead of just talking to someone by telephone, you are able to see them as well.

Benefits Include

Meetings can take place without leaving the office.

Travel costs and the time taken to travel can be reduced significantly. Meetings can be called instantly worldwide with little notice. Delegates can still attend meetings even if they are physically unable to.

Drawbacks Include

May not be as productive as a discussion around a table.

Confidential documents may need to be viewed and signed in person. There will always be times when you need to be able to meet face to face with another person.

How the Internet is Changing Our Lifestyle

Home Shopping

Home shopping options are many and varied and changing all the time. Most major supermarkets are now on-line, offering home delivery of goods and increasingly, the major high street stores are also competing for on-line trading. The Internet lends itself to shops selling goods which are easily portable, such as CDs and books.

Benefits of Home Shopping

- Avoid long queues
- Save time
- Shop from your own home.
- You can shop around for the best prices
- Travel abroad in cheaper goods.

Drawbacks of Home Shopping

- Security worries about payment by credit card over the Internet.
- You do not get to see the goods before purchase which may be defective.
- You may worry that the the goods will never arrive.
- There may be concerns over retailers collecting details about the buying habits of customers.

Benefits to the Company Include

- It opens the market to customers nationally and internationally.

- It enables smaller companies to compete with larger companies.
- There may be a possible reduction in staffing and/or shopping outlets, thereby reducing costs.
- You can offer 24 hour shopping at minimum cost.

Home Banking

Most major banks now offer online banking and some are offering only Internet banking. Without the overheads of running and staffing the high street branches they can offer higher rates of interest to customers.

Services Offered Include

- You can pay your bills from the comfort of your home or the workplace.
- It is possible to transfer money immediately to high interest accounts.
- You can check balances and daily transactions on line anytime.
- It is possible to set up direct debits and order stationery on line.

Benefits to the Customer Include

- All services are from the comfort of your home or workplace, 24 hrs a day, 365 days a year.
- Higher interest rates are available to Internet bankers.
- It is easy to shop around on line for the best interest rates and switch funds automatically.

Concerns Include

- Small branches are closing or having opening hours reduced.
- Reductions in staffing at the major banks.
- The move towards banking from your PC, digital TV or mobile phone will only increase these concerns.
- Some customers have worries about security because of possible credit card fraud.

Concerns About the Internet

- The Internet and freedom of speech
- No-one owns the Internet so anybody can post anything on it.
- The Internet is a great source of information but it has also become the home of political propaganda, racism, pornography and other controversial or illegal material.
- Apart from physically restricting access the only control is through some form of filtering software.
- Increasingly individuals and authorities are recommending some sort of control.

Arguments for Control

- To prevent illegal material being readily available, e.g. political propaganda, racism and pornography.
- To prevent young children accessing unsuitable material.
- To make the Web more efficient - at present there is too much useless information.
- To ensure copyright laws are maintained.

Arguments Against Control

- The aim of the Internet is to be a free source of information.
- Unsuitable material is easily available in other ways.
- Control would cost money and users would have to pay.
- Control would be very difficult to enforce.

Internet Crime

New technology brings with it new crimes and as a result some governments are setting up special units to deal with Internet crime. Concerns surround:

- The interception of credit card details and transactions online.
- Hacking into personal, private files with criminal intent.

- Fraudulent web sites taking credit card details from customers.
- The spreading of viruses thorugh the Internet.

Internet Security

A number of steps are being taken to reassure the general public that the Internet is safe:

- Data is encoded before transmission using encryption techniques which scramble the data. The data is then decoded at the receiving end (decryption).
- The use of passwords and access level restrictions.
- The use of firewalls (servers that filter incoming messages to protect LANs from viruses and hacking).
- Tough penalties for offenders under the Computer Misuse Act.

The Future

Increased speed of access combined with digital, satellite and wireless technologies will see Internet use and the resources on offer continue to expand.

In the home digital TV offering Internet access will enable home viewers to shop, bank, play games and send email. At work digital phone lines will offer companies high-speed communication enabling business to be conducted quickly, efficiently and with reduced costs.

Access to video conference links will become commonplace. Wireless technology (WAP) will support mobile phones offering hand-held Internet access.

Pocket-sized units will link email to weather, news, travel, entertainment listings and holiday information.

As connection speeds improve, banking, shopping and video conferencing will take place on the move, in the car on the bus, train or plane.

On the road new systems will be able to pinpoint your car on an onboard computer which will provide access to road and traffic information. Car phones will link to the Internet allowing drivers to check their email.

E LEARNING

DEFINITION OF E-LEARNING

A working definition adapted from the JISC is: 'Learning facilitated and supported through the use of information and communications technology (ICT)'. E-learning includes:

- Delivery of courses.
- On-line assessment.
- Student to student and student to teacher communications.
- Use of Internet resources.
- And other learning activities involving ICT and the Internet.

It can thus be thought of as a continuum, encompassing a broad range of activities across a spectrum from using e-learning for "smarter" learner support, through blended learning (the majority of activity) to learning that is delivered entirely online.

E-learning is a means of education that incorporates self-motivation, communication, efficiency, and technology. Because there is limited social interaction, students must keep themselves motivated. The isolation intrinsic to e-learning requires students to communicate with each other and the instructor frequently to accomplish their assigned tasks. E-learning is efficient as it eliminates distances and subsequent commutes. Distance is eliminated because the e-learning content is designed with media that can be accessed from properly equipped computer terminals, and other means of Internet accessible technology.

E-learning is a flexible term used to describing a means of teaching through technology.

TYPES OF E-LEARNING

The different types of e-learning are based on:

- Means of communication
- Schedule
- E-learning class structure
- Technologies used

E Learning Technology is used to implement instruction is not limited to web-based materials. E-learning can be achieved by utilizing any form of technology that sustains information yielding media. Video/Audio tape, aside from being an obsolete technology is a viable means to implement instruction. More current technology aids the learning experience because there are more means to convey the information. Technology is the most variable element in e-learning. The more advanced the technology becomes, the more options there are to further e-learning. The creation of the Internet subsequently created e-learning, as dial-up connections were replaced by cable modems, speed and bandwidth increased; correlatively the quality of on-line instruction improved because computers were able to support the media. As speed increases and devices become smaller and more mobile; training will become more flexible and further boost the growth and popularity of e-learning.

The topics mentioned previously are not mutually exclusive; they can be used in any combination to create the best instruction possible. Given e-learning's conceptual versatility and advancing technology, e-learning currently has increasingly limitless potential.

EVOLUTION

In the early 1990s, many companies were using videotape-based training for their employees. At this point, the industry "...represented a very small market and lacked the 'scalability' that is so important in today's applications." The idea of putting training on video was a good idea, though it was lacking in a few areas:

- Customization based on needs of users.
- Expensive to maintain.
- Could not be upgraded easily. There is also the issue of employees having to hunt down the proper equipment in order to watch the videos. These videos often had limited interactions which lead to the nearly impossible task of tracking progress and assessment.

Since it was obvious that video was not the best solution, a new form of training evolved, CBT or Computer Based Training. "Windows 3.1, Macintosh, CD-ROMs, PowerPoint marked the technological advancement of the Multimedia Era". CD-ROMs could be cheaply produced so that the problem of checking in and out videos was eliminated. Employees would also be able to simply pop in a CD to their personal computer at their desk and complete the training.

Although the CD-ROM Computer-Based Training made advances toward the better, it still lacked the ability to track employees' performance in a central database and was also not as easy to upgrade. All these problems would disappear with the use of the Internet as a means of delivering content. The problem was, when the content was placed on the web, it was simply text to begin with and maybe a few graphics. "No one really cared about the effectiveness of this new medium – it was just really cool."

People in the field of e-learning began to realise that you simply can not put information on the web without a learning strategy for the users. "...In order for technology to improve learning, it must 'fit' into students' lives...not the other way around. As a result, e-learning was born."

One of the first innovations in actual e-learning was the LMS or Learning Management System. "The first Learning Management Systems (LMS) offered off-the-shelf platforms for front-end registration and course cataloging, and they tracked skills management and reporting on the back-end."

This enabled schools and companies to place courses online and be able to track students' progress, communicate with students effectively and provide a place for real-time discussions.

The eClassroom evolved shortly after, which are "...web-based synchronous events with integrated CBT and simulations." Centra is a great example of an eClassroom that is used quite often today. eClassrooms are often called Live Instructor-Lead Training or ILT. "Live instructor-led training (ILT) via the Web can be combined with real-time mentoring, improved learner services, and up-to-date, engaging "born on the Web" content to create a highly-effective, multi-dimensional learning environment."

E-learning has come a very long way since its early days of being text-based via the Web or CD-ROM. So what does the future hold? There really is no saying where the field is headed. As long as training is continually geared towards the learners and strategies are used in the training, there is no end in sight for e-learning.

ADVANTAGES OF E-LEARNING

E-learning is beneficial to education, corporations and to all types of learners. It is affordable, saves time, and produces measurable results. E-learning is more cost effective than traditional learning because less time and money is spent traveling. Since e-learning can be done in any geographic location and there are no travel expenses, this type of learning is much less costly than doing learning at a traditional institute.

Flexibility is a major benefit of e-learning. E-learning has the advantage of taking class anytime anywhere. Education is available when and where it is needed. E-learning can be done at the office, at home, on the road, 24 hours a day, and seven days a week. . E-learning also has measurable assessments which can be created so the both the instructors and students will know what the students have learned, when they've completed courses, and how they have performed.

Students like e-learning because it accommodates different types of learning styles. Students have the advantage of learning at their own pace. Students can also learn through a variety of activities that apply to many different learning styles learners have. Learners can fit e-learning into their busy schedule. If they hold a job, they can still be working with e-learning. If the learner needs to do the learning at night, then this option is available. Learners can sit in their home in their pajamas and do the learning if they desire.

E-learning encourages students to peruse through information by using hyperlinks and sites on the worldwide Web. Students are able to find information relevant to their personal situations and interest. E-learning allows students to select learning materials that meet their level of knowledge, interest and what they need to know to perform more effectively in an activity. E-learning is more focused on the learner and it is more interesting for the learner because it is information that they want to learn. E-learning is flexible and can be customized to meet the individual needs of the learners.

E-learning helps students develop knowledge of the Internet. This knowledge will help learners throughout their careers. E-learning encourages students to take personal responsibility for their own learning. When learners succeed, it builds self-knowledge and self-confidence in them.

Educators and corporations really benefit from e-learning. Learners enjoy having the opportunity to learn at their own pace, on their own time, and have it less costly.

Advantages of eLearning Experienced by Instructional Developers Include

- Developers can develop training, demonstrating, in very specific details, how to perform a task such as repairing equipment.
- eLearning sets a framework for standardized course delivery.
- Facilitates modifying training and education materials, by using html.
- Allows developers to design once and use the same module in several programs, by using 'template-like' learning objects.
- Promotes the orderly layout of course materials, assignments and general administration through a Web site.

Advantages of eLearning for Training and Education Administrators Include

- eLearning accommodates automated, continuous assessment of student progress.
- Reduces capital costs associated with traditional bricks and mortar schools and training facilities.
- Can be accessed by a variety of platforms such as

Windows, UNIX and Mac because they all read html files.
- Template approach to developing online learning engenders consistency.
- Allows institutions to build the eLearning modules from courses of leading instructors.

DISADVANTAGES OF E-LEARNING

Next we look at the disadvantages of e-learning. One disadvantage of e-learning is that learners need to have access to a computer as well as the Internet. They also need to have computer skills with programs such as word processing, Internet browsers, and e-mail. Without these skills and software it is not possible for the student to succeed in e-learning. E-learners need to be very comfortable using a computer.

Slow Internet connections or older computers may make accessing course materials difficult. This may cause the learners to get frustrated and give up. Another disadvantage of e-learning is managing computer files and online learning software. For learners with beginner-level computer skills it can sometimes seem complex to keep their computer files organized. Without good computer organizational skills learners may lose or misplace reports causing them to be late in submitting assignments. Some of the students also may have trouble installing software that is required for the class.

E-learning also requires just as much time for attending class and completing assignments as any traditional classroom course. This means that students have to be highly motivated and responsible because all the work they do is on their own. Learners with low motivation or bad study habits may fall behind. Another disadvantage of e-learning is that without the routine structures of a traditional class, students may get lost or confused about course activities and deadlines causing the student to fail or do poorly.

Another disadvantage of e-learning is that students may feel isolated from the instructor. Instructions are not always available to help the learner so learners need to have discipline to work independently without the instructor's assistance. E-learners also need to have good writing and communication skills. When instructors and other learners aren't meeting face-to-face it is possible to misinterpret what was meant.

MODES OF E LEARNING

Just as there are many names for e-learning itself (e.g., online learning, web-based training, technology-based learning, etc.), there are many names for *types* of e-learning. For an analogy, consider how you might categorize a movie. Is it a blockbuster or an independent film, a psychological thriller or a comedy, a family film or an adult film, a short film or a long film, a good film or a bad film? It may be all, some, or none of these things. In this way, e-learning products are often segmented dependent on some sampling of their characteristics.

A number of fundamental modes of training or instructional models make up the backbone of valid and valuable training. While these can be used as guides no matter what type of technology is chosen, the specific strengths and weaknesses of a particular training mode should be considered in order to maximize learner benefits.

Tutorials

Tutorials are one of the most ancient and commonly used modes of education. A good tutorial presents information and guidance, makes sure the learner has an opportunity to understand the instruction, and only then continues on to new information. Many tutorials basically consist of a linear presentation of content. When implemented poorly, a tutorial can become what is derisively referred to as "an electronic page-turner," or if web-based, a "scroller."

This type of programme presents content directly without giving the learner any more opportunity to interact other than to call for the next screen. When implemented properly, using the classic principles of instructional systems design, guided tutorials can be engaging and effective. The key to useful tutorials in e-learning are interactions that establish pace, clarify content, provide for practice and instill confidence. Branching can greatly enhance the effectiveness of a tutorial, allowing it to operate in the way that a skilled teacher does.

A question posed following an instructional moment can determine if the student has mastered the content. If mastery is not achieved, one branch is followed and another approach is provided to eliminate confusion. Only after mastery is achieved is the branch containing the next piece of information followed.

Simulations

Simulations are often used to recreate lifelike job situations. Realism is the key to successful simulations but not every element of a simulation has to be realistic in order for it to be instructionally valid. While hearing a telephone ring in the background of an office simulation adds to the depth of the user experience, being able to answer that phone and talk with a customer adds value to the user's learning experience.

The best example of a simulation is the complex flight simulator employed by pilots. More commonly encountered simulations are the scenarios deployed in training classrooms as role-playing exercises within the group.

Current technology enables students to interact with on-screen participants in non-linear, discovery-learning scenarios. Sales calls, customer service scenarios, computer repairs, surgery, and the full responsibility of running a business can all be simulated. Simulations of software functionality are particularly prolific and have well documented learner benefits. Cutting-edge programs now exist using virtual reality that enable students wearing goggles and sensor gloves to actually be immersed in a digitally created environment. The challenge to the trainer is to isolate the elements of a situation that can be controlled and must be mastered by the learner in reality and put the learner in control of these elements in the simulation. All the realism in the world cannot make a simulation a valuable learning tool without the elements of guidance, remediation, or feedback.

True simulations and simulation-based drill and practice

exercises have in common the ability to reveal a learner's actions and reactions in a realistic, protected environment where time and distance are collapsed. In sales call simulations learners can try out various sales approaches without the jeopardy of awkward social situations.

Electronic Performance Support Systems

Electronic performance support systems (EPSSs) are created to give an individual the tool they need to perform a required task at the time they need it. A performance support system is in a way the opposite of a tutorial. Where a tutorial instructs the learner and then requires that the learner perform, a performance support system requires the learner to determine when they need assistance and then ask for the required guidance. The most ubiquitous example of a performance support system is the "Help" feature built into Microsoft's Office applications. A simple example of a non-e-learning performance support tool is an inventory checklist created for a grocery clerk.

A growing consensus in the industry is that e-learning should include imbedded support systems that provide instant guidance at the time and place of need. With the advent of Web-based training and the emergence of the hyperlink paradigm, the convergence of e-learning and electronic performance support systems is almost complete. Web-based tutorials can be completed independently as learning exercises for new users and yet be delivered as just-in-time chunks of information and interactive tools at the desktop.

The challenge of creating useful performance support systems obviously consists of determining what tools are needed by a population and providing those tools. In the context of e-learning, the further challenge is creating systems that allow an individual needing a tool to recognize that such a tool exists and then be able to use that tool.

Instructional Games

The inclusion of games has often been a hitch in getting management to agree to e-learning initiatives. Many learning theories contend, though, that games are essential to the learning exhibited by children and can be usefully extended into the realm of adult learning. Games can have great value, possibly greater value than any other mode of instruction, in reducing learner tension and increasing learner engagement. The reluctance toward employing games to teach is becoming less apparent as supervisors are educated in learning theory and many who have experience in gaming for educational purpose move into management roles.

Games in the style of TV game shows have long been used in the classroom to provide a fun and effective method for reinforcement and self-assessment. Instructional games are equally effective using the latest computer technologies. Games can run the gamut from simple speed and accuracy typing exercises to complex business simulators where a student might run an entire factory. Instructional games can also replicate classic, arcade, and game show styles such as tic-tac-toe, auto racing, and Jeopardy(TM).

The defining characteristic of instructional games is a set of goals or a competitor to provide motivation in addition to the learning. For maximum success, the motivational element of the game should run parallel to the overall motivation for the training. The game should have has instructional value aligned with the objectives of the overall course. There is little merit to using games as a reward for completing learning objectives exterior to the games themselves.

Tests, Record Keeping, and Guidance

Automated assessments are another commonly used facet of e-learning. When companies first adopt e-learning initiatives, testing and record-keeping systems are often accepted earlier than programs that integrate multiple training modes, due to their ease of implementation and their quickly recognizable returns.

Online tests can be used for self-assessment purposes, or can be computer graded and reported back to central administration. The explosion of enterprisewide networks now provides the power to assess thousands of individuals and track their progress against specific job competencies throughout their life within an organization. The latest and most sophisticated technology-based tests are tightly linked to learning objectives, which in turn can help create a completely personalized curriculum.

Combining the Modes

Maximum learner benefit can be typically achieved by combining several training modes in one project. The merit of each mode varies with training goals and some modes are ill suited to meet some needs. A solid and frequent model is to use tutorials to teach basic knowledge and concepts, use simulations for reinforcement and application of the knowledge (leading to skills), test or certify the comprehension, and finally provide an on-the-job performance support tool to aid in recall and application.

Unit IX

Science Teacher

INTRODUCTION

A Teacher who teaches courses in science has to be specialize in a field of science subjects, such as the design and function of science topics and chapters or operations and research analysis. Include both teachers primarily engaged in teaching and those who do a combination of both teaching and research.

For science teachers, the challenge of becoming and remaining exemplary educators is hampered by systems of pre-service education and teacher certification that are profoundly disconnected from the discipline of computer science and the needs of teachers and students. This white paper addresses a number of aspects of the crisis in high school computer science teacher certification. It includes a comprehensive description of the issues relating to certification, a review of the relevant research literature, a selection of examples of current teacher certification models, and a set of recommendations for a multi-level model that will provide detailed requirements for educators from multiple pathways, including new teachers, teachers from other disciplines with computer science experience, teachers with no computer science experience, and people transitioning to teaching from business and industry. *Click the image to download.*

AIM

Candidates interested to teach science subjects in schools

following ICSE/CBSE/State Syllabus are ready to work on a full time basis as per the school timings. Candidate should have good knowledge on science subjects. Selected candidates will be on the roles of the company and undergo one month training programme provided by the company. Candidates undergoing training need to take demo sessions both theory and practical and will be placed in schools based on their performance and location.

Postsecondary teachers are expected to grow by 23 per cent between 2006 and 2016, much faster than the average for all occupations. Because of the size of this occupation and its much faster than average growth rate, postsecondary teachers will account for 382,000 new jobs, which is among the largest number of new jobs for an occupation. Projected growth in the occupation will be primarlly due to increases in college and university enrollment over the next decade. This enrollment growth stems mainly from the expected increase in the population of 18- to 24-year-olds, who constitute the majority of students at postsecondary institutions, and from the increasing number of high school graduates who choose to attend these institutions. Adults returning to college to enhance their career prospects or to update their skills also will continue to create new opportunities for postsecondary teachers, particularly at community colleges and for-profit institutions that cater to working adults. However, many postsecondary educational institutions receive a significant portion of their funding from State and local governments, so expansion of public higher education will be limited by State and local budgets.

A significant number of openings in this occupation will be created by growth in enrollments and the need to replace the large numbers of postsecondary teachers who are likely to retire over the next decade. Many postsecondary teachers were hired to teach members of the baby boom generation, and they are expected to retire in growing numbers in the years ahead. As a result, Ph.D. recipients seeking jobs as postsecondary teachers will experience favorable job prospects over the next decade.

Although competition will remain tight for tenure-track positions at 4-year colleges and universities, there will be available a considerable number of part-time or renewable, term appointments at these institutions and at community colleges. Opportunities for master's degree holders are also expected to be favorable because there will be considerable growth at community colleges, career education programs, and other institutions that employ them.

Opportunities for graduate teaching assistants are expected to be very good, reflecting expectations of higher undergraduate enrollments coupled with more modest increases in graduate student enrollment. Constituting almost 9 per cent of all postsecondary teachers, graduate teaching assistants play an integral role in the postsecondary education system, and they are expected to continue to do so in the future. Teachers are licensed to teach in early pre-school grades, the elementary grades, and the middle grades. Teachers should also be licensed to teach secondary education subjects and special subjects including music. All states require that a teacher had finished a bachelor's degree and have had some training in teaching. Another requirement is that they should have finished a prescribed number of units in education. In addition, some also requires teachers to undergo a supervised teaching and have finished a prescribed number of teaching subjects. There are also some states that require teachers to have technology training and still some states had set a minimum limit on what your minimum grade point average should be. Meanwhile, some states also have a far stricter rule in their requirements than others, for example, in some states; a master's degree is a necessity after you had been given a teaching position. You should attain a master's degree within a specified number of years.

But the overall, the requirements for almost all of the states in America require that you have the basic skills and competencies in your chosen field including your proficiency in reading and writing but most especially in teaching. You should also have the needed expertise and knowledge in your chosen subject. Most schools are now in the process of executing a performance-based system as the basis for the said licensure. This system is an addition to passing the licensure examination in their chosen subject. You should demonstrate proficiency in teaching your subject. And your teaching performance should be acceptable as well. You should also note that some states have reciprocal agreements that lets teachers from one state to become licensed in another if that is what is agreed upon by the local government.

There is a shortage of mathematics and science teachers in most states, because of this problem, some states had come up with a method to entice people with a bachelor's degree but don't have the pre-requisite education units to become a teacher. This method is called the alternative licensure programs, this programme will enable people with a bachelor's degree to teach in their major. For example, if you are a math major, you can already become a teacher without any education units if your state implements this programme.

There are also other programs that try to fill up some vacancy in both urban and rural areas, and because of this, teachers that had difficulty in passing their licensure programs are provided with an alternative. One alternative is for teachers to take up only the course they failed or lack and they can become licensed. Some states even issue an emergency license if there is a severe shortage of teachers. But for teachers who really need to be licensed, there are other options like taking up a master's degree in education, taking up this course will grant a prospective teacher a license in teaching.

QUALIFICATION

There are varied requirements you must meet in order to become a teacher in India. Some states also have more strict training and qualifications that are required for you to be able to teach on their state. But the general requirement throughout the Country is that you need to have a license to teach in public schools. Generally though, a license is not required for you to teach in a private school. The teaching license is given by the State Board of Education as a rule even though a licensure committee is likewise able to provide the said license.

Employment of postsecondary teachers is expected to grow much faster than average as student enrollments continue to increase. However, a significant proportion of these new jobs will be part-time and non-tenure-track positions. Retirements of current postsecondary teachers should create numerous openings for all types of postsecondary teachers, so job opportunities are generally expected to be very good, although they will vary by the subject taught and the type of educational institution.

Overall Experience

Extensive skill, knowledge, and experience are needed for these occupations. Many require more than five years of experience. For example, surgeons must complete four years of medical school and up to an additional five to seven years of specialized medical training to do their job.

Education

At a minimum, a bachelor's degree is required for these occupations. However, many also require a graduate school degree such as a Master's, Ph.D., M.D., or J.D. (law degree).

Job Training

Employees may need some on-the-job training, but most of these occupations require that you already have the necessary skills, knowledge, work-related experience, and/or training.

QUALITIES

- Having Strong knowledge of subject areas in Science combined with a broad subject background enabling contributions to teaching programme.
- Excellent interpersonal, oral and written communication skills.
- Proven record of ability to conduct high quality research which is reflected in the authorship of high quality publications, and other research outputs, in the areas of computer science.

- Proven record of ability to manage time and work to strict deadlines.
- Exceptional ability to teach and to supervise academic work by undergraduates, masters, students.
- In-depth ability to work collaboratively.
- Great ability to perform research in science.
- Solid commitment to academic research, high quality teaching and fostering a positive l earning environment for students, continuous professional development, and to public communication.
- Strong ability to present technical material in a logical, coherent and interesting manner to students and specialists.
- Teach at undergraduate and graduate and master level in areas allocated by the Centre Manager and reviewed from time to time by the Centre Manager.
- Engage with the broader scholarly and professional communities.
- Supervise or assist with supervision of various Corporate Training in Software Engineering and QA Testing.
- Contribute to the development, planning and implementation of a high quality curriculum.
- Assist in the development of learning materials, preparing schemes of work and maintaining records to monitor student progress, achievement and attendance.
- Participate in departmental and faculty seminars aimed at sharing research outcomes and building interdisciplinary collaboration within and outside the department.
- Provide pastoral care and support to students.
- Maintained student attendance records, grades, and other required records.
- Prepared and delivered lectures to undergraduate and graduate students on topics such as physics, chemistry biology.

- Prepared and Delivered the lectures to Corporate people on topics such as Practical approach of science.
- Prepared course materials such as syllabi, homework assignments, and handouts.
- Kept abreast of developments in their field by reading current technology, talking with colleagues, and participating in professional conferences.
- Initiated, facilitated, and moderated classroom discussions.
- Supervised students' laboratory work.

TRAINING OF SCIENCE TEACHER

The training of Science Subjects is required in order to learn many thing what will be required in School as well as with dealing students. Following thing should be known to a Science Teacher:

TASKS

- Evaluate and grade students' class work, laboratory work, assignments, and papers.
- Maintain student attendance records, grades, and other required records.
- Prepare and deliver lectures to undergraduate or graduate students on topics such as programming, data structures, and software design.
- Prepare course materials such as syllabi, homework assignments, and handouts.
- Compile, administer, and grade examinations or assign this work to others.
- Keep abreast of developments in the field by reading current literature, talking with colleagues, and participating in professional conferences.
- Initiate, facilitate, and moderate classroom discussions.
- Plan, evaluate, and revise curricula, course content, and course materials and methods of instruction.
- Supervise students' laboratory work.

- Maintain regularly scheduled office hours to advise and assist students.

KNOWLEDGE

Science Subjects: Knowledge of diagrams, explanations, description, quizzes.

Education and Training: Knowledge of principles and methods for curriculum and training design, teaching and instruction for individuals and groups, and the measurement of training effects.

English Language: Knowledge of the structure and content of the English language including the meaning and spelling of words, rules of composition, and grammar.

Mathematics: Knowledge of arithmetic, algebra, geometry, calculus, statistics, and their applications.

Telecommunications: Knowledge of transmission, broadcasting, switching, control, and operation of telecommunications systems.

Engineering and Technology: Knowledge of the practical application of engineering science and technology. This includes applying principles, techniques, procedures, and equipment to the design and production of various goods and services.

Customer and Personal Service: Knowledge of principles and processes for providing customer and personal services. This includes customer needs assessment, meeting quality standards for services, and evaluation of customer satisfaction.

Communications and Media: Knowledge of media production, communication, and dissemination techniques and methods. This includes alternative ways to inform and entertain via written, oral, and visual media.

SKILLS

Instructing: Teaching others how to do something.

Critical Thinking: Using logic and reasoning to identify the strengths and weaknesses of alternative solutions, conclusions or approaches to problems.

Speaking: Talking to others to convey information effectively.

Learning Strategies: Selecting and using training/ instructional methods and procedures appropriate for the situation when learning or teaching new things.

Reading Comprehension: Understanding written sentences and paragraphs in work related documents.

Active Learning: Understanding the implications of new information for both current and future problem-solving and decision-making.

Active Listening: Giving full attention to what other people are saying, taking time to understand the points being made, asking questions as appropriate, and not interrupting at inappropriate times.

Complex Problem Solving: Identifying complex problems and reviewing related information to develop and evaluate options and implement solutions.

Writing: Communicating effectively in writing as appropriate for the needs of the audience.

Time Management: Managing one's own time and the time of others.

ABILITIES

Oral Expression: The ability to communicate information and ideas in speaking so others will understand.

Speech Clarity: The ability to speak clearly so others can understand you.

Written Comprehension: The ability to read and understand information and ideas presented in writing.

Oral Comprehension: The ability to listen to and understand information and ideas presented through spoken words and sentences.

Deductive Reasoning: The ability to apply general rules to specific problems to produce answers that make sense.

Inductive Reasoning: The ability to combine pieces of information to form general rules or conclusions (includes finding a relationship among seemingly unrelated events).

Written Expression: The ability to communicate information and ideas in writing so others will understand.

Information Ordering: The ability to arrange things or actions in a certain order or pattern according to a specific rule or set of rules (e.g., patterns of numbers, letters, words, pictures, mathematical operations).

Near Vision: The ability to see details at close range (within a few feet of the observer).

Problem Sensitivity: The ability to tell when something is wrong or is likely to go wrong. It does not involve solving the problem, only recognizing there is a problem.

WORK ACTIVITIES

Interacting With Computers: Using computers and computer systems (including hardware and software) to programme, developing contents in Science.

Training and Teaching Others: Identifying the educational needs of others, developing formal educational or training programs or classes, and teaching or instructing others.

Updating and Using Relevant Knowledge: Keeping up-to-date technically and applying new knowledge to your job.

Getting Information: Observing, receiving, and otherwise obtaining information from all relevant sources.

Thinking Creatively: Developing, designing, or creating new applications, ideas, relationships, systems, or products, including artistic contributions.

Communicating with Supervisors: Peers, or Subordinates: Providing information to supervisors, co-workers, and subordinates by telephone, in written form, e-mail, or in person.

Interpreting the Meaning of Information for Others: Translating or explaining what information means and how it can be used.

Making Decisions and Solving Problems: Analyzing information and evaluating results to choose the best solution and solve problems.

Processing Information: Compiling, coding, categorizing, calculating, tabulating, auditing, or verifying information or data.

Coaching and Developing Others: Identifying the developmental needs of others and coaching, mentoring, or otherwise helping others to improve their knowledge or skills.

WORK CONTEXT

Electronic Mail: How often do you use electronic mail in this job?

Indoors, Environmentally Controlled: How often does this job require working indoors in environmentally controlled conditions?

Freedom to Make Decisions: How much decision making freedom, without supervision, does the job offer?

Face-to-Face Discussions: How often do you have to have face-to-face discussions with individuals or teams in this job?

Structured versus Unstructured Work: To what extent is this job structured for the worker, rather than allowing the worker to determine tasks, priorities, and goals?

Public Speaking: How often do you have to perform public speaking in this job?

Contact With Others: How much does this job require the worker to be in contact with others (face-to-face, by telephone, or otherwise) in order to perform it?

Telephone: How often do you have telephone conversations in this job?

Coordinate or Lead Others: How important is it to coordinate or lead others in accomplishing work activities in this job?

Importance of Being Exact or Accurate: How important is being very exact or highly accurate in performing this job?

CLASSROOM CONDITIONS

OVERVIEW

Classroom conditions should not be confused with classroom culture or climate.

Certain classroom conditions are needed to enhance teaching and learning and could also enhance a positive classroom culture and climate, e.g.:

- Authentic relationships, based on quality, openness

and consistency which influence existing relationships in class
- Rules and boundaries, set by the educator, which inform learners what is expected of them in class
- Planning, resources and preparation, which include planning for a diverse group of learners, access to Learning and Teaching Support Material and the ability to use Learning And Teaching Support Material creatively in a variety of ways
- Educator repertoire, the variety of teaching styles and models the educator feels comfortable with and can apply in class in different contexts, with diverse learners to achieve the outcomes as stated in the Revised National Curriculum Statement
- Pedagogic partnerships, meaning the educator's ability to forge professional relationships with colleagues in order to better their own teaching practice
- Reflection on teaching, which points to the ability of the educator to reflect on own practice and to try out new styles and models recommended by other educators.

It is evident from the previous paragraphs that a positive classroom culture and climate could play a positive role in building a productive classroom. A positive classroom culture and climate conducive to an effective learning classroom requires however, classroom management practices to direct and manage the development of a productive classroom.

Classroom management is at the heart of the educator's work. The educator must be able to organize and manage learners in a confined space in order to enable learners to feel safe and concentrate on tasks.

Classroom management can be explained as:"what teachers do once they have considered their organization in order to ensure both the smooth running of the learning environment and fulfillment of intentions."

A classroom management includes all the activities needed for the main task, namely teaching and learning, to happen effectively. It deals with management of tasks as well as people. Effective classroom management helps to establish and maintain conditions in the classroom which enhances effective teaching and learning.

To succeed at this an educator will need good skills in long-term planning as well as short-term planning.

Unit X

Evaluation and its Statistic

TYPES OF TEST

CONSTRUCTION TESTING

This is used to describe the types of tests that follow how a unit or a component is constructed. There are several types of Construction tests:

Single Step Test: Most commonly found in integrated development environments where the developer steps through the programme using single steps and watches in a separate window key variables and how they change.

Bench Test: This is usually informal and carried out by the developer. It covers testing of a special feature just implemented. For example, a developer will setup a new button to print a single record. It can then be tested "on the bench" to see if it is working properly.

Unit Test: This tests a software unit independently from the rest of the system. A software unit can be an entry screen, a class component, an update procedure, etc. The behaviour of units is usually contained and can be subjected to different types of testing to be discussed later such as White or Black box testing.

Component Test: This is not to be confused with components currently known in the industry as COMs and relate to classes that are separately developed and accessed from different units. Components in this sense are groups of units or components that function together at a higher level than single units. For example, a unit could be the payment voucher posting screen. Others could be the receipt voucher, the journal voucher, the adjustment voucher, the debit note, etc.

The Component being tested may then be "all accounting transactions" or "all maintenance of employee allowances". It is assumed that unit testing would have been completed and that component testing is a streamlining test to ensure common behaviour.

SYSTEM TESTING

This takes place when all necessary units and components have been tested and released internally. System testing covers the behaviour of the whole system and encompasses all external software, hardware, operating environments, etc.

System testing is commonly known as QA Testing: This may be a misnomer because QA Testing involves a lot more as was mentioned earlier. However, the term has a meaning if System Testing is understood as a procedure to be carried out by third parties outside the development unit.

System testing consists of the following types of tests:

Integration Tests: Focuses on the functionality and stability of a system when all its units and components have been tested and passed. This is especially critical when the system is to be interfaced with other systems particularly third party systems.

Feature Tests: Focuses on specific features that may require full testing or additional testing. This is the type of test that traces back to the Requirements Definition Document.

Use Case tests: Since the UML models a system by its functions using Use Cases, the traceability of the Use Cases as identified in the very early Requirements Analysis and through to Technical Specifications allows the developers and QA Unit to specify tests based on Use Cases.

Release tests: Covers such requirements as installation, distribution and downloading from websites, etc.

Acceptance tests: Covers testing as per the delivery and acceptance criteria specified in agreement or contracts, internal or external.

Parallel Runs

These are actual runs of the system which are compared with the previous version be it manual or an earlier version of the same system. During this kind of test, key results are compared as it is not always possible to compare all results since the new system would include features not available in the earlier system.

SPECIAL TYPES OF TESTS

The following are special types of tests that take place under very specific conditions:

Regression Tests

when a system has been tested or is already operational and a feature is redeveloped, repaired or upgraded, that system may need to be retested from the start to ensure that it is still operating as required. This is known as regression testing.

Performance Tests

These are tests that cover the requirements placed on a system to perform within certain response parameters, loads and volumes. Performance testing is presented as a Standard Operating Procedure (SOP) in the Quality Management segment. The segment can be downloaded from OMSAR's website for ICT Standards and

Stress Tests

Much like the medical test from which it gets its name, stress testing tries the system under extreme conditions. It is not always performance that is being tested. Many systems fail because insufficient field lengths are used. Some fail because the database has a limited number of indices, records, etc. Stress testing investigates such "limits".

Configuration Tests

This type of testing evaluates the system behaviour under different types of configurations. There may be different network patterns, configuration settings, peripherals or even platforms. For example, if a system promises to run properly under both Oracle and Microsoft SQL Server, this type of testing ensures that the system works well with both database engines.

Compatibility Tests

This type of testing evaluates the system behaviour under different types of operating environments. It may be considered as similar to Configuration Testing, but it is more focused in scope. For example, a Microsoft Windows application can be tested for compatibility under both Arabic and English versions of Windows 2000 Professional and Windows XP Professional.

ACHIEVEMENT TEST

GENERAL STEPS

- Identify and define the learning outcomes to be measured.
- Prepare test specifications.
- Construct relevant test items.
- Review and edit the items.
- Arrange the items in the test.
- Prepare directions.

Step 1

- Identify and Define Learning Objectives (Outcomes).
- Begin each General Objective with one of the six cognitive domain headings of Bloom's Taxonomy.
- State the Specific Objectives.
- For each G.O., develop 3-5 Specific Objectives.
- Begin each S.O. with an action verb.

Step 2

Preparing Test Specifications

- Select the Specific Outcomes to be tested
- Outline the subject matter by listing topic and subtopic areas in the lesson plan.

- Make a two-way Table of Specifications.

Step 3

Construct Relevant Test Items and Consider:

- Selecting the type of test items to use.
- Selection Type Items (e.g., multiple choice, true-false, matching, interpretive exercises.
- Supply Type Items (e.g., short answer, essay (restricted response), essay (extended response).
- Matching items to Specific Objectives.
- For each S.O., write one or more related items.

Nature of Multiple-Choice Items

- Parts of an Item:
  - Stem - the question or incomplete sentence.
  - Alternatives - the choices.
  - Distractors - the incorrect choices.

Uses Of Multiple-Choice Items

- Knowledge Items.
  - Measures the degree to which material is remembered.
- Comprehension Items.
  - Measures the degree to which material is remembered and understood.
- Application Items.
  - Measures the degree to which material is remembered, understood, and can be applied.

Writing Multiple-Choice Items

General Rules

Nothing in the item should prevent an informed student from answering correctly.

Nothing in the item should increase the probability that an uninformed student will answer correctly.

True-False Items

- Students identify whether a statement of fact is correct.

- Most effective when there are only two possible responses.

Variations of True-False Items

- Supply-Type.
  - For statements that are false, the student must underline the part of the statement that is false and change the false statement so it is true.
- Cluster-Type.
  - The student judges whether a series of items based on a common stem are true or false.

Matching Items

- When the same alternatives are repeated in several multiple-choice items, combine in a matching item.

Parts of A Matching Item

Premises: A series of stems.
Responses: A series of alternative answers.
Interpretive Exercises.

- An introductory paragraph, table, chart, graph, map or picture is provided and the student answers a series of items related to specific objectives.

Types of Supply-Type Items

Short-Answer Items.
Restricted-Response Essay.
Extended-Response Essay.
Short-Answer Items

- Requires the student to supply the appropriate words, numbers or symbols to complete a statement.

Restricted-Response Essays

- The student supplies a response to a narrowly defined problem and directions.

Extended-Response Essays

- Student supplies a response to a problem with few boundaries.

Guidelines for Effective and Fair Grading

- Inform students of grading procedures
- Base grades on student achievement only
- Base grades on a variety of valid assessment data
- When combining scores, use proper weighting

Select an appropriate frame of reference (I.e., absolute or relative)

ACHIEVEMENT TEST

Any test designed to evaluate a person's current state of knowledge or skill. Contrast with aptitude test, which is designed to evaluate potentialities for achievement independent of current knowledge.

Achievement tests are exams that are designed to determine the degree of knowledge and proficiency exhibited by an individual in a specific area or set of areas. An achievement test is sometimes administered as part of the acceptance process into an educational programme or to qualify an individual for employment or a promotion with a current employer.

In other applications, the achievement test serves as a tool to measure current knowledge levels for the purpose of placing students in an educational environment where they have the chance to advance at a pace that is suitable for their abilities.

It is not unusual for public school systems to utilize achievement testing to identify students who are prepared to move on to more advanced courses of study or who need some type of remedial instruction.

The idea behind using an achievement test format to measure the grade level for each student is not intended to reflect on the general intelligence of the individual. Rather, the purpose of the testing is to ensure each student is placed in a classroom situation where there is the best opportunity for learn and assimilate data in an organized fashion that prepares them for moving on to more advanced material.

For example, a student who does not do well with basic mathematics on an achievement test is likely to be placed in a remedial learning situation. Doing so provides the student with the opportunity to master the basics before attempting to learn more advanced mathematical concepts like algebra or geometry. At a later date, the student will have the chance to take a second test; should the results indicate that the student is sufficiently prepared to move on to something more complicated, he or she can be reassigned to a more challenging course of study.

While utilized widely, not all educators universally support tests of achievement. Proponents point to the success of the tests in placing students into learning situations that are more in line with their current level of knowledge rather than overwhelming them with additional information that they may or may not be able to assimilate. Individuals and groups that oppose the use of an achievement test claim that the exams are not structured in a manner that accounts for the general aptitude of each student, resulting in the creation of an overall learning environment.

BLUE PRINT

BLUEPRINTING

Blueprint is a lightweight way to manage releases of your software and to track the progress of features and ideas, from initial concept to implementation. Using Blueprint, you can encourage contributions from right across your project's community, while targeting the best ideas to future releases.

With very little administrative overhead, Blueprint helps you to create a roadmap for your project and shepherd individual features through to release.

To enable Blueprint for your project, follow the Change details link on your project overview page and select the This project uses Blueprint option.

Blue print is the older method, invented in 1842. The drawing to be copied, drawn on translucent paper, is placed against paper sensitized with a mixture of ferric ammonium citrate and potassium ferricyanide. The sensitized paper is then exposed to light. Where the areas of the sensitized paper are not obscured by the drawing, the light makes the two chemicals react to form blue. The exposed paper is then washed in water. This produces a negative image, with the drawing appearing in white against a dark blue background.

In the diazotype method, the paper is light-sensitized with a mixture of a diazonium salt (used in the manufacture of dyes), a reactant, and an acid that keeps the diazonium salt and the reactant from reacting with each other. The semi-transparent original is placed on top of the sensitized paper, and a copy of the same size as the original is made by direct contact. Light destroys the diazonium salt. Ammonia gas or solution is used as a developer after exposure — it neutralizes the acid and allows the remaining diazonium salt to combine with the reactant to create a blue dye. The chemicals on the paper acquire colour only in the areas not exposed to light. This diazotype method produces dark lines on a white background, and is the popular method used today for reproduction of large-format drawings.

A blueprint is a simple specification. It describes an idea - such as a feature or process - and tracks enough metadata to show its implementation status and who's involved.

Let's take a look at what information makes up a blueprint:

- *Title and summary*: some ideas are simple enough to express fully in the summary.
- *Link to further information:* this can be any URL and is usually a wiki page where the idea or feature is fully explored. Launchpad doesn't provide a wiki facility.
- *People*: who's working on this blueprint? You can optionally track the person drafting the blueprint, the assignee and the reviewer.
- *Drafting status*: how well has this been discussed? Is it still just an idea or is it ready to code?
- Implementation status.
- *Related bugs*: link to any bug reports tracked in Launchpad that will be fixed or otherwise affected by this feature.
- *Code branches*: while you're working on the

implementation, you can upload/register branches your code branches in Launchpad and link to them from the blueprint.

- *Subscribers*: people can subscribe to receive email updates when the blueprint changes.
- *Dependencies*: which other blueprints must be implemented before this one?

Launchpad Blueprint leaves you to manage your project in the way that you want. It imposes no project management structure but instead makes it easy for you, and your project's community, to suggest, develop and implement ideas and features.

PEOPLE: ROLES AND RESPONSIBILITIES

We saw above that there are certain roles associated with each blueprint. Anyone can take any of these roles and anyone can set who is in any of those roles for a particular blueprint. That makes it very easy for members of your community to suggest new features and track their progress for everyone else to see, without requiring special permission.

However, to allow projects to plan future releases, Launchpad restricts who can prioritise and target blueprints and bugs. As you'd expect, the project-group and project owner have these permissions but Launchpad also allows owners to grant them to other individuals and teams. They take role that, in effect, is a release manager and that Launchpad calls the "driver".

DRIVERS

Drivers come in three flavours:

- project group
- project/distribution
- project/distribution series.

Each driver's permission to target and prioritise trickles down the hierarchy, so, for example, project-group drivers also have driver permissions for each project within the group and each series in each of those projects.

As a project-group, project or distribution owner, you can

set drivers by following the Appoint driver link on the relevant project-group, project, distribution or series overview page.

TARGETING WORK

Launchpad Blueprint helps you to plan future release with two tools:

- Milestones: points in time, such as a future release or development sprint
- Series goals: a statement of intention to work on the blueprint for a particular series.

Although only drivers can target blueprints to milestones and set them as series goals, anyone can propose a blueprint as a series goal. As a driver or owner, you can review proposed goals by following the Set goals link on your project's Blueprint overview page.

YOUR PROJECT ROADMAP

As we saw earlier, you can tell Launchpad which other blueprints must be implemented before the blueprint you're working on.

Launchpad uses this information to recommend the order in which you might implement your project's blueprints. Take a look at the Ubuntu roadmap for an example.

SUBSCRIBING TO BLUEPRINTS

By following the Subscribe yourself link on a blueprint page, you can ask Launchpad to send you email notification of any changes to the blueprint. In most cases, you'll receive notification only of changes made to the blueprint itself in Launchpad and not to any further information, such as in an external wiki.

However, if the wiki software supports email change notifications, Launchpad can even notify you of changes to the wiki page.

If you're a blueprint owner and want Launchpad to know about updates to the related wiki page, ask the wiki admin how to send email notifications. Notifications should go to notifications@specs.launchpad.net.

SPRINTS

Many free software projects find that face to face meetings are a useful opportunity to make plans. They're also usually a great way to get to know your fellow project members.

Launchpad helps you plan development sprints by:

- Allowing you to register and publicise the meeting
- Track who's attending and allow people to register their intention to attend
- Mark specific blueprints for discussion at a meeting, thereby creating an agenda.

As a meeting organiser, you can download a file of all the attendees. When subscribing to a blueprint, individuals can request that they're listed as an attendee of any meeting at which that blueprint is discussed by selecting the Participation essential option.

PRINCIPLE OF TEST CONSTRUCTION

Writing items requires a decision about the nature of the item or question to which we ask students to respond, that is, whether discreet or integrative, how we will score the item; for example, objectively or subjectively, the skill we purport to test, and so on. We also consider the characteristics of the test takers and the test taking strategies respondents will need to use. What follows is a short description of these considerations for constructing items.

TEST ITEMS

A test *item* is a specific task test takers are asked to perform.Test items can assess one or more points or objectives, and the actual item itself may take on a different constellation depending on the context. For example, an item may test one point (understaning of a given vocabulary word) or several points (the ability to obtain facts from a passage and then make inferences based on the facts). Likewise, a given objective may be tested by a series of items. For example, there could be five items all testing one grammatical point. Items of a similar kind may also be grouped together to form *subtests* within a given test.

CLASSIFYING ITEMS

Discrete

A completely discrete-point item would test simply one point or objective such as testing for the meaning of a word in isolation. For example:

Choose the correct meaning of the word *paralysis*.

- Inability to move
- State of unconscious
- State of shock
- Being in pain

Integrative

An integrative item would test more than one point or objective at a time.

For example:

Demonstrate your comprehension of the following words by using them together in a written paragraph: "paralysis," "accident," and "skiing."

Sometimes an integrative item is really more a procedure than an item, as in the case of a free composition, which could test a number of objectives; for example, use of appropriate vocabulary, use of sentence level discourse, organization, statement of thesis and supporting evidence. For example:

Write a one-page essay describing three sports and the relative likelihood of being injured while playing them competitively.

Objective

A multiple-choice item, for example, is objective in that there is only one right answer.

Subjective

A free composition may be more subjective in nature if the scorer is not looking for any one right answer, but rather for a series of factors (creativity, style, cohesion and coherence, grammar, and mechanics).

Writing items requires a decision about the nature of the

item or question to which we ask students to respond, that is, whether discreet or integrative, how we will score the item; for example, objectively or subjectively, the skill we purport to test, and so on.

We also consider the characteristics of the test takers and the test taking strategies respondents will need to use. What follows is a short description of these considerations for constructing items.

THE SKILL TESTED

The language skills that we test include the more receptive skills on a continuum – listening and reading, and the more *productive* skills – speaking and writing. There are, of course, other language skills that cross-cut these four skills, such as vocabulary. Assessing vocabulary will most likely vary to a certain extent across the four skills, with assessment of vocabulary in listening and reading – perhaps covering a broader range than assessment of vocabulary in speaking and writing. We can also assess nonverbal skills, such as gesturing, and this can be both receptive (interpreting someone else's gestures) and productive (making one's own gestures).

THE INTELLECTUAL OPERATION

Items may require test takers to employ different levels of intellectual operation in order to produce a response. Following levels of intellectual operation have been identified:

- Knowledge (bringing to mind the appropriate material);
- Comprehension (understanding the basic meaning of the material);
- Application (applying the knowledge of the elements of language and comprehension to how they interrelate in the production of a correct oral or written message);
- Analysis (breaking down a message into its constituent parts in order to make explicit the relationships between ideas, including tasks like recognizing the connotative meanings of words and

correctly processing a dictation, and making inferences);

- Synthesis (arranging parts so as to produce a pattern not clearly there before, such as in effectively organizing ideas in a written composition); and
- Evaluation (making quantitative and qualitative judgments about material).

It has been popularly held that these levels demand increasingly greater cognitive control as one moves from knowledge to evaluation – that, for example, effective operation at more advanced levels, such as synthesis and evaluation, would call for more advanced control of the second language. Yet this has not necessarily been borne out by research. The truth is that what makes items difficult, sometimes defies the intuitions of the test constructors.

THE TESTED RESPONSE BEHAVIOUR

Items can also assess different types of response behaviour. Respondents may be tested for accuracy in pronunciation or grammar. Likewise, they could be assessed for fluency, for example, without concern for grammatical correctness. Aside from accuracy and fluency, respondents could also be assessed for speed – namely, how quickly they can produce a response, to determine how effectively the respondent replies under time pressure.

In recent years, there has also been an increased concern for developing measures of performance – that is, measures of the ability to perform real-world tasks, with criteria for successful performance based on a needs analysis for the given task.

Performance tasks might include "comparing credit card offers and arguing for the best choice" or "maximizing the benefits from a given dating service." At the same time that there is a call for tasks that are more reflective of the real world, there is a commensurate concern for more *authentic* language assessment. At least one study, however, notes that the differences between authentic and pedagogic written and spoken texts may not be readily apparent, even to an audience specifically listening for differences. In addition, test takers may not necessarily concern themselves with task authenticity in a test situation. Test familiarity may be the overriding factor affecting performance.

CHARACTERISTICS OF RESPONDENTS

Items can be designed to be appropriate for groups of test-takers with differing characteristics.

- The personal characteristics of the respondents – for example, their age, gender, and native language;
- The knowledge of the topic that they bring to the language testing situation;
- Their affective schemata (that is, their prior likes and dislikes with regard to assessment); and
- Their language ability.

Research into the impact of these characteristics continues. For example, with regard to the age variable, researchers have suggested that educators revisit this issue and perhaps conceive of new ways to consider the impact of the age variable in assessing language ability.

With regard to performance on language measures, it would appear that age interacts with other variables such as attitudes, motivation, the length of exposure to the target language, as well as the nature and quality of language instruction.

With regard to language ability, detail the many types of knowledge that respondents may need to draw on to perform well on a given item or task:

- World knowledge and culturally-specific knowledge.
- Knowledge of how the specific grammar works.
- Knowledge of different oral and written text types.
- Knowledge of the subject matter or topic.
- Knowledge of how to perform well on the given task.

ITEM-ELICITATION FORMAT

The format for item elicitation has to be determined for any given item. An item can have a spoken, written, or visual stimulus, as well as any combination of the three. Thus, while an item or task may ostensibly assess one modality, it may also be testing some other as well.

So, for example, a subtest referred to as "listening" which has respondents answer oral questions by means of written multiple-choice responses is testing *reading* as well as listening.

It would be possible to avoid introducing this reading element by having the multiple-choice alternatives presented orally as well. But then the tester would be introducing yet another factor, namely, short-term memory ability, since the respondents would have to remember all the alternatives long enough to make an informed choice.

ITEM-RESPONSE FORMAT

The item-response format can be fixed, structured, or open-ended. Item responses with a fixed format include true/false, multiple-choice, and matching items.

Item responses, which call for a structured format include ordering (where respondents are requested to arrange words to make a sentence, and several orders are possible), duplication – both written (such as., dictation) and oral (for example, recitation, repetition, mimicry), identification (explaining the part of speech of a form), and completion.

Those item responses calling for an open-ended format include composition – both written (for example, creative fiction, expository essays) and oral (such as a speech) – as well as other activities, such as free oral response in role-playing situations.

GRAMMATICAL COMPETENCE

Grammatical competence includes phonology, morphology, syntax, knowledge of lexical items, and semantics, as well as matters of mechanics (spelling, punctuation, capitalization, and handwriting). It would seem that this definition is perhaps too broad for practical purposes.

A truly perplexing issue is determining what constitutes a *grammatical error*, as well as determining the severity of this error. In other words, will the use of the error stigmatize the speaker? Let us say that we are using a *grammatical* scale which deals with how acceptably words, phrases, and sentences are formed and pronounced in the respondents' utterances. Let us assume that the focus is on both of the following:

- Clear cases of errors in form, such as the use of the present perfect for an action completed in the past (e.g., "We have had a great time at your house last night.").
- Matters of style, such as the use of a passive verb form in a context where a native would use the active form (e.g., Question - "What happened to the CD I lent you, Jorge?" Reply - "The CD was lost." vs. "I lost your CD.").

Major grammatical errors might be considered those that either interfere with intelligibility or stigmatize the speaker. Minor errors would be those that do not get in the way of the listener's comprehension nor would they annoy the listener to any extent.

ESSAYS

Many assignments need to be written in the form of an essay. There are four main types of essay: argument essays; discussion essays; comparison essays and multi-task essays. The structure of essay-style assignments is very open but generally includes an introduction, a main body and a conclusion.

MULTIPLE CHOICE TESTS

DEFINITION

Probably the most common way of testing grammatical knowledge is the multiple choice test. These tests have the advantage of being easy to grade and being able to cover a lot of grammatical points quickly.

TYPES OF MULTIPLE CHOICE TEST

The most common type of multiple choice grammatical item is one in which the test maker gives the testee a sentence with a blank and four or five choices of a word or phrase which completes the sentence correctly. For example,

Because my mother was sick, I _____ to go home last week.

- Had
- Have
- Has
- Hadn't

To give slightly more context, this type of question sometimes makes use of a short dialogue, with one person saying something and the other person responding.

A way of testing short answers and responses is to give the testees an utterance, and have them decide which of four or five utterances is an appropriate response. This can be either a test of comprehension or a test of grammar. For example,

"I think that tuition is much too high here."

- I do so.
- Do I so.
- I so do.
- So do I.

Another way to test grammatical knowledge using multiple choice items is to give testees a sentence and ask them to choose which of four or five alternatives has the same meaning.

"The school should have expelled him."

- The school didn't expel him, which was wrong.
- The school expelled him, because it was necessary.
- The school might have expelled him, if it had known.
- The school will probably expel him in the near future.

Again this is a test of reading comprehension as well as grammar, but in order to understand the meaning of the sentence, the reader does have to understand the grammar.

The test maker must find a balance between giving enough context and giving too much. One way to give more context and make the language more natural is to give the items in the form of a short reading passage rather than individual sentences. This gives the testees more context and, if the passage is chosen carefully, is also much more interesting than reading individual, uncontextualized sentences. However, it may be more difficult to test a range of grammatical points, since the grammatical points are restricted by the content of the passage.

A variation on this idea is to use a piece of prose written by a non-native English speaker. This is particularly useful for making a grammar test for testees who are all of the same language group, since the errors made by the writer can be used as distracters.

Error Correction

Error correction items are also useful for testing grammar. An error correction item is one in which the testee is given a sentence with an error. Four words or phrases in the sentence marked with letters, and the testee needs to decide which of the words or phrases has the error. For example,

- Most of students
- Believe that they
- Should be getting better grades
- Than they are.

The teacher may also mix in some sentences that have no errors, and students are required to indicate that there is no error. In addition, the students might be required to correct the error. Errors from students' actual writing are a good source of ideas for this type of exercise.

Items to Test Knowledge of Word/Sentence Order

Other types of items can be used to test testees' knowledge of word order. The traditional way is to present the testee with four alternative word orders. For example,

I wonder how she knows ______.

- How it costs much.
- How much it costs.
- It costs how much.
- It how much costs.

Another possibility is to give testees the four words and ask them to put the words in order. For example,

I wonder how she knows __________

- How
- It

- Much
- Costs

/__/__/__/__/

This can also be done in a way that actually requires the writer to do some writing. For example,

I wonder how she knows ______________.

how / it /much / costs

Understanding of appropriate sentence order can also be tested in a similar way by giving testees several sentences and asking them to put them in order. This type of test tests knowledge of references, cohesive devices, etc.

Completion Items

Completion items are items in which the testees are asked to fill in blanks in sentences.

For example:

Give the book to ______ woman in the blue dress.

For the purpose of a grammar test, the words which fit in the blanks should be function words, such as articles and prepositions.

The advantage of completion items is that they test production, not just recognition. The disadvantage is that they need to be marked by hand and there will be some cases where the marker needs to make judgements about whether a response is correct.

It is not always easy to write items for which there is only one possible answer. Using a piece of continuous prose rather than disconnected sentences is one way of cutting down on possible different interpretations of what goes into a particular blank, but it is probably impossible to entirely eliminate the possibility of different answers.

Also, it is possible to require a phrase instead of a word in each blank. However, while this method presents a more realistic situation, it does become more difficult to mark. While it is probably not realistic for large- scale testing situations, it is something that is useful for classroom teachers who want to help their students develop an ability to produce appropriate grammatical forms in context.

Transformation Items

Another type of grammar item makes use of transformations. In this type of item, testees are given a sentence and the first few words of another sentence to change the original sentence without changing the meaning. For example,

- Jim hasn't been home in a long time.
  It's been a long time ______________.
- I don't need to go to the grocery store this week.
  It isn't ______________.
- It is difficult to study when it is so noisy.
  Studying ______________.

There are variations on this type of item in which the word which starts the transformed sentence is underlined, or the testee is given one word to use in the new sentence. For example,

I don't need to go to the grocery store this week. (necessary)

Again, this type of test is difficult to grade because the teacher has to be aware of the variety of possible answers. Another problem is that it does not in any way test the testees' knowledge of when each of the possible transformations would be most appropriate. For example, the testee might be perfectly able to transform an active sentence to a passive sentence but not know when to use passive rather than active. However, it is still sometimes a useful test of grammatical knowledge.

Word Changing Items

Another type of item is one in which the testees are given a sentence and a word which they need to fit into the sentence by changing the form of the word. For example,

- I have never ____ to Australia. (be)
- I will be with you __________. (moment)

This type of grammar test item tests students' knowledge of different word forms and how they are used in sentences.

Sentence Combining Exercises

Sentence combining exercises can play a part in testing

grammar as well as its more traditional use as part of composition testing and training. For example, testees might be instructed to combine the following sentences using a relative pronoun.

I met a man.

The man went to the same high school I did.

I met a man who went to the same high school I did.

MEASURE OF CENTRAL TENDENCY

INTRODUCTION

One of the most common quantities used to summarize a set of data is its centre. The centre is a single value, chosen in such a way that it gives a reasonable approximation of normality. There are many ways to approximate the centre of a set of data. One of the most familiar and useful measures of centre is the mean, however, using only the mean to approximate normality can often be misleading. To obtain a better understanding of what is considered normal, other measures of central tendency such as the median, the trimmed mean, and the trimean may be utilized in addition to the mean.

Measures of central tendency, or "location", attempt to quantify what we mean when we think of as the "typical" or "average" score in a data set. The concept is extremely important and we encounter it frequently in daily life. For example, we often want to know before purchasing a car its average distance per litre of petrol.

Or before accepting a job, you might want to know what a typical salary is for people in that position so you will know whether or not you are going to be paid what you are worth. Or, if you are a smoker, you might often think about how many cigarettes you smoke "on average" per day. Statistics geared toward measuring central tendency all focus on this concept of "typical" or "average." As we will see, we often ask questions in psychological science revolving around how groups differ from each other "on average". Answers to such a question tell us a lot about the phenomenon or process we are studying.

MODE

By far the simplest, but also the least widely used, measure of central tendency is the mode. The mode in a distribution of data is simply the score that occurs most frequently. In the distribution of sexual partners data, the mode is "1" because it is the most frequently occurring score in the data set. If you have had only one sexual partner in the last year, it would be reasonable therefore to say that you are fairly typical of UNE students (or at least of those students who responded to the question).

Importantly, you cant necessarily claim that "most" UNE students had only one sexual partner last year. From the frequency distribution, notice that actually fewer than half of the respondents reported having only one sexual partner. So "most" students reported having something different to 1 sexual partner. Still the most frequent single response to this question, and so it is the mode or modal response. In some cases, however, such a conclusion would be justified.

Recall that one way of describing a distribution is in terms of the number of modes in the data. A unimodal distribution has one mode. In contrast, a bimodal distribution has two. Now this might seem odd to you. How can there be more than one "most frequently occurring" score in a data set? I suppose statisticians are a bit bizarre in this way. We would accept that a distribution is bimodal if it seems that more than one score or value "stands out" as occurring especially frequently in comparison to other values. But when the data are quantitative in nature, we also want to make sure that the two more frequently occurring scores are not too close to each other in value before we accept the distribution as one that could be described as "bimodal." So there is some subjectivity in the decision as to whether or not a distribution is best characterised as unimodal, bimodal, or multimodal.

MEDIAN.

Technically, the median of a distribution is the value that cuts the distribution exactly in half, such that an equal number of scores are larger than that value as there are smaller than that value. The median is by definition what we call the 50th percentile. This is an ideal definition, but often distributions can be cut exactly in half in this way, but we still can define the median in the distribution. Distributions of qualitative data do not have a median.

The median is most easily computed by sorting the data in the data set from smallest to largest. The median is the "middle" score in the distribution. Suppose we have the following scores in a data set: 5, 7, 6, 1, 8. Sorting the data, we have: 1, 5, 6, 7, 8. The "middle score" is 6, so the median is 6. Half of the (remaining) scores are larger than 6 and half of the (remaining) scores are smaller than 6.

To derive the median, using the following rule. First, compute (n+1)/2, where n is the number of data points. Here, there are 5, so n = 5. If (n+1)/2 is an integer, the median is the value that is in the (n+1)/2 location in the sorted distribution. Here, (n+1)/2 = 6/2 or 3, which is an integer. So the median is the 3rd score in the sorted distribution, which is 6. If (n+1)/2 is not an integer, then there is no "middle" score. In such a case, the median is defined as one half of the sum of the two data points that hold the two nearest locations to (n+1)/2.

For example, suppose the data are 1, 4, 6, 5, 8, 0. The sorted distribution is 0, 1, 4, 5, 6, 8. n = 6, and (n+1)/2 = 7/2 = 3.5. This is not an integer. So the median is one half of the sum of the 3rd and 4th scores in the sorted distribution. The 3rd score is 4 and the firth score is 5.

One half of 4 + 5 is 9/2 or 4.5. So the median is 4.5. Here, notice that half of the scores are above 4.5 and half are below. In this case, the ideal definition is satisfied. Also, notice that the median may not be an actual value in the data set. Indeed, the median may not even be a possible value.

The median number of sexual partners last year is 1. Here, n = 177, and (n+1)/2 = 178/2 = 89, an integer. So in the sorted distribution, the 89th data point is the median. In this case, the 89th score is a 1. Notice that this doesnt meet the ideal definition, but we still call it the median. It certainly isnt true that half of the people reported having fewer than 1 sexual partner, and half reported having more than 1. Violations of the ideal definition will occur when the median value occurs more than once in the distribution, which is true here. There are many "1"s in the data.

Computing the median seems like a lot of work. But computers do it quite easily. In real life, you rarely have to compute the median by hand but there are some occasions where you might, so you should know how.

MEAN

The mean, or "average", is the most widely used measure of central tendency. The mean is defined technically as the sum of all the data scores divided by n (the number of scores in the distribution). In a sample, we often symbolize the mean with a letter with a line over it. If the letter is "X", then the mean is symbolized as $\overline{X}$ pronounced "X-bar." If we use the letter X to represent the variable being measured, then symbolically, the mean is defined as.

$$\frac{\sum x}{n}$$

For example, using the data from above, where the n = 5 values of X were 5, 7, 6, 1, and 8, the mean is (5 + 7 + 6 + 1 + 8) / 5 = 5.4. The mean number of partners reported by UNE students who responded to the question is (1 + 0 + 2 + 4 + . . . + 0 + 6 + 2 + 2)/ 177 = 1.864. Note that this is higher than both the mode and the median. In a positively skewed distribution, the mean will be higher than the median because its value will be dragged in the direction of the tail. Similarly in a negatively skewed distribution, the mean will be dragged lower than the median because of the extra large values in the left-hand tail. Distributions of qualitative data do not have a mean.

While probably not intuitively obvious, the mean has a very desirable property: it is the "best guess" for a score in the distribution, when we measure "best" as LEAST IN ERROR. This might seem especially odd because, in this case, no one would report 1.864 partners, so if you guessed 1.864 for someone, you always be wrong! But if you measure how far off your guess would tend to be from the actual score that you are trying to guess, 1.864 would produce the smallest error in your guess. It is worth elaborating on this point because it is important.

Suppose you put the data into a hat, and pulled the scores out of the hat one by one, and each time you to guess the score out of the hat. After each guess, you record how far off your guess was, using the formula: error = actual score - guess. Repeating this procedure for all 177 scores, we can compute your mean error.

Now, if you always guessed 1.864, your mean error would be, guess what? ZERO! Any other guessing strategy you used would produce a mean error different from zero. Because of this, the mean is often used to characterize the "typical" value in a distribution. No other single number we could report would more accurately describe EVERY data point in the distribution.

MEASURE OF VARIABILITY

VARIABILITY

Variability refers to how "spread out" a group of scores is. To see what we mean by spread out, consider graphs in Figure. These graphs represent the scores on two quizzes. The mean score for each quiz is 7.0. Despite the equality of means, you can see that the distributions are quite different. Specifically, the scores on Quiz 1 are more densely packed and those on Quiz 2 are more spread out. The differences among students was much greater on Quiz 2 than on Quiz 1.

Quiz 1

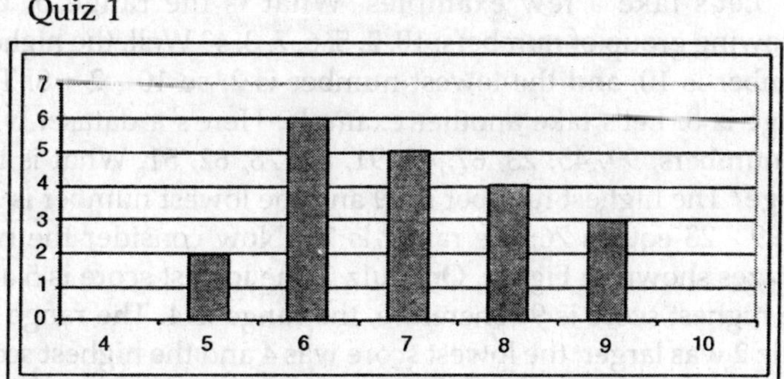

Quiz 2

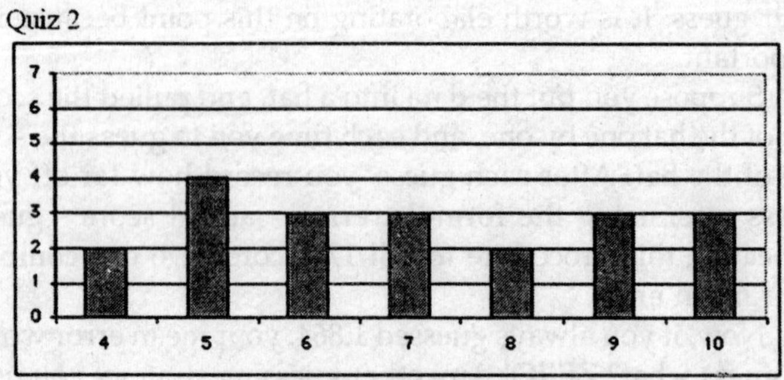

Fig. Bar Charts of Two Quizzes.

The terms variability, spread, and dispersion are synonyms, and refer to how spread out a distribution is. Just as in the section on central tendency we discussed measures of the centre of a distribution of scores, in this chapter we will discuss measures of the variability of a distribution.

There are four frequently used measures of variability, the range: interquartile range, variance, and standard deviation. In the next few paragraphs, we will look at each of these four measures of variability in more detail.

RANGE

The range is the simplest measure of variability to calculate, and one you have probably encountered many times in your life. The range is simply the highest score minus the lowest score.

Let's take a few examples. What is the range of the following group of numbers: 10, 2, 5, 6, 7, 3, 4? Well, the highest number is 10, and the lowest number is 2, so 10 - 2 = 8. The range is 8. Let's take another example. Here's a dataset with 10 numbers: 99, 45, 23, 67, 45, 91, 82, 78, 62, 51. What is the range? The highest number is 99 and the lowest number is 23, so 99 - 23 equals 76; the range is 76. Now consider the two quizzes shown in Figure. On Quiz 1, the lowest score is 5 and the highest score is 9. Therefore, the range is 4. The range on Quiz 2 was larger: the lowest score was 4 and the highest score was 10. Therefore the range is 6.

Interquartile Range

The interquartile range (IQR) is the range of the middle 50% of the scores in a distribution. It is computed as follows:

IQR = 75th percentile - 25th percentile

For Quiz 1, the 75th percentile is 8 and the 25th percentile is 6. The interquartile range is therefore 2. For Quiz 2, which has greater spread, the 75th percentile is 9, the 25th percentile is 5, and the interquartile range is 4. Recall that in the discussion of box plots, the 75th percentile was called the upper hinge and the 25th percentile was called the lower hinge. Using this terminology, the interquartile range is referred to as the H-spread.

A related measure of variability is called the semi-interquartile range. The semi-interquartile range is defined simply as the interquartile range divided by 2. If a distribution is symmetric, the median plus or minus the semi-interquartile range contains half the scores in the distribution.

VARIANCE

Variability can also be defined in terms of how close the scores in the distribution are to the middle of the distribution. Using the mean as the measure of the middle of the distribution, the variance is defined as the average squared difference of the scores from the mean. The data from Quiz 1 are shown in Table 1. The mean score is 7.0. Therefore, the column "Deviation from Mean" contains the score minus 7. The column "Squared Deviation" is simply the previous column squares.

One thing that is important to notice is that the mean deviation from the mean is 0. This will always be the case. The mean of the squared deviations is 1.5. Therefore, the variance is 1.5. Analogous calculations with Quiz 2 show that it's variance is 6.7. The formula for the variance is:

$$\sigma^2 = \frac{\sum(x-\mu)^2}{N}$$

where σ^2 is the variance, ? is the mean, and N is the number of numbers. For Quiz 1, ? = 7 and N = 20.

Table. Calculation of Variance for Quiz 1 scores.

Scores	Deviation from Mean	Squared Deviation
9	2	4
9	2	4
9	2	4
8	1	1
8	1	1
8	1	1
8	1	1
7	0	0
7	0	0
7	0	0
7	0	0
7	0	0
6	-1	1
6	-1	1
6	-1	1
6	-1	1
6	-1	1
6	-1	1
5	-2	4
5	-2	4
7	0	1.5

If the variance in a sample is used to estimate the variance in a population, then the previous formula underestimates the variance and the following formula should be used:

$$s^2 = \frac{\sum (X - M)^2}{N - 1}$$

where s2 is the estimate of the variance and M is the sample mean. Note that M is the mean of a sample taken from a population with a mean of ?. Since, in practice, the variance is usually computed in a sample, this formula is most often used. The simulation "estimating variance" illustrates the bias in the formula with N in the denominator.

Let's take a concrete example. Assume the scores 1, 2, 4, and 5 were sampled from a larger population. To estimate the variance in the population you would compute s2 as follows:

M = (1 + 2 + 4 + 5)/4 = 12/4 = 3.

s2 = [(1-3)2 + (2-3)2 + (4-3)2 + (5-3)2]/(4-1)

= (4 + 1 + 1 + 4)/3 = 10/3 = 3.333

There are alternate formulas that can be easier to use if you are doing your calculations with a hand calculator:

$$\sigma^2 = \frac{\sum x^2 - \frac{(\sum x)^2}{N}}{N}$$

and

$$s^2 = \frac{\sum x^2 - \frac{(\sum x)^2}{N}}{N-1}$$

For this example, $\sum x^2$

= 12 + 22 + 42 + 52 = 46$(\sum x)^2$

= (1 + 2 + 4 + 5)2/N = 144/4 = 36 σ^2

= (46 - 36)/4 = 2.5 and

s2 = (46 - 36)/3 = 3.333 as with the other formula.

STANDARD DEVIATION

The standard deviation is simply the square root of the variance. This makes the standard deviations of the two quiz distributions 1.225 and 2.588. The standard deviation is an especially useful measure of variability when the distribution is normal or approximately normal because the proportion of the distribution within a given number of standard deviations from the mean can be calculated.

For example, 68% of the distribution is within one standard deviation of the mean and approximately 95% of the distribution is within two standard deviations of the mean. Therefore, if you had a normal distribution with a mean of 50 and a standard deviation of 10, then 68% of the distribution would be between 50 - 10 = 40 and 50 +10 =60.

Similarly, about 95% of the distribution would be between 50 - 2 x 10 = 30 and 50 + 2 x 10 = 70. The symbol for the population standard deviation is ?; the symbol for an estimate computed in a sample is s. Figure shows two normal distributions.

Both distributions have means of 50. The blue distribution has a standard deviation of 5; the red distribution has a standard deviation of 10. For the blue distribution, 68% of the distribution is between 45 and 55; for the red distribution, 68% is between 40 and 60.

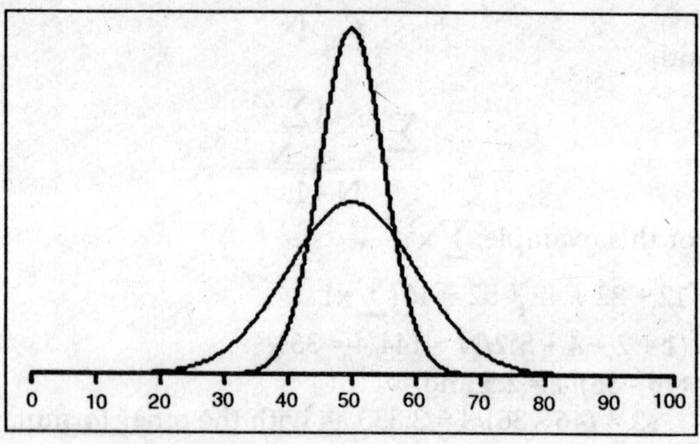

Fig. Normal Distributions with Standard Deviations of 5 and 10.

CORRELATION

The correlation is one of the most common and most useful statistics. A correlation is a single number that describes the degree of relationship between two variables. Let's work through an example to show you how this statistic is computed.

EXAMPLE

Let's assume that we want to look at the relationship between two variables, height (in inches) and self-esteem. Perhaps we have a hypothesis that how tall you are effects your self esteem. Height is measured in inches. Self esteem is measured based on the average of 10 1-to-5 rating items (where higher scores mean higher self esteem). Here's the data for the 20 cases (don't take this too seriously -- I made this data up to illustrate what a correlation is):

Person	*Height*	*Self Esteem*
1	68	4.1
2	71	4.6
3	62	3.8
4	75	4.4
5	58	3.2
6	60	3.1
7	67	3.8
8	68	4.1
9	71	4.3
10	69	3.7
11	68	3.5
12	67	3.2
13	63	3.7
14	62	3.3
15	60	3.4
16	63	4.0
17	65	4.1
18	67	3.8
19	63	3.4
20	61	3.6

Now, let's take a quick look at the histogram for each variable:

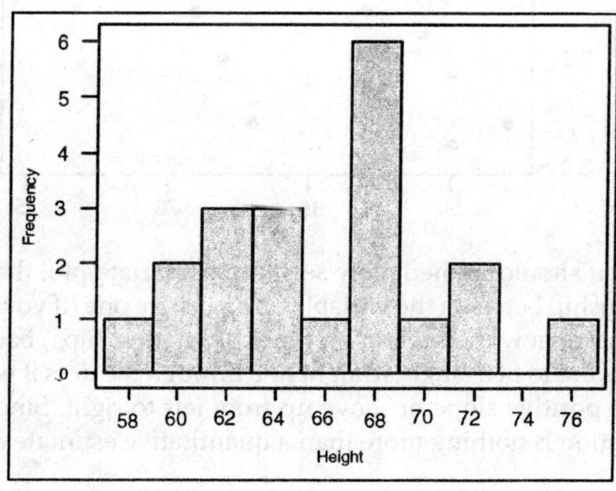

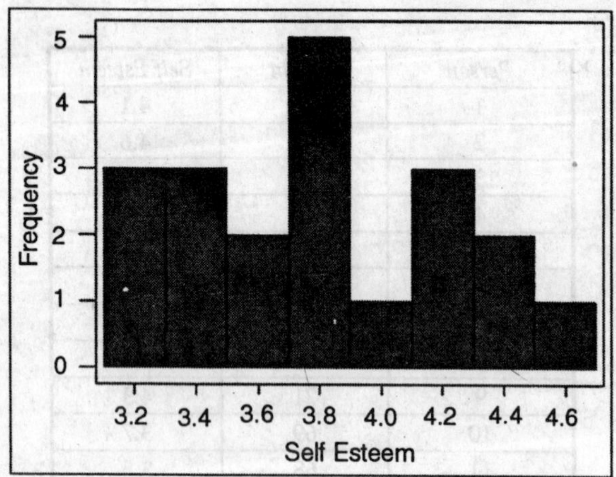

And, here are the descriptive statistics:

Variable	*Mean*	*StDev*	*Variance*	*Sum*	*Minimum*	*Maximum*	*Range*
Height	65.4	4.40574	19.4105	1308	58	75	17
Self Esteem	3.755	0.426090	0.181553	75.1	3.1	4.6	1.5

Finally, we'll look at the simple bivariate (i.e., two-variable) plot:

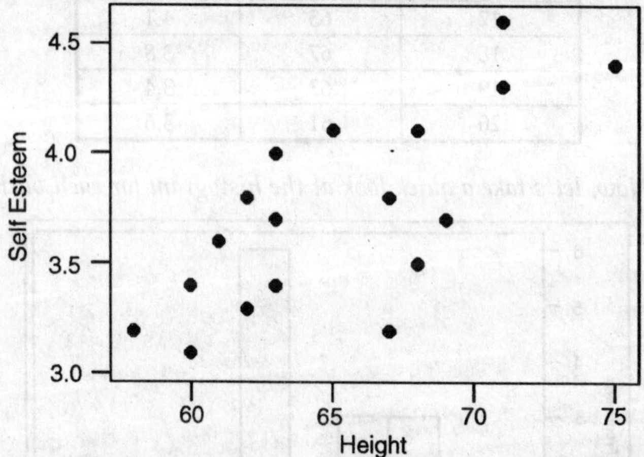

You should immediately see in the bivariate plot that the relationship between the variables is a positive one (if you can't see that, review the section on types of relationships) because if you were to fit a single straight line through the dots it would have a positive slope or move up from left to right. Since the correlation is nothing more than a quantitative estimate of the relationship, we would expect a positive correlation. What does a "positive relationship" mean in this context? It means that, in general, higher scores on one variable tend to be paired with higher scores on the other and that lower scores on one variable tend to be paired with lower scores on the other. You should confirm visually that this is generally true in the plot above.

CALCULATING THE CORRELATION

Now we're ready to compute the correlation value. The formula for the correlation is:

$$r = \frac{N\sum xy - (\sum x)(\sum y)}{\sqrt{[N\sum x^2 - (\sum x)^2][N\sum y^2 - (\sum y)^2]}}$$

where:

N = number of pairs of score

$\sum xy$ = sum of the products of scores

$\sum x$ = sum of x scores

$\sum y$ = sum of y scores

$\sum x^2$ = sum of squared x scores

$\sum y^2$ = sum of squared y scores

We use the symbol r to stand for the correlation. Through the magic of mathematics it turns out that r will always be between -1.0 and +1.0. if the correlation is negative, we have a negative relationship; if it's positive, the relationship is positive.

You don't need to know how we came up with this formula unless you want to be a statistician. But you probably will need to know how the formula relates to real data -- how you can use the formula to compute the correlation. Let's look at the data we need for the formula. Here's the original data with the other necessary columns:

The first three columns are the same as in the table above. The next three columns are simple computations based on the height and self esteem data. The bottom row consists of the sum of each column. This is all the information we need to compute the correlation. Here are the values from the bottom row of the table (where N is 20 people) as they are related to the symbols in the formula:

$$N = 20$$
$$\sum xy = 4937.6$$
$$\sum x = 1308$$
$$\sum y = 75.1$$
$$\sum x^2 = 85912$$
$$\sum y^2 = 285.45$$

Person	*Height (x)*	*Self Esteem (y)*	*x*y*	*x*x*	*y*y*
1	68	4.1	278.8	4624	16.81
2	71	4.6	326.6	5041	21.16
3	62	3.8	235.6	3844	14.44
4	75	4.4	330	5625	19.36
5	58	3.2	185.6	3364	10.24
6	60	3.1	186	3600	9.61
7	67	3.8	254.6	4489	14.44
8	68	4.1	278.8	4624	16.81
9	71	4.3	305.3	5041	18.49
10	69	3.7	255.3	4761	13.69
11	68	3.5	238	4624	12.25
12	67	3.2	214.4	4489	10.24
13	63	3.7	233.1	3969	13.69
14	62	3.3	204.6	3844	10.89
15	60	3.4	204	3600	11.56
16	63	4	252	3969	16
17	65	4.1	266.5	4225	16.81
18	67	3.8	254.6	4489	14.44
19	63	3.4	214.2	3969	11.56
20	61	3.6	219.6	3721	12.96
Sum =	1308	75.1	4937.6	85912	285.45

Now, when we plug these values into the formula given above, we get the following (I show it here tediously, one step at a time):

$$r = \frac{20(4937.6) - (1308)(75.1)}{\sqrt{[20(85912) - (1308 * 1308)][(75.1 * 75.1)]}}$$

$$r = \frac{98752 - 98230.8}{\sqrt{[1718240 - 1710864)][(5709 - 5640.01)]}}$$

$$r = \frac{521.2}{\sqrt{[7376)][(68.99)]}}$$

$$r = \frac{521.2}{\sqrt{508870.2}}$$

$$r = .73$$

So, the correlation for our twenty cases is .73, which is a fairly strong positive relationship. I guess there is a relationship between height and self esteem, at least in this made up data!

SIGNIFICANCE OF A CORRELATION

Once you've computed a correlation, you can determine the probability that the observed correlation occurred by chance. That is, you can conduct a significance test. Most often you are interested in determining the probability that the correlation is a real one and not a chance occurrence. In this case, you are testing the mutually exclusive hypotheses:

Null Hypothesis:	r = 0
Alternative Hypothesis:	r < > 0

The easiest way to test this hypothesis is to find a statistics book that has a table of critical values of r. Most introductory statistics texts would have a table like this. As in all hypothesis testing, you need to first determine the significance level. Here, I'll use the common significance level of alpha = .05. This means that I am conducting a test where the odds that the correlation is a chance occurrence is no more than 5 out of 100. Before I look up the critical value in a table I also have to compute the degrees of freedom or df. The df is simply equal to N-2 or, in this example, is 20-2 = 18. Finally, I have to decide whether I am doing a one-tailed or two-tailed test. In this example, since I have no strong prior theory to suggest whether the relationship between height and self esteem would be positive or negative, I'll opt for the two-tailed test.

With these three pieces of information — the significance level (alpha = .05)), degrees of freedom (df = 18), and type of test (two-tailed) — I can now test the significance of the correlation I found. When I look up this value in the handy little table at the back of my statistics book I find that the critical value is .4438.

This means that if my correlation is greater than .4438 or less than -.4438 (remember, this is a two-tailed test) You can conclude that the odds are less than 5 out of 100 that this is a chance occurrence. Since my correlation 0f .73 is actually quite a bit higher that it is not a chance finding and that the correlation is "statistically significant" (given the parameters of the test). I can reject the null hypothesis and accept the alternative.

CORRELATION MATRIX

All I've shown you so far is how to compute a correlation between two variables. In most studies we have considerably more than two variables. Let's say we have a study with 10 interval-level variables and we want to estimate the relationships among all of them (i.e., between all possible pairs of variables). In this instance, we have 45 unique correlations to estimate (more later on how I knew that!). We could do the above computations 45 times to obtain the correlations. Or we could use just about any statistics programme to automatically compute all 45 with a simple click of the mouse.

I used a simple statistics programme to generate random data for 10 variables with 20 cases (i.e., persons) for each variable. Then, I told the programme to compute the correlations among these variables. Here's the result:

C1 C2 C3 C4 C5 C6 C7 C8 C9 C10
C1 1.000
C2 0.274 1.000

C3 -0.134 -0.269 1.000
C4 0.201 -0.153 0.075 1.000
C5 -0.129 -0.166 0.278 0.011 1.000
C6 -0.095 0.280 -0.348 -0.378 -0.009 1.000
C7 0.171 -0.122 0.288 0.086 0.193 0.002 1.000
C8 0.219 0.242 -0.380 -0.227 -0.551 0.324 -0.082 1.000
C9 0.518 0.238 0.002 0.082 -0.015 0.304 0.347 -0.013 1.000
C10 0.299 0.568 0.165 -0.122 -0.106 -0.169 0.243 0.014 0.352 1.000

This type of table is called a *correlation matrix*. It lists the variable names (C1-C10) down the first column and across the first row. The diagonal of a correlation matrix (i.e., the numbers that go from the upper left corner to the lower right) always consists of ones. That's because these are the correlations between each variable and itself (and a variable is always perfectly correlated with itself). This statistical programme only shows the lower triangle of the correlation matrix. In every correlation matrix there are two triangles that are the values below and to the left of the diagonal (lower triangle) and above and to the right of the diagonal (upper triangle). There is no reason to print both triangles because the two triangles of a correlation matrix are always mirror images of each other (the correlation of variable x with variable y is always equal to the correlation of variable y with variable x). When a matrix has this mirror-image quality above and below the diagonal we refer to it as a *symmetric matrix*. A correlation matrix is always a symmetric matrix.

To locate the correlation for any pair of variables, find the value in the table for the row and column intersection for those two variables. For instance, to find the correlation between variables C5 and C2, look for where row C2 and column C5 is (in this case it's blank because it falls in the upper triangle area) and where row C5 and column C2 is and, in the second case, you find that the correlation is -.166.

OK, so how did you know that there are 45 unique correlations when we have 10 variables? There's a handy simple little formula that tells how many pairs (e.g., correlations) there are for any number of variables:

$$\frac{N*(N-1)}{2}$$

where N is the number of variables. In the example, you had 10 variables, so you know you have (10 * 9)/2 = 90/2 = 45 pairs.

GRAPHICAL REPRESENTATION OF DATA

INTRODUCTION

Most people show lack of interest or have no time to go through facts and figures given in a daily newspaper or a magazine. But if these figures are graphically presented, they become easier to grasp and catch the eye and have a more lasting effect on the reader's mind.

The graphical representation of data makes the reading more interesting, less time-consuming and easily understandable. The disadvantage of graphical presentation is that it lacks details and is less accurate.

GRAPHICAL REPRESENTATION OF DATA

In Graphical Representation there are two methods, histograms and cumulative frequency diagrams, are described in detail for presenting frequency data.

Other presentation methods are: barcharts, piecharts, boxplots, frequency polygons, dotplots, and stem-and-leaf diagrams.

FREQUENCY DISTRIBUTION

A frequency distribution is simply a grouping of the data together, generally in the form of a frequency distribution table, giving a clearer picture than the individual values. The most usual presentation is in the form of a histogram and/or a frequency polygon.

HISTOGRAM

A Histogram is a pictorial method of representing data. A histogram is used to graphically summarize and display the distribution of a process data set.

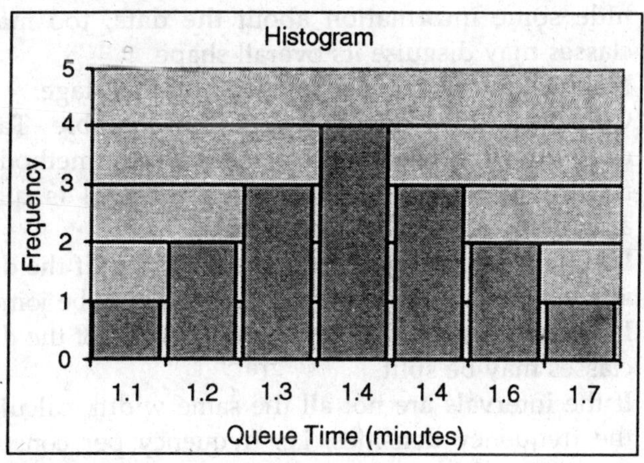

Constructing the above Histogram

A histogram can be constructed by segmenting the range of the data into equal sized bins (also called segments, groups or classes). For example, if your data ranges from 1.1 to 1.8, you could have equal bins of 0.1 consisting of 1 to 1.1, 1.2 to 1.3, 1.3 to 1.4, and so on. The vertical axis of the histogram is labeled Frequency (the number of counts for each bin), and the horizontal axis of the histogram is labeled with the range of your response variable. You then determine the number of data points that reside within each bin and construct the histogram. The bins size can be defined by the user, by some common rule, or by software methods

It appears similar to a Bar Chart but has two fundamental differences:

- The data must be measurable on a standard scale; e.g. lengths rather than colours.
- The Area of a block, rather than its height, is drawn proportional to the Frequency, so if one column is twice the width of another it needs to be only half the height to represent the same frequency.

Method

- Construct a Frequency Distribution Table, grouping the data into a reasonable number of classes, (somewhere in the order of 10). Too few classes may hide some information about the data, too many classes may disguise its overall shape.

- Make all intervals the same width at this stage.
- Construct the frequency distribution table. Tally charts may be used if preferred, but any method of finding the frequency for each interval is quite acceptable.
- Intervals are often left the same width but if the data is scarce at the extremes then classes may be joined. If frequencies are very high in the middle of the data classes may be split.
- If the intervals are not all the same width, calculate the frequency densities, i.e. frequency per constant interval. (Often the most commonly occurring interval is used throughout.) If some intervals are wider than others care must be taken that the areas of the blocks and not their heights are proportional to the frequencies.
- Construct the histogram labelling each axis carefully. For a given frequency distribution, you may have to decide on sensible limits if the first or last Class Interval is specified as 'under ....' or 'over....', i.e. is open ended.
- Hand drawn histograms usually show the frequency or frequency density vertically. Computer output may be horizontal as this format is more convenient for line printers.

FREQUENCY POLYGON

A frequency polygon is constructed by joining the midpoints at the top of each column of the histogram. The final section of the polygon often joins the mid point at the top of each extreme rectangle to a point on the x-axis half a class interval beyond the rectangle. This makes the area enclosed by the rectangle the same as that of the histogram.

Example: You are working for the Transport manager of

a large chain of supermarkets which hires cars for the use of its staff. Your boss is interested in the weekly distances covered by these cars. Mileages recorded for a sample of hired vehicles from 'Fleet 1' during a given week yielded thc following data:

138 164 150 132 144 125 149 157 161 150
146 158 140 109 136 148 152 144 145 145
168 126 138 186 163 109 154 165 135 156
146 183 105 108 135 153 140 135 142 128

Minimum = 105 Maximum = 186 Range = 186 - 105 = 81

Nine intervals of 10 miles width seems reasonable, but extreme intervals may be wider.

Next calculate the frequencies within each interval.

Frequency distribution table

Class interval	Tally	Frequency	Frequency density
100 and < 110	||||	4	2.0
110 and < 120		0	
120 and < 130	|||	3	3.0
130 and < 140	||||| ||	7	7.0
140 and < 150	|||||||||||	11	11.0
150 and < 160	||||| |||	8	8.0
160 and < 170	||||	5	5.0
170 and < 180		0	1.0
180 and < 190	||	2	
	Total	40	

The data is scarce at both extremes so join the extreme two classes together. This doubles the interval width so the **frequency** needs to be halved to produce the frequency per 10 **miles,** i.e. the frequency density. Calculate all the frequency densities. Next draw the histogram and add the frequency polygon. Freq. per 10 mile interval Histogram and frequency polygon

CUMULATIVE FREQUENCY

A Cumulative Frequency Diagram is a graphical method of representing the accumulated frequencies up to and including a particular value - a running total. These cumulative frequencies are often calculated as percentages of the total frequency. This method, as we shall see next week, is used for estimating median and quartile values and hence the interquartile or semi-interquartile ranges of the data. It can also be used to estimate the percentage of the data above or below a certain value.

Method

- Construct a frequency table as before.
- Use it to construct a cumulative frequency table noting that the end of the interval is the relevant plotting value.
- Calculate a column of cumulative percentages.
- Plot the cumulative percentage against the end of the interval and join up the points with straight lines. N.B. Frequencies are always plotted on the vertical axis.

Cumulative Frequency Table

Interval less than	Frequency	Cumulative frequency	% cumulative frequency
100	0	0	0.0
120	4	4	10.0
130	3	7	17.5
140	7	14	35.0
150	11	25	62.5
160	8	33	82.5
170	5	38	95.0
190	2	40	100.0

Using the data in the section on Histograms, we work

through the above method for drawing the cumulative frequency diagram. Next week you will use it to estimate the median mileage, the interquartile range and the semi-interquartile range of the data.

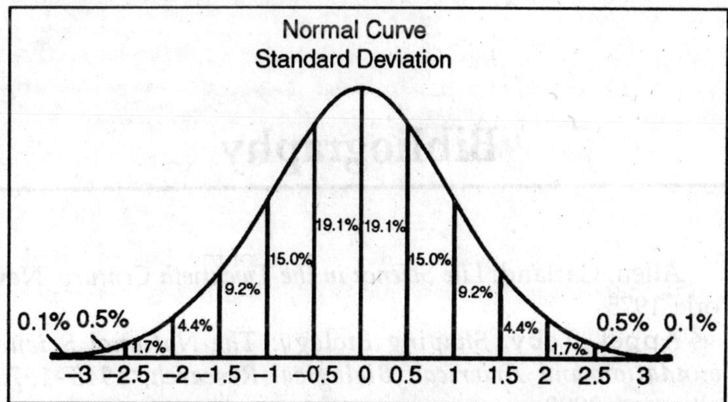

Fig. Normal Probability Curve.

Bibliography

Allen, Garland. *Life Science in the Twentieth Century*. New York: 1975.

Appel, Toby. *Shaping Biology: The National Science Foundation and American Biological Research, 1945–1975*. Baltimore: 2000.

Caron, Joseph. "'Biology' in the Life Sciences: A Historiographical Contribution." *History of Science* 26 (1988): 223–268.

Coleman, William. *Biology in the Nineteenth Century: Problems of Form, Function, and Transformation*. New York: 1971.

Dobzhansky, Theodosius. "Nothing in Biology Makes Sense Except in the Light of Evolution." *American Biology Teacher* 35 (1973): 125–129.

Farley, John. *Gametes and Spores: Ideas about Sexual Reproduction, 1750–1914*. Baltimore: 1982.

The Spontaneous Generation Controversy from Descartes to Oparin. Baltimore: 1977.

Lenoir, Timothy. *Strategy of Life*. Chicago: 1989.

Loeb, Jacques. *The Mechanistic Conception of Life*. Chicago: 1912.

Lovelock, James. *The Ages of Gaia: A Biography of Our Living Earth*. New York: 1988.

Mayr, Ernst. "Cause and Effect in Biology." *Science* 1961.

The Growth of Biological Thought: Diversity, Evolution, and Inheritance. 1982.

This Is Biology: The Science of the Living World. 1997.

Moore, John A. *Science as a Way of Knowing: The Foundations of Modern Biology*. 1993.

Index

A

B

C

L

M

O

P

R